D1216501

C# .NET
Illuminated

Art Gittleman
California State University, Long Beach

JONES AND BARTLETT PUBLISHERS
Sudbury, Massachusetts
BOSTON   TORONTO   LONDON   SINGAPORE

World Headquarters
Jones and Bartlett Publishers
40 Tall Pine Drive
Sudbury, MA 01776
978-443-5000
info@jbpub.com
www.jbpub.com

Jones and Bartlett Publishers
Canada
2406 Nikanna Road
Mississauga, ON L5C 2W6
CANADA

Jones and Bartlett Publishers
International
Barb House, Barb Mews
London W6 7PA
UK

Copyright © 2005 by Art Gittleman

Cover Image © Photodisc

Library of Congress Cataloging-in-Publication Data
Gittleman, Art.
  C# .Net illuminated / Art Gittleman.
      p. cm.
  Includes bibliographical references and index.
  ISBN 0-7637-2593-5 (pbk.)
  1. C# (Computer program language) 2. Microsoft .NET. I. Title.
  QA76.73.C154G52 2004
  005.13'3—dc22

                              2004004572

All rights reserved. No part of the material protected by this copyright notice may be reproduced or utilized in any form, electronic or mechanical, including photocopying, recording, or any information storage or retrieval system, without written permission from the copyright owner.

Microsoft® and Windows® are registered trademarks of the Microsoft Corporation in the USA and other countries. Screen shots and icons reprinted with permission of Microsoft Corporation. This book is not sponsored or endorsed by or affiliated with the Microsoft Corporation.

Acquisitions Editor: Stephen Solomon
Production Manager: Amy Rose
Editorial Assistant: Caroline Senay
Marketing Manager: Matthew Bennett
Sales Manager: Jennifer Corr
Manufacturing Buyer: Therese Bräuer
Composition: Northeast Compositors
Technical Artist: George Nichols
Text and Cover Design: Kristin E. Ohlin
Printing and Binding: Courier Westford
Cover Printing: John Pow Company

Printed in the United States of America
08 07 06 05 04   10 9 8 7 6 5 4 3 2 1

In memory of my Uncle Julius who
always volunteered his help

PREFACE

I designed this text to teach programmers and aspiring programmers how to build applications using the C# language and Visual Studio .NET. These tools facilitate building applications for desktop computers, the Internet, and mobile devices. The text provides a thorough introduction to C#, and carefully shows how to exploit the power of the Visual Studio .NET environment to minimize the coding a developer needs to do "by hand."

The text starts by introducing the event-driven programming style, in which we write code to respond to users interacting with the forms we create. The second chapter goes through the steps of building an application using Visual Studio .NET, while the third presents user interface controls. Chapters 4, 5, and 6 cover the basics of C#.

In Chapter 7 we access a database, and in Chapters 8 and 9 we build Web applications, which are an ever-increasing part of the computing landscape. Chapters 10 and 11 cover XML and Web services, the technologies that allow applications to communicate and integrate functions and data. The concluding chapters, 12 and 13, treat mobile applications for handheld computers and other devices and the Crystal Reports report writing tool included with Visual Studio .NET.

The Visual Studio .NET platform makes rapid application development possible for those with a wide range of interests. This text will be useful to those preparing to become developers, as well as to those who use computers as a tool to enhance their productivity in their major areas of interest.

Visual Studio .NET incorporates all of the capabilities of the .NET class framework library. It generates much of the code we need, leaving only the event-handling code to be written by the developer. For those who want to look behind the scenes and do all the programming without the aid of application building tools, the author's book *Computing with C# and the .NET Framework* (Jones and Bartlett, 2003) uses the .NET class framework directly, covering many of the same topics as in this text.

Software

Microsoft Visual Studio .NET 2003 or later will handle all the examples in this text. Visual C# .NET, which can be bundled with this text, will handle the examples in the first 11 chapters.

In the text, we deploy Web applications (Chapter 8 and later) locally using Microsoft Internet Information Server. If IIS is not installed, Web Matrix is available at no cost from Microsoft and will run Web applications locally while not permitting connections from other sites. Once Web Matrix is installed, its readme file will show how to use it.

The database examples use the Microsoft Access database. If Access is not installed, the SQL Server Desktop Engine is available at no cost from Microsoft.

Resources

All of the applications are included on the publisher's website at `http://computerscience.jbpub.com`, so readers have the complete code for each example. Answers to the odd-numbered Test Your Understanding exercises appear at the end of the book.

Acknowledgments

I thank the following reviewers for their helpful comments and suggestions on an earlier draft. I found their feedback to be extremely valuable.

> Corinne Hoisington, Northern Virginia Community College
>
> Sheila Sicilia, Onondaga Community College
>
> Ron Greenwald, Saint Petersburg Community College
>
> Gerald Baumgartner, The Ohio State University
>
> Ayad Boudiab, Georgia Perimeter College

I am thankful for the dedicated assistance and support from the Jones and Bartlett staff, including Stephen Solomon, Caroline Senay, Amy Rose, Matthew Bennett, Kristin Ohlin, Anne Spencer, and Tracey Chapman, and Mike Wile of Northeast Compositors.

Errata

Please e-mail any errors or typos to me at `artg@csulb.edu`. I will post them on my website at `http://www.cecs.csulb.edu/~artg/csharp/errata1.txt`

CONTENTS

Chapter 1   **Introduction   1**

Event-Driven Programming   1
   Windows Applications   2
   Using a Database   4
   Web Applications   5
   Web Services   6
   Mobile Applications   6
   Crystal Reports   7

Computing with C#   8
   Hardware   8
   Software   9
   History   10
   Features   12

Visual Studio .NET   12

Summary   14

Chapter 2   **Creating an Application   15**

Creating a Windows Application   15
   The Start Page   15
   Creating a Project   16
   The Properties Window   17
   Changing Properties   18

Adding Controls   19
   The Toolbox   19
   TextBox   20
   Label   21
   Code for an Event   22
   IntelliSense   23
   Running an Application   24
   Closing the Project   25
   Test Your Understanding   25

Positioning and Sizing Controls   25
   Anchoring   27
   Aligning Text   28

Docking   31
Moving and Sizing Controls   33

Using a Button   34
Setting Properties   35
Handling the Click Event   37
Context-Sensitive Help   37

Summary   38

Programming Exercises   39

Chapter 3   **Controls for Windows Forms   41**

Using Radio Buttons and Link Labels   41
Radio Buttons   41
Adding a Link   45
Grouping Radio Buttons   47
Adding Another Group   51

More Boxes   52
Picture Boxes   52
Check Boxes   53
List Boxes   58
Combo Boxes   61

Keeping Track   62
DateTimePicker   63
NumericUpDown   65
Enabling the Display   65
StatusBar   66
Timer   66

Menus and Dialogs   68
MainMenu   68
RichTextBox   70
File Dialogs   72
A Print Dialog   75
A Color Dialog   75
A Font Dialog   77

Summary   78

Programming Exercises   79

Chapter 4   **Variables and Types   81**

Variables and the Assignment Operator   81
Identifiers   81

Keywords   82
The Character Set   82
Variables   82
The Assignment Operator   83
Illustrating Variables   84
Constants   87

Types   87
Formatting   89
Format Specifiers   90
Field Width   92

Operators and Expressions   96
Precedence of Arithmetic Operators   97
Increment and Decrement Operators   99
Relational Operators and Expressions   100
The AND, OR, and NOT Operators   101
Conditional AND   101
Conditional OR   102
Logical Complement   102
Operator Precedence   103
Combining AND with OR   103

Summary   106

Programming Exercises   107

Chapter 5   Selection and Repetition   109

The if and if-else Statements   110
The if Statement   110
The if-else Statement 111
Blocks   112

Nested ifs and the switch Statement   116
Nested if Statements   117
Pairing else with if   119
The switch Statement   122

Repetition   126
The while Statement   126
Loop Termination   127
The for Statement   128
The do Statement   133

Summary   136

Programming Exercises   137

Chapter 6   **Reference Types   139**

Arrays   139

Multiple ListBox Selections   141
Using the Documentation   142
A CheckBox Array   143
A Search Game   144
Random Numbers   145
Array Variables and Values   148

Strings   150

Visualizing a String   150
Creating a String   151
A String Property   152
A String Indexer   152
String Methods   152
Overloaded Methods   154
Class Methods   156
Using StringBuilder   158

Library Classes   162

Namespaces   162
Control Objects   163

Summary   164

Programming Exercises   165

Chapter 7   **Using a Database   169**

The Northwind Database   170

Relational Databases   170
Queries   171

The Connected Model   173

Connecting to a Database   173
Building a Command   175
Reading and Displaying the Data   176

The Disconnected Model   179

The Data Adapter Configuration Wizard   180
A Query Builder   181
A Data Set   182
Using the Data Form Wizard   183

Using Multiple Tables   187

Building the Query   188
Displaying the Query Results   190

Summary   192

Programming Exercises   191

Chapter 8   **Web Applications**   **195**

HTML   196
   Some HTML Tags   196

Web Server Controls and Code Behind   200
   Hosting a Web page   200
   Server Controls   202
   Code Behind   202
   More Web Controls   204

Accessing a Database   208
   Adding a Connection   209
   Configuring a Command   209
   Displaying in a DataGrid   209
   Writing the Event Handler   210
   Choosing Data to Display   211

Using Multiple Web Forms   216
   Redirecting a Response   216
   The AutoPostBack Property   217
   Adding a Web Form to a Project   218
   Initializing the Page   219
   Hidden State   220
   Initializing the Page   223

Summary   224

Programming Exercises   225

Chapter 9   **Validation Controls**   **227**

Checking Required Fields   227

Range Checking   231
   String Values   232
   Integer Values   233
   Dates   233
   Currency   234

Comparing Values   235
   Client-Side Versus Server-Side Validation   237

Validating Expressions and Summarizing   239
   Validating Expressions   239

Summarizing Validation Errors   243

Summary   244

Programming Exercises   244

Chapter 10   **XML   247**

XML and Its Syntax   247
   The Limitations of HTML   247
   XML Syntax   248

Schemas   251
   Building a Schema in Visual Studio .NET   252
   Valid Documents   255
   Using a Schema to Create an XML Document   256

From Data to XML   258
   Northwind Data to XML   258
   The Document Object Mode (DOM)   260
   Processing an XML Document   261

Transforming XML   263
   XSLT (Extensible Stylesheet Language for
      Transformations)   263

Summary   272

Programming Exercises   273

Chapter 11   **Web Services   275**

Web Service Clients   275
   Adding a Web Reference   276
   Asynchronous Calls   279
   The Event Handler and the Callback Methods   280

Creating a Web Service   282
   Testing the Web Service   284
   A Client for the Reverse Service   285

Accessing Data   286
   Creating the Web Service   286
   Creating a Client   290

Summary   292

Programming Exercises   292

Chapter 12   **Mobile Applications   295**

Introduction   295
  Mobile Devices   295
  Operating Systems   296
  The .NET Compact Framework   297
  Mobile Web Applications   298

A Simple Mobile Web Application   301
  Creating a Web Application   301
  The Windows CE .NET Emulator   302
  The Pocket PC 2002 Emulator   304

A Smart Device Application: Appointment List   306
  Using Tabs   307
  Saving the Appointment List   309
  Initializing the Appointment List   310

Accessing Web Services   311
  Adding Web References   313

Summary   315

Programming Exercises   316

Chapter 13   **Crystal Reports   317**

Creating a Simple Report   317
  Adding and Creating a Report   317
  Viewing the Report   320
  Filtering   321

Adding Features to a Report   323
  The Data Tab   323
  The Fields Tab   324
  The Group Tab   325
  The Total Tab   325
  The Remaining Tabs   326
  Viewing the Report   326

Reports via the Web   327
  Viewing a Report in a Web Form   327
  A Web Service Report   328
  Accessing the Web Service   329

Summary   330

Programming Exercises   330

Appendix A   C# Keywords   331

Appendix B   Operator Precedence Table   333

Appendix C   The ASCII Character Set   335

Answers to Odd-Numbered Test Your Understanding Exercises   337

Index   343

CHAPTER 1

Introduction

Sending e-mail, playing games, and buying books are just a few of the many uses for our computer. With powerful tools we can learn to create computer applications ourselves. The C# language and Visual Studio .NET are two such powerful tools, both of which are introduced in this chapter. C# is a general-purpose programming language that lends itself to many programming styles. Visual Studio .NET is a development environment that makes it easy to develop applications for desktop computers, mobile devices, and the Web. The style of these applications frequently is event-driven, presenting an interface with which the user interacts.

Chapter Objectives:

- Explain event-driven programming
- Introduce the C# language
- Introduce Visual Studio .NET

1.1 Event-Driven Programming

User-generated events control an event-driven program. A simple example appears in Figure 1.1.

The application shown in Figure 1.1 waits for the user to enter a name in the text box. As the user enters a name, the name replaces the initial message in the label. If the user does not enter a name or even goes away, then no code is executed. The system executes code when the user enters text.

Using Visual Studio .NET means that we have very little C# code to write ourselves. For an event-driven application, the code we need to write consists of event handlers. Event handlers respond to an event generated by the user.

In the application shown in Figure 1.1 we need to handle the event that occurs when the user enters text in the text box. Our code will consist of

Figure 1.1   A simple form.

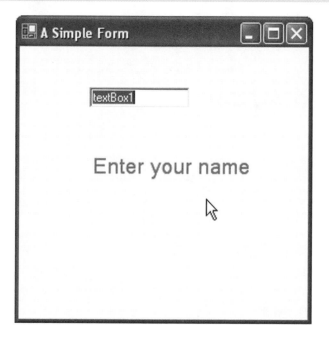

only one line used to copy the text from the text box to the label. Visual Studio .NET writes the code to create the text box and label, position them in the form, and make the label color red. It provides the code structure needed to run the application.

In this text we will create several types of event-driven applications. They include Windows applications, ASP.NET Web applications, ASP.NET Web services, and mobile Web applications.

1.1.1   Windows Applications

A Windows application runs on a computer using the Windows operating system. Currently, Windows XP is the latest version. The application starts by displaying a user interface, such as the simple one shown in Figure 1.1. It waits for the user's actions and responds to them. In Chapter 2 we carefully go through the steps necessary to create a Windows application.

A form represents a window for a user interface. Controls are components with a visual representation that we can add to a form to build a user interface. Chapter 3 presents a wide variety of Windows application controls.

Figure 1.2   Using list box and combo box controls.

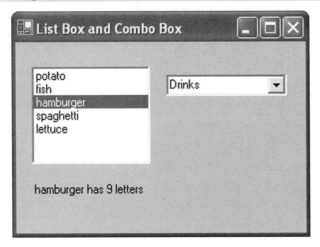

Figure 1.3   A form to calculate the change from a dollar.

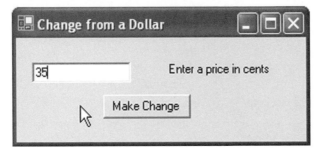

For example, Figure 1.2 shows a screen that contains a list box, a combo box, and a label. When the user selects a drink from the combo box, the event handler that we wrote displays the food and drink that the user selected in the label.

Because we have not really begun to explore the C# language, we only do simple things in the event-handling code that we write. We only allow the user to select one food and one drink because we need to cover more C# concepts to allow multiple selections.

Chapters 4, 5, and 6 introduce the C# language, presenting the features we need to write various types of event-driven applications. Chapter 4 uses C# for simple computations, introducing arithmetic expressions and basic data types. Figure 1.3 shows the screen for an application that finds the coins needed to make change from a dollar given the purchase amount the user enters in a text box. We respond to the event the user generates by pressing a button. We use the button to allow the user to complete the entry in the text box before calculating the change. Had we responded to the user entering text in the text box, we would have responded after each digit was entered, which is not what we want.

Figure 1.4
Change from a dollar.

Figure 1.4 shows the result of the calculation display in a message box. It is correct mathematically, but not grammatically. The display shows "1 dimes", but would be better as "1 dime". Similarly, "1 nickels" should be "1 nickel". To correct the grammar we need to learn how to make choices, which is the subject of Chapter 5.

In Chapter 5 we cover the C# statements needed to select from among alternatives and to repeat steps. Figure 1.5 shows a form in which the user enters a test score in a text box and presses a button to find out the letter grade assigned to that score. The event-handling code selects the grade based on the range of values in which the grade lies. It makes choices depending on the results of comparisons.

Chapter 6 covers arrays and strings. Array notation lets us use collections of data conveniently. We use character strings in each chapter, and then we take the time in Chapter 6 to cover important details about them that we will use in later examples. Applications can handle multiple selections in a list box and can produce the grammatically correct response shown in the text box of Figure 1.6.

1.1.2   Using a Database

Chapter 7 continues Windows applications, adding the use of a database. Many applications use and create data that needs to be saved. A database

Figure 1.5   Assigning a letter grade.

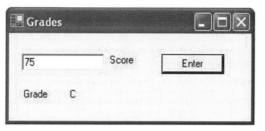

Figure 1.6   Choosing animals and a thing.

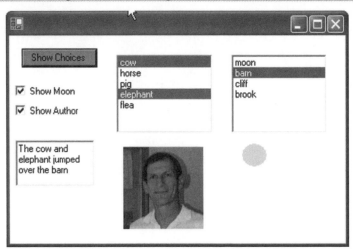

system uses efficient methods to save possibly large sets of data. Figure 1.7 shows a screen that displays the products from the Northwind database included with the Microsoft Access database program.

1.1.3   Web Applications

The World Wide Web is becoming the platform of choice for many applications. Users can browse sites all over the world with Internet Explorer or other similar software. Web pages are written in HTML, the hypertext markup language. Chapter 8 introduces HTML, but in our application Visual Studio .NET writes the HTML we need.

Visual Studio .NET provides Web forms and Web controls to enable us to build Web applications. We host these applications on our Web site. Users browse our site and download our application to their own computers. They may submit information that they enter on forms to our server. Web server controls, covered in Chapter 8, execute on our server and send responses back to the users who submitted requests. Figure 1.8 shows a Web form that confirms the user's choices for ordering an ice cream sundae.

Chapter 9 continues discussion of building Web applications. It illustrates validation controls that make sure the user does not leave a field blank. These controls can also check that a value is in a correct range or that it compares correctly with another value such as a password. They can also

Figure 1.7   Displaying database data.

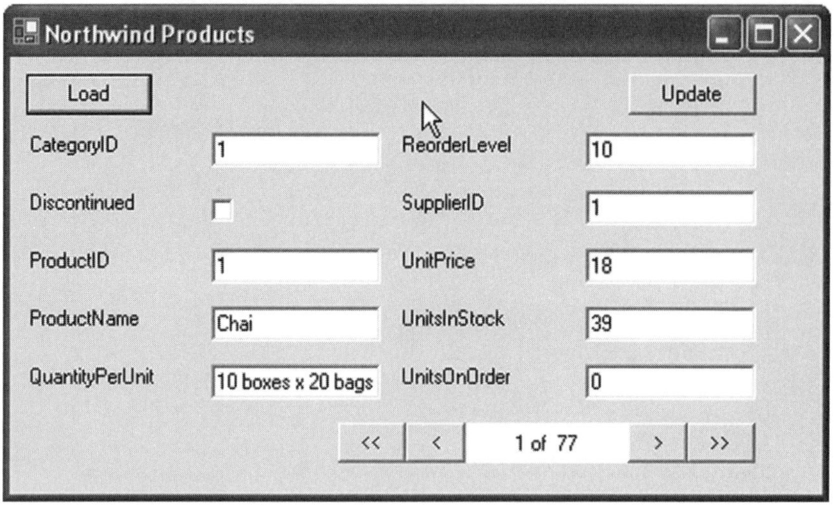

check for valid formats of common data items such as telephone numbers and zip codes. Checking correct data entry is an important part of building a robust application. Figure 1.9 shows a screen indicating that the user has failed to enter a name or an address in the Web form.

1.1.4   Web Services

The Web applications covered in Chapters 8 and 9 let a user access and interact with forms downloaded from a remote site. More generally, Web services allow programs to access other sites without depending on a human user with a browser. Web services use XML, a general notation for expressing information, which we cover in Chapter 10. In Chapter 11 we access and build Web services.

Figure 1.10 shows an interface to a weather-temperature Web service. In this case we provided a user interface. The user enters a zip code, and then the Web service returns the temperature in that zip code.

1.1.5   Mobile Applications

Mobile devices, including handheld computers, personal digital assistants, and cell phones, have installed applications and may access Web applications hosted on servers. Visual Studio .NET, starting with the 2003 version,

Figure 1.8 A Web application.

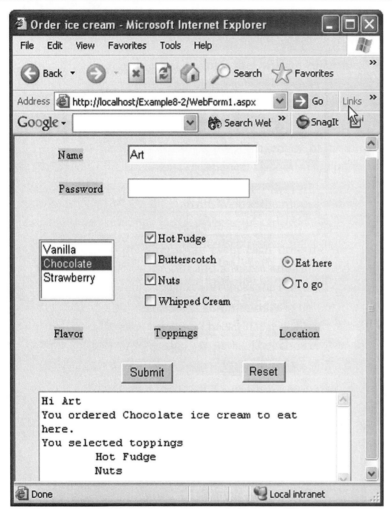

allows us to develop applications for these devices. We introduce application development for mobile devices in Chapter 12.

1.1.6 Crystal Reports

Visual Studio .NET includes the Crystal Reports package that enables us to create a variety of reports to present the data and results of .NET applications. In Chapter 13 we show how to create reports and to access them on the Web.

Figure 1.9   Validating entries in a Web form.

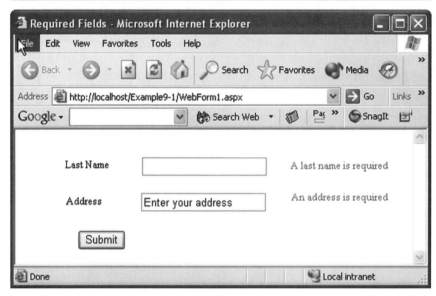

Figure 1.10   Using a Web Service.

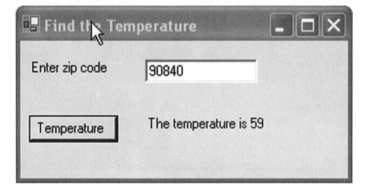

1.2   Computing with C#

Microsoft created the C# language along with the .NET platform. We start with some basic computing concepts and then trace the evolution of C# and highlight its features.

1.2.1   Hardware

A computer has several basic components. The processor executes programs stored in memory, using the memory to store data needed in the

Figure 1.11   A computer system.

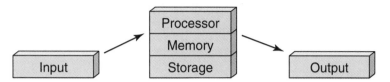

computation. External storage, including disk drives, holds programs and data. Input devices such as a keyboard and a mouse allow user interaction. Output devices display results. Figure 1.11 illustrates this system. Changing technology continually improves the performance of these components and provides new types, but current commercial computers are structured in this manner.

1.2.2   Software

Software consists of the programs that the computer executes. The operating system software makes it much easier for us to use the computer. It provides an interface to the hardware so that we do not have to write programs to read input from the keyboard, write output to the screen, or create files on the hard disk. An operating system can be relatively simple, providing few services, or it can be a huge program with many bells and whistles.

Programmers appreciate utility programs such as editors that allow us to create or modify programs, and compilers that translate programs from one language to another to facilitate their execution. End users run word processors, spreadsheets, games, and browsers, among many other applications. Businesses rely on computer software to serve customers and for their own accounting, payroll, and other management needs.

The processor executes software using its specially designed instruction set. Each instruction is simple, so it may take hundreds, thousands, or millions of instructions to implement the tasks we want our software to perform. Each instruction has several parts. These parts specify the operation—addition, for example—that the instruction performs and any operands that it uses, such as the numbers to add. Each memory location has a numerical address. High-level languages such as C# provide instructions that perform the equivalent of many low-level machine instructions.

High-Level Languages

Each processor has its own instruction set that uses numerical codes for the operators and numerical addresses for the operations. Each instruction performs one basic step such as an addition, a load, or a store. Programming using a processor's instruction set would make it difficult to accomplish anything more than the simplest tasks. Moreover, we would have to write such a program all over again for the instruction set of a different processor. A program using processor ABC's instruction set will not run on processor XYZ, and vice versa.

A high-level language allows us to express the computation in a more understandable form, combining several steps into one expression, and to write a program that we can implement on many different types of processors. For example, we can express an addition as

```
totalSalary = baseSalary + bonus;
```

and write more complicated statements such as

```
totalScore =
    (judge1Score + judge2Score + judge3Score) * difficulty;
```

which represents the total score obtained by first adding the scores of three judges and then multiplying that sum by a difficulty factor. We use the star, *, to denote multiplication.

1.2.3   History

FORTRAN and COBOL were among the first high-level languages, introduced in the late 1950s. Both are still used today, FORTRAN for scientific applications and COBOL for business. Smalltalk, released around 1980, is a fully object-oriented language that influenced its successors, including Java and C#.

Systems programmers who needed access to the machine hardware used assembly languages, which are very low-level and specific to the hardware. The C language, developed in the early 1970s, is sometimes described as a portable assembly language. It is a high-level language, like FORTRAN and COBOL, but provides access to machine hardware. The UNIX operating system, developed for the then new minicomputers, was mostly written in C, and both C and UNIX rapidly grew in popularity.

Although good for systems programming, C is a small language that does not facilitate the development of large software systems. Introduced in the late 1960s, object-oriented programming started to become popular in the mid 1980s. Languages that support object-oriented programming do facilitate the development of large software systems. C++ extends C to include constructs that support object-oriented programming, while still including those that access machine hardware. Consequently, C++ grew in popularity.

Meeting a different need, BASIC was developed in the 1960s as an easier way for students to learn to program. It used an interpreter so that students could immediately see the results of execution. Originally, personal computers had very limited memory chips in which to hold programs, so BASIC, which did not require compilation to a larger low-level representation, became the main language used on early PCs. As memory became cheaper and graphics capabilities grew, BASIC morphed to Visual Basic, an extremely popular language for the rapid development of user applications.

With the introduction of the .NET Framework, Visual Basic has evolved to Visual Basic .NET, a cousin of C#. One way we might describe C# is as a language that tries to combine the rapid application development of Visual Basic with much of the power of C++.

With the rise of desktop computers and the rapid growth of the Internet in the mid 1990s came the need for a language to support programming by allowing users on vastly different systems to interact in a secure way. Java, introduced in 1995, uses a Java Virtual Machine to provide security and enable programs developed on different systems to interact. A large library extends its capabilities for Internet programming. Because it suited the new demands placed on developers, Java has become very popular.

The goals of C# are similar to those of Java. Those versed in one of these languages can rapidly convert to using the other. C# had the advantage of seeing the Java approach and how it might enhance it. C# adds features for the easy development of components to make it simpler for developers to combine programs from different sources. One can annotate a C# program with attributes that are available when the application is running. This metadata describes the program so that other programs can use it. C#, newly developed in the 21st century, promises to become very popular as the primary .NET programming language.

1.2.4   C# Features

Microsoft identifies C# as a modern, object-oriented language that allows programmers to quickly build .NET components from high-level business objects to system-level applications. These components can easily be converted to Web services to be used over the Internet. Important characteristics are:

- Productivity and Safety

  — C# uses the .NET platform supporting Web technologies. C# works well with XML, the emerging standard way to pass structured data over the Internet.

  — The C# design eliminates many costly programming errors. It includes automatic memory management and initialization of variables. It checks types to avoid run-time errors.

  — C# reduces updating costs by supporting versioning in the language, making it easier and less costly to introduce a new version of a product.

- Power, Expressiveness, and Flexibility

  — C# allows a close connection between the abstract business process and its software implementation. The developer can associate metadata with a program that will allow tools to determine whether a component is correctly identified as part of a business object or to create reports.

  — To avoid the need to use C++ to access basic machine functions, C# permits carefully identified low-level access to machine resources.

1.3   Visual Studio .NET

Visual Studio .NET is a complete set of development tools for building desktop applications, ASP Web applications, XML Web services, and mobile applications. In Chapter 2 we carefully detail the steps needed to create a Windows application. In this section we illustrate some of the features of Visual Studio .NET.

Figure 1.12 shows Visual Studio .NET opened to the design view with a form. The Toolbox on the left show the controls that we can drag onto the form. The form currently contains a TextBox and a Label. The selected tab at

Figure 1.12   Using Visual Studio .NET.

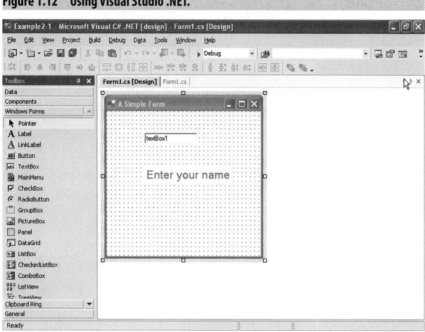

the top of the left side has the label Form1.cs [design]. Visual Studio .NET creates the default name Form1. The extension .cs denotes a C# application.

The form contains the user interface design that we create by dragging controls from the Toolbox. The rightmost tab, Form1.cs, is not selected. It contains the C# code that Visual Studio .NET has written to implement our design. We never need to select it. The only C# code we will need to write to make this application work will be one line to copy the text that the user enters in the text box to the label below it. To write event-handling code, we double click on the control in which the event occurs. In the design shown in Figure 1.12, we will double click the TextBox and add that one line of code inside the template that appears.

Similarly, we use Visual Studio .NET forms and a Toolbox to design Web applications and mobile applications. We use a similar process to write event-handling code for these types of applications. Visual Studio .NET is a powerful tool that minimizes the amount of C# code the developer needs to write.

1.4 Summary

- With powerful tools we can learn to create computer applications ourselves. The C# language and Visual Studio .NET are two such powerful tools.

- User-generated events control an event-driven program. Types of event-driven applications include Windows applications, ASP.NET Web applications, ASP.NET Web services, and mobile Web applications.

- Using Visual Studio .NET means that we have very little C# code to write ourselves. For an event-driven application, the code we need to write consists of event handlers.

CHAPTER 2

Creating an Application

We start by building a simple application illustrating the use of Visual Studio .NET. Controls are components with visual representations that we add to a form to make a user interface. We discuss placing controls in a form, configuring controls by setting properties, and writing code to make a control respond to the user's actions.

Chapter Objectives:

- Create a simple Windows application
- Add controls using the Toolbox
- Configure controls using Properties
- Write code to respond to user actions
- Use context-sensitive help

2.1 Creating a Windows Application

We show how to use Visual Studio .NET to begin creating a simple Windows application.

2.1.1 The Start Page

Visual Studio .NET opens by default with a Start Page, as shown in Figure 2.1.

We can change the default by choosing the *Tools, Options* menu item. In the upper-right corner, we can pop up the following choices:

Show *Start Page*
Load last loaded solution
Show *Open Project* dialog box

Figure 2.1   The Start Page.

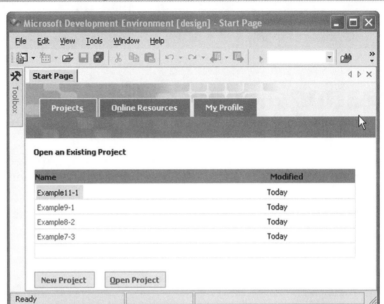

Show *New Project* dialog box

Show empty environment

2.1.2   Creating a Project

To create a new project we click the *New Project* button, choosing `Visual C#`
`Projects` as the project type and the `Windows Application` template. Templates
provide the correct starting environment for the type of project we are
building. The various project types with their accompanying descriptions
are:

`Windows Application`	A project for creating an application with a Windows user interface
`Class Library`	A project for creating classes to use in other applications
`Windows Control Library`	A project for creating controls to use in Windows applications
`Mobile Web Application`	A project for creating an application viewable on PDAs, cell phones, and other mobile devices

`ASP.NET Web Application`	A project for creating an application with a Web user interface
`ASP.NET Web Service`	A project for creating XML Web services to use from other applications
`Web Control Library`	A project for creating controls to use in Web applications
`Console Application`	A project for creating a command-line application
`Windows Service`	A project for creating services for Windows
`Empty Project`	An empty project for creating a local application
`Empty Web Project`	An empty project for creating a Web Application
`New Project in Existing Folder`	An empty project created in an existing folder

We will use some of these templates later in the text. Later versions of Visual Studio .NET include a few additional choices. The `Mobile Web Application` template requires a separate download to install in earlier versions. For the Windows application we are creating, we choose the name `Example2-1` and the location `c:\booknet\ch2`, and click *OK*. The location is the folder in which all the files for this project will be stored.

2.1.3 The Properties Window

Figure 2.2 shows the form on the left with the `Properties` window on the right. If the `Properties` window does not appear, we can view it by clicking the *View, Properties Window* menu item.

The form in Figure 2.2 has a grid of dots that we can use to align controls that we add to the form. Using the scroll bar in the `Properties` window, we can explore the various properties that we can use to configure the form. The main `Properties` categories for a `Form` are `Accessibility`, `Appearance`, `Behavior`, `Configurations`, `Data`, `Design`, `Focus`, `Layout`, `Misc`, and `Window Style`. If they show with a plus sign (+) at the left, clicking on the plus sign will open a list of properties in that category. Figure 2.2 shows the `Appearance` properties. The highlighted property, `Text`, has its description below the `Properties` window.

In the `Properties` windows, the row just below the name, `Form1`, contains five buttons. The leftmost two, separated by a vertical bar from the rest, allow us to choose to arrange the properties by category or alphabetically. The left button of these two, for categories, is the default. The second group of two buttons lets us choose this window to display property values or event

Figure 2.2   A Windows application.

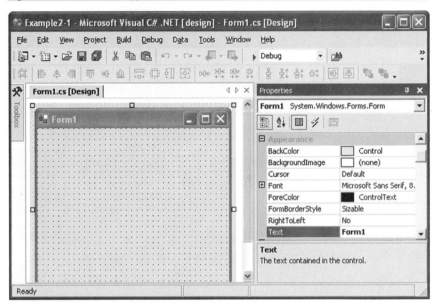

methods. The default is property values. We will discuss event methods later and use another approach to define them. We stick with the default choice of property values. The rightmost button, for Property Pages, is disabled.

2.1.4   Changing Properties

The Text property contains the title of the application. It appears in the frame of the form. We can replace the default text, Form1, with our own title. We type *A Simple Form*, and after pressing the *Enter* key this text appears as the new title in the form.

We use the BackColor property to change the background color of the form. The current color is a gray, which is the default for a Control. If we click on this current BackColor value we get a combo box with an arrow to allow us to pop up a window with three tabs, Custom, Web, and System. The System tab is on top and shows the default color for various system elements. We could select ControlLight or ControlLightLight to get a lighter color for the form background, but we select the Custom tab to get a grid of custom color selections. We choose the fourth color in the top row, which is a light pinkish yellow. The numbers 255, 255, and 192 associated with this color represent its red, green, and blue components on a scale from 0 to 255, with 255 being the most intense.

We can use properties to specify the size and the location of the form. We use pixels to indicate size and location. A pixel is a picture element, a single dot on the screen. The screen resolution determines the number of pixels for the full screen. Some usual configurations are 800 by 600 or 1024 by 768, where the first measurement is the number of pixels making up the width and the second is the height.

Test Your Understanding

1.   Using Visual Studio .NET, find the property to set the size of a form. What is the default size?

2.   Using Visual Studio .NET, in what property group is the Location property? At which corner of the form does it specify the position?

2.2   Adding Controls

Controls are components that we can add to a form. They enable us to create rich user interfaces.

2.2.1   The Toolbox

The Visual Studio .NET Toolbox contains controls that we can add to a form. To view the Toolbox, we click on the *View, Toolbox* menu item. The main window is getting crowded with the form, the Properties window, and the Toolbox. The Properties window in Figure 2.2 shows a pushpin in the vertical position just to the left of the **X** that allows the user to close that window. Clicking on the pushpin turns it to the horizontal position and hides the Properties window in a bar on the right side. It reappears when we move the mouse over the bar. By auto-hiding the Properties window we can have it readily available without cluttering the screen. We could auto-hide the Toolbox but leave it showing as in Figure 2.3, so that we can refer to it. Figure 2.3 shows the form with its new title and background color.

The Toolbox groups controls into the following categories:

Data   Controls to represent database data

Components   Nonvisual components such as a timer or report document

Windows Forms   Controls that make up the visual interface

The BIG Picture

Visual Studio .NET opens with a Start page that we can configure in various styles. We begin by creating a project of which there are several types. A Windows application provides a Form for creating a user interface. A Properties window lists properties of the form, such as its background color, that we can customize with our choices.

Figure 2.3   The Toolbox.

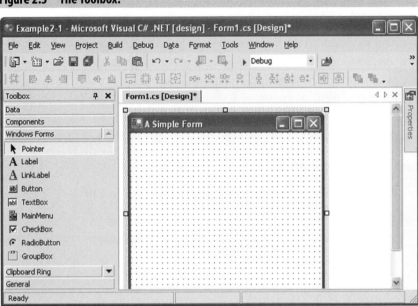

Clipboard Ring   Used to copy text

General   Used to add additional controls

In Figure 2.3, the opened Windows Forms tab shows the first of the user interface controls. Notice that the controls are not in alphabetical order, but rather are in order of expected frequency of use. The commonly used Label, LinkLabel, Button, and TextBox controls appear first. Clicking once on a control will enable it, so that clicking the mouse in the form will place that control on the form in the position of the mouse click. The Pointer option appears in every category. Clicking on it releases the mouse to function normally. We could click Pointer if we had clicked Button but changed our mind about adding a button to the form.

For our application, we will use two of most frequently used controls, TextBox and Label. A TextBox allows the user to enter text and displays it, while a Label is just for display.

2.2.2   TextBox

The TextBox control allows the user to enter text in an application. We click the mouse on the TextBox entry under the Windows Forms tab in the Toolbox, and click the mouse again at the location in the form where we want to add the text box. We can also drag the TextBox from the Toolbox to the form.

When we add the TextBox to the form or later select it by clicking on it, the Properties window shows its properties. The Properties window always shows the values of the properties for the selected control. The categories for a TextBox are Accessibility, Appearance, Behavior, Configurations, Data, Design, Focus, and Layout.

Properties may be relevant for one control and not another. For example, the Appearance category for a TextBox includes a Lines property that contains the lines of text in the text box. The Form control does not have a Lines property. The default text, textBox1, appears in the text box initially. It is the default value of the Text property. To allow the user to enter text without having to erase, we could delete the value textBox1 from the Text property field in the Properties window.

Visual Studio .NET generates default names for each control that it uses in the code it generates. It generates the name textBox1 for the TextBox that we include in Example2-1. We prefer to change the names of our controls to be more meaningful. This makes the programs easier to understand. To change the variable name, we look for the (Name) property in the Design section of the Properties window for the text box. We change the default name, textBox1, to nameEntry because the user should enter his or her name.

Note that properties refer to the control when the application is running, not while using Visual Studio .NET to design the application. For example, the Cursor property indicates the style of cursor that will appear when the user passes the mouse over the control when the application is running. The TextBox is initially configured with the IBeam cursor that looks like the letter I. This IBeam cursor will appear when the user passes the mouse over it in the running application. During the design, the cursor is either the default Arrow or the SizeAll cursor pointing in all four directions.

2.2.3 Label

Labels are often used to provide descriptive text for controls. We add a Label to the form by clicking Label in the Toolbox and then clicking at the location where we wish to place the label. Using the grid of dots, we can align the label in the same column below the text box already on the form. The default text in the label is *label1*, but we use the Text property in the

Figure 2.4   Adding a Label.

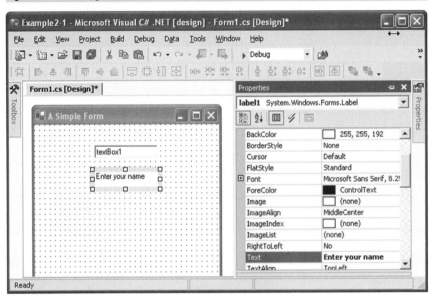

Properties window to change it to *Enter your name*. We also change the (Name) property value from label1 to display in order to make it more meaningful. Figure 2.4 shows the form so far.

2.2.4   Code for an Event

To make a complete application we ask the user to input his or her name in the text box and then display it in color in a larger font in the label. The user's action of entering a name in the text box generates an event. Visual Studio .NET generates code to register an event handler for the text box. The event handler uses a C# method. (We will discuss methods in detail later.) A method performs an operation. The operation we want to perform is to take whatever the user enters in the text box and display it larger and in color in the label.

We know that both the TextBox and the Label have a Text property. We can get and set the values of these properties in our C# code. The line

```
display.Text = nameEntry.Text;
```

will copy the text from the text box to the label. It is an example of an assignment statement that we will discuss later.

Not only does Visual Studio .NET generate code to register an event handler, it generates the outline of the method needed, and we only have to fill in the specific action we want to happen. To see the template that Visual Studio .NET provides, we double-click on the TextBox and another tab appears with the code for our application. The template is

```
private void nameEntry_TextChanged
                    (object sender, System.EventArgs e)
{

}
```

For now all we need to observe about this method is that its name, nameEntry_TextChanged, identifies it as the method that will be called automatically when the user changes the text in the nameEntry text box. This is where we want to add the line that copies the text from the text box to the label. After adding this line, the code is

```
private void nameEntry_TextChanged
                    (object sender, System.EventArgs e)
{
  display.Text = nameEntry.Text;
}
```

We terminate the line with a semicolon.

2.2.5   IntelliSense

Visual Studio .NET is very helpful when coding. The IntelliSense feature pops up a list of possible continuations of the code we are entering. For example, as soon as we type the period after display, a menu pops up that lists all the Label properties, and we can just choose Text from that menu rather than typing it. This has the advantage of saving typing and reducing spelling errors as well as of reminding us of all the possibilities in this context. A similar menu pops up after we type the period following nameEntry.

Our project now has two tabs. One is Form1.cs[Design], that shows our application window. The other is Form1.cs, that shows the C# code, most of which has been generated by Visual Studio .NET. Let's return to the design tab, because we need to set some properties for the label to make it use a larger font and display in color.

To set properties for the label we first select it by clicking on it with the mouse. Now the Properties window will display the properties for the label.

Figure 2.5   Executing the application.

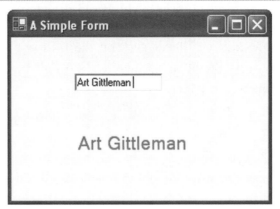

Clicking on the ForeColor property whose default is black, normally used for ControlText, pops up a color editor. We choose the Custom tab and select the second color in the third row, which is Red. Doing that changes the color of the text in the label to red.

A FontDialog window pops up when we click on the Font value in the Properties window. We change the size from 8 to 16. Making the font size larger changes the display in the label from *Enter your name* to *Enter you* because the label is not large enough to hold the original text. To fix this, we find the AutoSize property under the Behavior category in the Properties window for the label and change its value to True. This will allow the label to change its size automatically to accommodate the text we place in it.

2.2.6   Running an Application

Our application is very simple, but before going any further we want to execute it. The easiest way to execute an application is to click the *Debug, Start* menu item. This will compile the code and execute it. We could compile the code first by clicking *Build, Build Solution* and then run it by clicking *Debug, Start*. Figure 2.5 shows the application window. Notice that the label has the same indentation as the text box, because we use the grid in Visual Studio .NET to align them.

The name that the user enters appears in the label in a larger size and in red. Each character appears in the label as soon as the user enters it in the text box because the event handler responds to each entry. Another approach, which we explore later, would add a button and copy the text from the text box to the label when the user clicks the button. This alternative would allow the user to finish the entry and make any necessary corrections before the result appears in the label.

Notice that the application window in Figure 2.5 has three buttons in the upper-right corner. Clicking on the leftmost button, the minus sign, minimizes the application as an icon on the taskbar. Clicking on the middle button, the screen, maximizes the window to fill the screen. When we maximize the window, the text field and the label remain in their original locations with respect to the upper-left corner. Thus they appear in the upper-left corner of the maximized window. We will see later how to allow these positions to change when the window is maximized. Clicking on the rightmost button, the X, closes the window and terminates the execution of the application.

2.2.7 Closing the Project

We want to save this project as it stands to compare it with later extensions. We click *File, Close Solution*. A window pops up asking us whether we want to save those parts of the project that have changed. We click *Yes*. All the files pertaining to this project are located in the folder `c:\booknet\ch2\Example2-1`.

Test Your Understanding

3. Using Visual Studio .NET, find the properties in the `Appearance` category for each of the three controls, `Form`, `TextBox`, and `Label`. Which appear in one `Control` and not in one of the others?

4. What happens if you click `Label` in the `Toolbox` and then click `Pointer` before clicking in the `Form`?

5. Describe how the running Example2-1 application looks when you maximize it by clicking the middle button in the upper-right corner.

2.3 Positioning and Sizing Controls

We will use anchoring to position a control appropriately when the user resizes the form containing it. We will dock a control to an edge of the form. We can use the mouse to drag a control to a new location or to resize it. The keyboard can also be used to resize a control.

The BIG Picture

The `Toolbox` contains controls that we can drag onto a form. It groups controls by categories. The `TextBox` control allows the user to enter text in an application. Labels are often used to provide descriptive text for controls. Double-clicking on a `TextBox` displays the template for an event handler that will be called to respond when the user changes the text in the box. We enter the C# code to perform the desired action to respond to this event. We can execute the application from Visual Studio .NET.

Figure 2.6   Creating a new project.

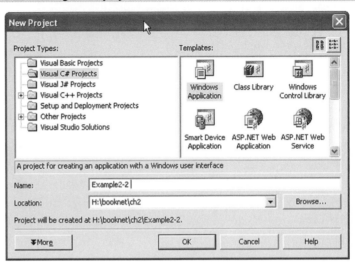

To illustrate, we start a new Visual Studio .NET project. After Visual Studio .NET opens, we click the New, Project menu item to pop up the New Project window. We choose Visual C# Projects on the left and Windows Application on the right. Then we enter *Example2-2* as the project name, as Figure 2.6 shows.

Clicking *OK* opens the design for Example2-2 with a blank form. We add a TextBox to the form. Under it we add a Label, and under the Label we add another TextBox. We align all three the same distance from the left of the form and roughly centered horizontally.

First we want to choose more meaningful names for each control and change the default display messages. (Figure 2.11 shows how the running application will look.) Because this example illustrates the different anchoring positions, we name the upper text box topText, name the label middleDisplay, and name the lower text box bottomText. To assign these names we select each control by clicking on it and changing the value of its (Name) property from the default name to the desired name. The default Text property of the form itself is Form1. This text appears in the title of the form at the top. We change the Text property of the form to *Anchor and Align*.

The default display message for a TextBox or a Label just displays its name. To prompt the user, we change the Text properties of topText and bottomText to *Enter a message*. We change the Text property of the middle-Display label to *Display here*.

Figure 2.7   Selecting a control in the Properties window.

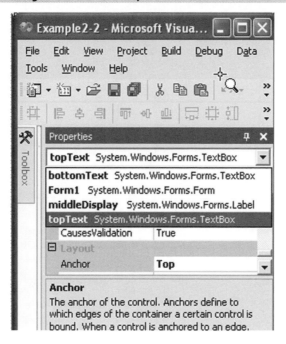

2.3.1   Anchoring

The default anchor for a control is top and left. This means that the control will maintain the same distance from the top and the left of the form as the user resizes the form. The Anchor property allows us to change this default. To balance the appearance of the form, we can anchor some controls to the top and some to the bottom, or some to the right and some to the left.

Because the default anchor is Top, Left, if we run this application and maximize the form by clicking the middle button on the upper left of the form, all three controls will appear in the top left part of the form, not centered as we originally placed them. To change the Anchor property, we find it in the Properties window toward the bottom in the Layout category.

The Properties window has a combo box at the top that allows us to select the control whose properties we wish to view. Pressing the arrow button at the right pops up all the choices, as shown in Figure 2.7. Choosing topText and clicking its Anchor value pops up a diagram with rectangles pointing up, right, down, and left, and a larger rectangle in the center, as shown in Figure 2.8. We can choose from 0 to 4 of the four outer rectangles for the Anchor

Figure 2.8   Choices for the Anchor property.

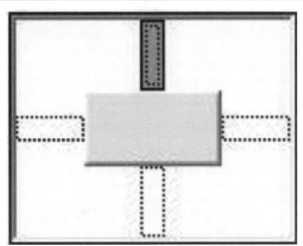

value. For topText, we select the rectangle pointing up to set its Anchor to Top. We do not use the center rectangle for a TextBox.

We set the Anchor property for middleDisplay to Left, Right by selecting both the left and right rectangles in the window similar to Figure 2.8, but for middleDisplay. This will force middleDisplay to keep the same distance from the left and right edges of the form when the form is resized. If the user maximizes the form, middleDisplay will have to expand horizontally because its distance from either edge cannot increase and the form gets much wider. Finally, we set the Anchor property of bottomText to Bottom.

2.3.2   Aligning Text

If we click *Debug, Start* to execute this application and click the middle button on the upper right to maximize the window, we see that upperText and lowerText remain in the center of the form because they are no longer anchored to the left edge. But the text *Display here* still appears near the left edge, which at first glance looks inconsistent with the new anchoring of Left, Right for middleDisplay. But we cannot see the boundaries of middleDisplay because its default color is the same as the color of the form. To see the extent of middleDisplay, we change its BackColor to pink using the color dialog that pops up in the Properties window, as shown in Figure 2.9.

Rerunning the application now shows that middleDisplay remains centered in the form, but expanded in width so that its left and right edges remain

Figure 2.9   Setting the `BackColor` property.

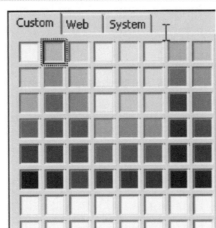

the same distance from the left and right edges of the form. The text, *Display here*, appears at the upper-left edge of `middleDisplay` because its alignment is `TopLeft`. To change the alignment we click on the value of the `TextAlign` property in the `Appearance` category in the `Properties` window, bringing up the choices shown in Figure 2.10. Selecting the center rectangle will change `TextAlign` to `MiddleCenter`. Rerunning the application again will show the text in the center of the label.

Figure 2.10   `TextAlign` choices.

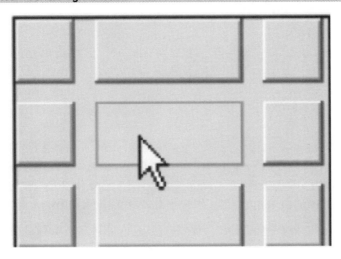

Now that we have used anchoring to position the controls, we can respond to user actions. For Example2-2, we let the user enter a message in the upper text box, which we display in middleDisplay. When the user enters a message in bottomText we copy it to topText. Whenever the text in topText changes, the event handler for topText displays the new text in middleDisplay. So as the user enters text in bottomText, it winds up being copied to both topText and middleDisplay.

Next, we need to write the event-handling code. We handle topText events just as we did in Example2-1. Double-clicking on topText brings up a code template to which we add one line, copying the text from topText to middleDisplay. As in Example2-1, the result is

```
private void topText_TextChanged
                    (object sender, System.EventArgs e)
{
  middleDisplay.Text = topText.Text;
}
```

We want to copy the text the user enters in bottomText into topText. Double-clicking on bottomText brings up the template

```
private void bottomText_TextChanged
                    (object sender, System.EventArgs e)
{

}
```

We add the line

```
topText.Text = bottomText.Text;
```

giving

```
private void bottomText_TextChanged
                    (object sender, System.EventArgs e)
{
topText.Text = bottomText.Text;
}
```

Running Example2-2 produces the application of Figure 2.11. We widen the form by placing the cursor on the right edge until the cursor changes to horizontal arrows, and then dragging the right edge to the right. The label widens to keep the same distance from the left and right edges, and the text remains centered in it. When we enter Hi there in bottomText it appears in topText and middleDisplay. Figure 2.12 shows the result.

Figure 2.11   Executing Example2-2.

Figure 2.12   Widening the form of Example2-2.

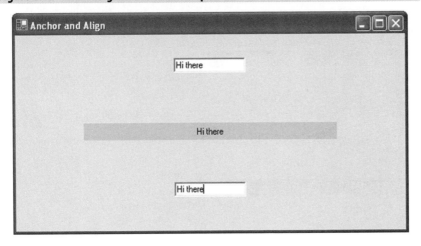

2.3.3   Docking

Docking a control attaches it to an edge of the form, or to all edges. To illustrate, in Example2-3 we will dock a TextBox to the top of the form and allow a Label to fill the rest. The width of the text box must expand to match the edge of the form. The text box will remain docked to the top edge of the form when the form is resized.

Figure 2.13   Setting the Dock property.

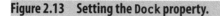

Figure 2.13   Setting the Dock property.

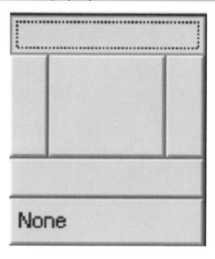

We create the Example2-3 project, add a TextBox to the form, and add a Label below the TextBox. First we choose meaningful names for the controls by using the Properties window of each control to set the following (Name) property values:

Default name	Meaningful name
textBox1	enterMessage
label1	display

We also change the Text property of each control to something more descriptive.

Default text	Descriptive text
Form1	Dock
textBox1	Enter a message
label1	Display here

To dock the enterMessage text box to the top of the form, we find the Dock property of the enterText text box in the Layout section of the Properties window. Clicking on the Dock value pops up the window shown in Figure 2.13. Selecting the top rectangle will set the Dock property for enterMessage to Top.

When setting the Dock property for the display label, we select the middle rectangle. This sets the Dock property to Fill, indicating that all four edges

Figure 2.14   Illustrating docking.

will be docked to the form and fill the remaining space. To continue config-uring display, we set BackColor to green, ForeColor to purple, and TextAlign to MiddleCenter. We click on the Font value to open a Font dialog, and we change the size to 14 and the style to Bold.

When we add code to handle the user's text entries, we not only copy the text to the label, but use the ToUpper method to change it to uppercase. The event-handling method is

```
private void enterMessage_TextChanged
              (object sender, System.EventArgs e)
{
     display.Text = enterMessage.Text.ToUpper();
}
```

The parentheses after the method name contain information we pass to the method. We do not pass any information, so we leave that position empty. We will discuss methods later in the text. Figure 2.14 shows Example2-3.

2.3.4   Moving and Sizing Controls

We do not have to place our controls in exactly the right location initially. If we click the mouse in the center of the control and hold the mouse button down, we can drag the control to a new location.

We can make the control larger or smaller using the mouse. When we select a TextBox or a Label in the form that we are designing in Visual Studio .NET, eight small squares appear around the boundary, as we saw earlier in Figure 2.4. For a TextBox, when we point the mouse over the middle square on the left or right edge, the cursor changes to a horizontal line with arrows pointing left and right. This signifies that if we press the mouse and drag the control, we can expand or contract it horizontally. None of the other squares on the selected TextBox box provide resizing starting points.

By contrast, each of the eight squares around a selected label provides a resizing starting point. Placing the cursor on the squares in the middle of the left and right sides of the label allows horizontal resizing. When we put the cursor on one of the middle squares on the top or bottom side of the label, the cursor changes to a vertical bar with an arrow pointing up or down. This signifies that we can resize the label vertically. Placing the cursor on one of the four corners changes the cursor to a diagonal bar with arrows pointing in both diagonal directions. This indicates that we can resize diagonally, changing both the vertical and horizontal dimensions of the label as we drag the mouse.

The BIG Picture

The Anchor property determines which edges of a control are anchored to the edges of its container. The TextAlign property of a Label positions its text. The Dock property specifies an edge on which to attach the control. We use the mouse to move a control or resize it.

Test Your Understanding

6. If the Anchor property of a control has the value Top, Right, what can we conclude about the distances of the control to the edges of the form?

7. What value does the Dock property have when the control attaches to all four edges of the form?

8. The Multiline property of a TextBox is False by default. How do you think changing its value to True would affect the resizing capability of that text box?

2.4   Using a Button

The applications so far have copied the text from the text box to the label character by character as the user types it. We might prefer to wait until the user has completed the entry, making any necessary corrections, before copying that text. We can do that by using a button. Only when the user clicks the button will the application copy the text from the text box to the label.

Figure 2.15   Some form properties.

We create an Example2-4 project with a text box, a label, and a button. After opening Visual Studio .NET, we click on the *File*, *New*, *Project* menu item to display the New Project window. We choose Visual C# Projects and Windows Application and then enter *Example2-4* in the Name text box. Clicking *OK* displays an empty form.

If the Toolbox is not visible we click on the View, Toolbox menu item to display it. We drag a TextBox, a Label, and a Button from the Toolbox to the form.

2.4.1   Setting Properties

Our next objective is to customize these controls by changing various property values. We start with the form itself. To display its Properties window we first select the form by clicking on it. Next we click the *View*, *Properties* menu item to display the long list of properties that we are able to modify. Figure 2.15 shows a portion of that list of properties for the form. The Text property, highlighted in Figure 2.15, has the default value Form1 that will be displayed in the title of the application. We prefer a more meaningful title, so we change that property value to *Using a Button*. As soon as we key in this new title and press the *Enter* key, the changed title appears at the top of the form.

Figure 2.16   Changing the background color.

The BackColor property specifies the color of the background of the control. For a form, the default background color is a gray, called Control in Figure 2.15. To change this color to white we click on the BackColor property, causing it to display an arrow on the right. Clicking on the arrow will display the list of colors shown in Figure 2.16. Because the System tab is showing, the list shows colors that were predefined for various features. We prefer a lighter color, so we choose ControlLightLight. We could also click on the Custom tab to display a grid of colors, from which we can choose one color to be the new background color for this form.

We follow a similar procedure to change some properties for the TextBox, Label, and Button controls. We list the changes that we made with each property name and new value.

```
TextBox
     Text      Enter a message
     Anchor    Top
     (Name)    enterMessage
Label
     BackColor  Red
     Font
     Size       14
     Text       Display here
     TextAlign  MiddleCenter
```

```
    Anchor    Left, Right
    (Name)    displayLabel
Button
    BackColor Yellow
    Text      Copy
    Anchor    Bottom
    (Name)    copyButton
```

2.4.2   Handling the Click Event

For Example2-4, we write code to handle the event generated when the user clicks the button. Double-clicking the button brings up the following template:

```
private void copyButton_Click
            (object sender, System.EventArgs e)
{

}
```

We add our usual line to copy the text giving the completed method

```
private void copyButton_Click
            (object sender, System.EventArgs e)
{
    displayLabel.Text = enterMessage.Text;
}
```

Notice that the name of this method is copyButton_Click, while the method name for the TextBox event handler of Example2-3 was enter-Message_TextChanged. These names chosen by Visual Studio .NET reflect the difference between entering text in a text box, which generates a TextChanged event, and clicking a button, which generates a Click event.

Running Example2-4 produces the form of Figure 2.17. If we enter a message in the text box and click the *Copy* button, this application will display the message in a larger font in the center label.

2.4.3   Context-Sensitive Help

We conclude this chapter by describing a useful Visual Studio .NET feature that we can use to get information about buttons or about any part of the design or code we are creating. Pressing the *F1* function key at the top of the keyboard brings up help information about the currently selected item. For example, selecting button1 in Example2-4 in the Visual Studio .NET

Figure 2.17   Using a button.

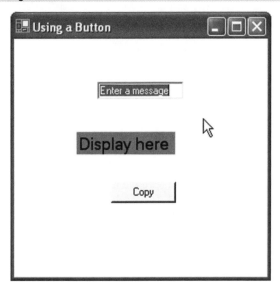

The BIG Picture

Rather than responding to an event each time the user makes a change in a TextBox, we can add a Button and only respond when the user finishes entering text and clicks the button. Pressing the *F1* key provides context-sensitive help on the selected control.

design and clicking the *F1* key brings up a full description of button members from the .NET Framework Class Library. A link near the top of that screen directs us to a button overview. We can get the same information by pressing the *F1* key when selecting *Button* in the Toolbox. We will study many other controls in later chapters. Selecting any of them and pressing the *F1* key will bring up descriptive information about that control.

Test Your Understanding

9.   How would the form of Example2-4 appear if we change the Auto-Size property of label1 to True?

10.   Is Button resizing behavior more like a TextBox or a Label? Explain.

2.5   Summary

- Visual Studio .NET opens with a Start page that we can configure in various styles. We begin by creating a Project of which there are several types. A Windows Application provides a Form in which we can create a user interface. A Properties window lists properties of the form, such as its background color, that we can customize with our choices.

- The Toolbox contains controls that we can drag onto a form. It groups controls by categories. The TextBox control allows the user to enter text in an application. Labels are often used to provide descriptive text for controls. Double-clicking on a TextBox displays the template for an event handler that will be called to respond when the user changes the text in the box. We enter the C# code to perform the desired action to respond to this event. We can execute the application from Visual Studio .NET.

- The Anchor property determines which edges of a control are anchored to the edges of its container. The TextAlign property of a Label positions its text. The Dock property specifies an edge on which we can attach the control. We use the mouse to move a control or resize it.

- Rather than responding to an event each time the user makes a change in a TextBox, we can add a Button and only respond when the user finishes entering text and clicks the button. Pressing the *F1* key provides context-sensitive help on the selected control.

2.6   Programming Exercises

2.1   Modify Example2-1 to make the background color of the form white.

2.2   Reset the Anchor of each control in Example2-2 to the default of Top, Left. Rerun the example and maximize the form that appears. Compare the positioning of the controls here with that of the original when the form is maximized.

2.3   Restore the TextAlign property of the label in Example2-2 to the default of TopLeft. Rerun the example and indicate how its appearance changes.

2.4   Change the Dock property of the Label in Example2-3 to Bottom. Rerun the example and describe how its appearance changes.

2.5   Create a Windows application that includes a TextBox, two Label controls, and two Button controls. Clicking one button will display the text in the text box in a small size in the first label. Clicking the other button will display it in a large size in the other label.

2.6   Redo Exercise 2.5 to anchor each control to a different edge of the form.

2.7 Create a Windows application that includes a TextBox, Label, and two Button controls. Clicking one button will display the textbox's contents as red in the label field. Clicking the other button will display it in blue.

2.8 Redo Exercise 2.7 so that the controls stay in the center of the form when it is maximized.

CHAPTER 3

Controls for Windows Forms

Visual Studio .NET provides many controls to build user interfaces for Windows applications. We have already used `TextBox`, `Label`, and `Button` in Chapter 2. In this chapter, we introduce radio buttons, more boxes, bars, dates, timers, menus, and dialogs.

Chapter Objectives:

Add controls to

- make selections
- add links
- add images
- choose a date or number
- time events
- make menu choices
- respond to dialogs

3.1 Using Radio Buttons and Link Labels

Several controls allow the user to make selections. Radio buttons require an exclusive choice, while check boxes allow multiple selections. We can add a larger number of selections to a list box, or, to save space, to a combo box that shows one choice and pops up others. We use a link label to display a hyperlink.

3.1.1 Radio Buttons

A `RadioButton` may display text, an image, or both. By default the radio buttons on a form comprise a group, and the user must select exactly one. This explains the name `RadioButton`. Older radios used to have buttons set to different stations. Pushing in a button would tune the radio to the preset station, releasing the previously pushed button. The selected button would remain depressed until another button was pushed. Car radio buttons work similarly, but they do not remain depressed. By using a `GroupBox` or a `Panel` we can create groups of radio buttons where exactly one button in each group must be selected.

Example3-1 contains three radio buttons, each representing a color, and a label. When the user selects a color, the text in the label changes to the selected color. The text of the label also changes to reflect the selection. We open Visual Studio .NET and click on the *File*, *New*, *Project* menu to display the `New Project` window. We select `Visual C# Projects` as the project type, select the `Windows Application` template, enter Example3-1 in the `Name` field, and click *OK*.

The design will show a blank form with the default title, `Form1`, showing at its top. We change this default to the more meaningful *Select a Color*. To make this change we select the form by clicking on it. Then we click the *View*, *Properties* menu item to display the `Properties` window. Now we can change the `Text` property.

We use the Toolbox to add controls to the form. To display the Toolbox we click the *View*, *Toolbox* menu item. To add the controls to the form, we select each from the Toolbox and drag it to the form. Figure 3.1 shows the Toolbox with the `RadioButton` control selected.

We use the `Properties` window to configure each of the three radio buttons and the label that we added to the form. Our three radio buttons will represent the colors red, green, and blue, so we will set their background colors and their text to show the user the color in two ways. To make the text more visible we will change the font style to `Bold`. As usual, we give each control a more meaningful name. Finally, we change the anchor of each radio button to `Top` to allow them to remain centered should the user maximize the form.

The list below shows the properties we configure for each radio button. It shows the values for the topmost button.

```
BackColor       Red
Font
   Bold             True
Text            Red
Anchor          Top
(Name)          redButton
```

Figure 3.1   Selecting `RadioButton`.

To see the `Font.Bold` property in the `Properties` window we click on the plus sign to the left of the `Font` property. Figure 3.2a shows part of the `Properties` window before we click on the plus sign, and Figure 3.2b shows that window after the click.

Figure 3.3 shows the form of Example3-1 after we have configured the remaining controls. The application is running and the user has selected the color red.

The list that follows shows the properties we configure for the `Label` control. The `BorderStyle` can be the default of `None`, or `FixedSingle` that frames it

Figure 3.2a   Before expanding the `Font` properties.   **Figure 3.2b   After expanding the `Font` properties.**

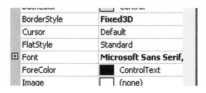

Figure 3.3   Using radio buttons.

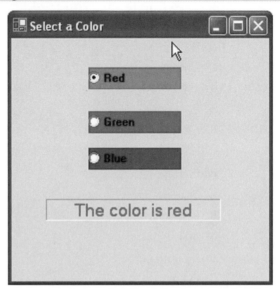

with a black rectangle, or Fixed3D that recesses it. We chose Fixed3D. The form displays the initial message in the label before the user chooses a color. It will be in the default color of black, so we set the initial message to state that the color is black. Giving the text a MiddleCenter alignment will center it in the label for a nicer appearance. Choosing Left, Right for the Anchor property will keep the label centered in the form even if the user resizes it.

```
BorderStyle       Fixed3D
Font
  Size            14
Text              The text color is black
TextAlign         MiddleCenter
Anchor            Left, Right
Name              display
```

We need to code the event handlers to make the radio buttons respond to the user's selection. When the user checks a radio button it generates a CheckedChanged event. Double-clicking the topmost radio button in Example3-1 displays the template

```
private void redRadio_CheckedChanged
                         (object sender, System.EventArgs e)
{

}
```

We add code to change the label's foreground color to the one shown in the radio button. We also change the label's text to describe the chosen color. The completed event handlers for all three radio buttons are

```
private void redRadio_CheckedChanged
                         (object sender, System.EventArgs e)
{
    display.ForeColor = Color.Red;
    display.Text = "The color is red";
}
private void greenRadio_CheckedChanged
                         (object sender, System.EventArgs e)
{
    display.ForeColor = Color.Green;
    display.Text = "The color is green";
}
private void blueRadio_CheckedChanged
                         (object sender, System.EventArgs e)
{
    display.ForeColor = Color.Blue;
    display.Text = "The color is blue";
}
```

3.1.2 Adding a Link

The LinkLabel control lets us add links to Web sites to our form. In Example3-2, we start by adding a link to a White House site giving a short biography of George Washington. Then we will enhance this application to include three radio buttons to allow the user to choose a president. When the user chooses a president, the link changes to point to the site for that president's biographical information. Clicking on the link will open an Internet Explorer window displaying the selected president's biography.

By default, radio buttons form a group. The user can only choose one radio button from the group. The final enhancement to Example3-2 will include a second group of two radio buttons to choose the border style for the LinkLabel control. Figure 3-4 shows how the application appears when running.

Figure 3.4   A form with two radio button groups and a link label.

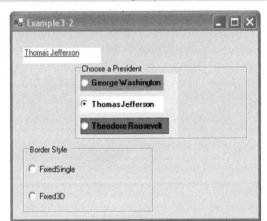

To start building Example3-2, we create a new project named Example3-2 and drag a LinkLabel control from the Toolbox to the design form. Before adding any radio buttons, we will configure the link to access a Web site for George Washington. Building an application one step at a time and testing it is much more effective than trying to build it in one big step.

We use the Text property to change the default link text, linkLabel1, to George Washington. We also change the (Name) property of the LinkLabel from linkLabel1 to presidentLink. When the user clicks on this link, we want to have Internet Explorer appear showing George Washington's biography. The user click generates a LinkClicked event. Our job as developers is to write the code to open Internet Explorer.

To start Internet Explorer, we use the Process class of the System.Diagnostics namespace. The Process class is useful for starting, stopping, controlling, and monitoring applications. We use its Start method to start the Internet Explorer browser, passing it the address of the site we seek, which is

http://www.whitehouse.gov/history/presidents/gw1.html

The code to open Internet Explorer displaying George Washington's biography is

```
System.Diagnostics.Process.Start("IEExplore",
  "http://www.whitehouse.gov/history/presidents/gw1.html");
```

Figure 3.5   Adding a link.

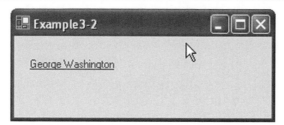

We need to place this code inside the event handler that will be called when the user clicks the `presidentLink` link label. Double-clicking the link in the Visual Studio .NET design displays the template for the event handler.

```
private void presidentLink_LinkClicked(object sender,
    System.Windows.Forms.LinkLabelLinkClickedEventArgs e)
{

}
```

We add code to open Internet Explorer, so the completed event handler becomes

```
private void presidentLink_LinkClicked(object sender,
    System.Windows.Forms.LinkLabelLinkClickedEventArgs e)
{
  System.Diagnostics.Process.Start("IEExplore",
  "http://www.whitehouse.gov/history/presidents/gw1.html");
}
```

Figure 3.5 shows the link in Example3-2. We changed the `Text` property of the form to show `Example3-2` rather than `Form1`.

3.1.3   Grouping Radio Buttons

By default, all radio buttons on a form are in one group, and the user selects one of them. We can use `GroupBox` controls to let the user choose one radio button from each group.

We add a `GroupBox` to Example3-2 to hold radio buttons that allow us to choose the president whose biography we wish to view. A `GroupBox` displays a border with the default title `groupBox1`. To make this title more meaningful, we change the `Text` property of this `GroupBox` to *Choose a President*, which describes the function of the radio buttons that we will add to it.

The user can select only one of the RadioButton controls in a GroupBox. Using the Toolbox, we add three radio buttons to this group box, one for each president: George Washington, Thomas Jefferson, and Theodore Roosevelt. We set the Text property for each radio button to a president's name and change their (Name) properties to george, tom, and teddy. Initially we have no president selected, so we change the Text property of presidentLink to *Select a president first*.

To give our form the familiar colors of the U.S. flag, we set the BackColor property of the radio buttons to Red, White, and Blue. We set Font.Bold to True for each radio button to make the text stand out more.

Because we cannot link until the user chooses a president, we use the Properties window to set the LinkBehavior property of presidentLink to NeverUnderline. The choices for LinkBehavior are

SystemDefault	Use default system underlining rules
AlwaysUnderline	Always underline
HoverUnderline	Underline when mouse hovers over the link
NeverUnderline	Never underline

Figure 3.6 shows how Example3-2 now looks when it starts.

Figure 3.6   Adding a group of radio buttons.

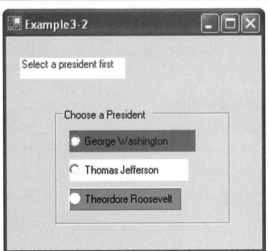

To make the links function, we need to change the approach we used when we had only one radio button. When the user selects a radio button, we want to do three things:

1. Show the president's name in the link.
2. Underline the link.
3. Associate the link with the site containing the president's biography.

Double-clicking on the George Washington radio button in the Visual Studio .NET design displays the template for the CheckedChanged event handler. We add three lines to it, resulting in the following code:

```
private void george_CheckedChanged
                    (object sender, System.EventArgs e)
{
    presidentLink.Text = "George Washington";
    presidentLink.LinkBehavior =
                    LinkBehavior.AlwaysUnderline;
    presidentLink.Links[0].LinkData =
        "http://www.whitehouse.gov/history/presidents/gw1.html";
}
```

The first line

```
presidentLink.Text = "George Washington";
```

sets the text of the link. The second statement

```
presidentLink.LinkBehavior = LinkBehavior.AlwaysUnderline;
```

sets the LinkBehavior property. Note that in the code we need to prefix the value AlwaysUnderline with its type, LinkBehavior. When we set LinkBehavior during design, Visual Studio .NET remembered this detail for us.

The third statement

```
presidentLink.Links[0].LinkData =
  "http://www.whitehouse.gov/history/presidents/gw1.html";
```

associates the site for George Washington's biography with the link. A Link-Label has a Links property that holds a collection of the links that the LinkLabel contains. A LinkLabel may contain more than one link, although we only use one in Example3-2.

The collection of links is indexed by integers starting with index 0 for the first link. To access an element of a collection using an index, we place the index in square brackets so that the Link in the presidentLink is

presidentLink.Links[0]

Each link has a LinkData property that we set to associate the George Washington site with the link.

Writing the event handlers for the other two radio buttons is just a matter of changing the president's name and the biography site. The other two event-handling methods are

```
private void tom_CheckedChanged
                    (object sender, System.EventArgs e)
{
    presidentLink.Text = "Thomas Jefferson";
    presidentLink.LinkBehavior =
        LinkBehavior.AlwaysUnderline;
    presidentLink.Links[0].LinkData =
        "http://www.whitehouse.gov/history/presidents/tj3.html";
}


private void teddy_CheckedChanged
                    (object sender, System.EventArgs e)
{
    presidentLink.Text = "Theodore Roosevelt";
    presidentLink.LinkBehavior =
                        LinkBehavior.AlwaysUnderline;
    presidentLink.Links[0].LinkData =
                "http://www.whitehouse.gov/history/presidents/tr26.html";
}
```

To make the link work, we use the event-handling code

```
private void presidentLink _LinkClicked(object sender,
  System.Windows.Forms.LinkLabelLinkClickedEventArgs e)
{
    System.Diagnostics.Process.Start
                    (e.Link.LinkData.ToString());
}
```

Because the link site depends on which radio button the user clicks, we do not want to hard code the link in this event-handling method. When .NET calls an event handler, it passes information to it about the event. For the LinkClicked event it uses an object with type LinkLabelLinkClickedEventArgs, which we refer to as e in the code. This long name identifies itself as the EventArgs of the LinkClicked event of the LinkLabel.

The object e has a Link property describing the link. The Link has a LinkData property, which in general is an object, so we use the ToString method to get the string representing the link to pass to the Start method. Because the string has the .html extension, the Start method will start Internet Explorer.

3.1.4   Adding Another Group

We add another group box, this time including two radio buttons. The radio buttons will give the user a choice of border styles for presidentLink. We set the group box Text property to Border Style, the Text of one radio button to FixedSingle, and the Text of the other to Fixed3D. We change the names of these two radio buttons to singleBorder and threeDBorder.

To make the form balance the controls when the user resizes it, we set the Anchor property of the upper GroupBox for choosing a president to Top and the Anchor of the lower GroupBox for choosing a border style to Right. Figure 3.4 shows the final version of Example3-2.

To make the added radio buttons implement the user's choice, we double-click each to display its event-handling template and add code to set the border style of linkLabel1. The event-handling code is

```
private void singleBorder_CheckedChanged
                (object sender, System.EventArgs e)
{
    presidentLink.BorderStyle = BorderStyle.FixedSingle;
}

private void threeDBorder_CheckedChanged
                (object sender, System.EventArgs e)
{
    presidentLink.BorderStyle = BorderStyle.Fixed3D;
}
```

Test Your Understanding

1. Name the event that occurs when the user checks a RadioButton.

2. Name the event that occurs when the user clicks a LinkLabel.

3. Which property of a LinkLabel do we set to specify how the link is underlined?

The BIG Picture

Exactly one RadioButton of a group can be selected. By default, all RadioButton controls belong to one group. We can use a GroupBox to create another group. The BorderStyle property specifies the type of border for a Label.

The LinkLabel control lets us add links to our form. A LinkLabel may contain more than one link. The Links property holds the collection of links. The first link is at index 0. The LinkBehavior property specifies the underline rule for the link. To start Internet Explorer we use the Process class of the System.Diagnostics namespace.

4. Which property of a `LinkLabel` holds the collection of links it contains?

5. How would the application of Example3-2 work if we just added the five radio buttons but omitted the two group boxes?

3.2   More Boxes

A `PictureBox` displays an image. We use `CheckBox` controls when the user can select zero or more items, in contrast to `RadioButton` controls that are mutually exclusive. A `ListBox` conveniently holds a list of choices. A `ComboBox` holds a list of choices but saves space by showing only one. It also allows the user to enter additional choices.

3.2.1   Picture Boxes

We can display graphics in a `PictureBox`. Example3-3, shown in Figure 3.7, includes four picture boxes. To create this application we dragged four `PictureBox` controls to the form. The user does not interact with this application. It simply illustrates the use of the `PictureBox` control.

To place an image in a `PictureBox`, we click on the `PictureBox` and display its `Properties` window. Clicking on the `Image` property lets us search for an image file to display. Three of the `PictureBox` controls use a picture, `amanda.jpg`, of the author's daughter. The other `PictureBox` uses an image of the author, `gittleman.gif`.

Figure 3.7   Using `PictureBox` controls.

The SizeMode property specifies how the image will be displayed. It has four modes of type PictureBoxSizeMode. They are:

Normal   Places the image in the upper-left corner, clipped if too large

StretchImage   Stretches or shrinks the image to fit

AutoSize   Resizes the PictureBox to the size of the image

CenterImage   Displays the image in the center if the PictureBox is larger than the image. Centers and clips the image if it is larger.

In Example3-3, the large picture on the left, of the author's daughter Amanda, uses AutoSize mode to adjust the size of the PictureBox. The upper-right PictureBox uses the Normal mode to show the same image placed in the upper-left corner and clipped to fit. The middle-right image uses the CenterImage mode to clip the center of the image to fit. The lower-left image uses the StretchImage mode that distorts the image to fit. The author felt it prudent to use his own image rather than his daughter's in this case.

The BorderStyle property lets us choose one of the three styles: None, Fixed-Single, or Fixed3D. The upper-right image has the Fixed3D border, the middle-right image has None, while the lower-right uses the FixedSingle border style.

3.2.2 Check Boxes

Using CheckBox controls, we can make multiple selections or select nothing. In Example3-4 we add four CheckBox controls and a Label. Each CheckBox names a type of food. The Label displays the result of the last change the user made. Figure 3.8 shows Example3-4 running when the user has

Figure 3.8   Illustrating check boxes.

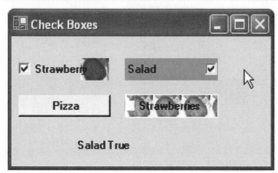

checked the upper two CheckBox controls. The user's last change was to check the *Salad* box, so the label contains the message *Salad true*. If the user next removes the *Strawberry* box check, the message will read *Strawberry false*.

Each CheckBox in Figure 3.8 has a different appearance. The Appearance property determines the form of the check box. A Normal value displays a CheckBox with a small square for the user to check or uncheck. A Button value makes the check box appear like a button. Checking it in this mode depresses it. In Example3-4 we set the Appearance property for the *Pizza* check box to Button. The other three check boxes have a Normal appearance with a square box for the user to check or uncheck.

The BackColor property lets us specify a background color for a CheckBox. As we see from Figure 3.8, we changed the BackColor property of the *Salad* check box to green and that of the *Pizza* check box to yellow.

We can set the Image property to add an image or set the BackgroundImage property to have an image cover the background. In Example3-4 we added an image of a strawberry to the *Strawberry* check box. The steps needed to add an image are:

1. Click on the View, Properties menu item to show the list of properties.
2. Click on the Image property to display a small button at the right.
3. Click on the small button to pop up a window to open a file.
4. Browse to locate the desired image, and click the *Open* button.

Setting the BackgroundImage property follows similar steps. We set the same strawberry image, a file named straw.jpg, as the Image property for the *Strawberry* check box and as the BackgroundImage for the *Strawberries* check-box. As a background image it repeats to cover the check box. As an image it appears only once.

The ImageAlign property lets us place the image at different positions within a CheckBox. The CheckAlign property functions in the same way for the position of the box that the user checks. The TextAlign property determines the placement of the text. The steps to set any of these three alignment properties are

1. Click on the View, Properties menu item to show the list of properties.
2. Click on the ImageAlign, CheckAlign, or TextAlign property to display a small button at the right.

3. Click on the small button to pop up a grid of three rows and three columns that allows us to choose the alignment position.

4. Click to choose one of the nine positions. The three vertical positions, Top, Middle, and Bottom, combine with the three horizontal positions, Left, Center, and Right, to give the nine choices.

In the *Salad* check box we changed the TextAlign property value from its default of MiddleLeft to MiddleRight. We changed the ImageAlign property to MiddleRight in the *Strawberry* check box so the image would not cover the text.

The FlatStyle property determines the flat style appearance of the square box holding the check. Its possible values are

Flat	The box appears flat.
Popup	The box appears flat until the mouse passing over makes it appear three-dimensional.
Standard	The box appears three-dimensional.
System	The appearance of the box is determined by the user's operating system.

In Example3-4 we set the FlatStyle property of the *Strawberries* check box to Popup. The others are Standard.

Figure 3.8 shows the form of Example3-4. Each time the user selects a CheckBox, the name of the food appears in the label followed by the word True. When the user deselects a CheckBox, the name of the food appears followed by False. Only the last change appears in the label. We set the Anchor property of each control to Top to allow the controls to adjust during resizing.

Selecting or deselecting a CheckBox generates a CheckChanged event. If we want an immediate response to a selection or deselection, we write an event handler for the CheckChanged event. Another approach would be to use a button to generate an event and get the state of each check box in the button's event handler. We can determine whether the user checked the box by getting the Checked property.

In Example3-4 we handle each CheckedChanged event. Double-clicking on a check box in the Visual Studio .NET design displays the template shown in Figure 3.9.

We add a line to the event handler to set the text of the label to show the current status of the check box after it has just been checked. In that line of

Figure 3.9   The CheckedChanged event-handling template.

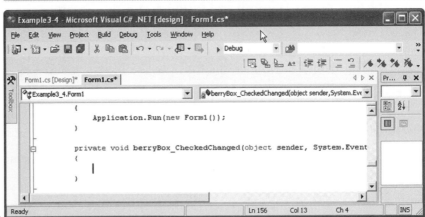

code, we concatenate the status of the check box to the food name using the + operator. Similarly, we click on each of the other three check boxes to display the event-handling template and add a line of code to each. The code for the event handlers is

```
private void berryBox_CheckedChanged
                  (object sender, System.EventArgs e)
{
    display.Text = "Strawberry " + berryBox.Checked;
}

private void pizzaBox_CheckedChanged
                  (object sender, System.EventArgs e)
{
    display.Text = "Pizza " + pizzaBox.Checked;
}

private void saladBox_CheckedChanged
                  (object sender, System.EventArgs e)
{
    display.Text = "Salad " + saladBox.Checked;
}

private void berriesBox_CheckedChanged
                  (object sender, System.EventArgs e)
{
```

```
        display.Text = "Strawberries " + berriesBox.Checked;
}
```

To summarize, we set the following properties for the controls in Example3-4.

berry

Image	straw.jpg
ImageAlign	MiddleRight
Text	Strawberry
Anchor	Top
Font	
Bold	True
(Name)	berry

pizza

Appearance	Button
BackColor	Yellow
Text	Pizza
TextAlign	MiddleCenter
Anchor	Top
Font	
Bold	True
(Name)	pizza

salad

BackColor	0, 192, 0
CheckAlign	MiddleRight
Text	Salad
Anchor	Top
Font	
Bold	True
(Name)	salad

berries

BackgroundImage	straw.jpg
FlatStyle	Popup

Figure 3.10   Selecting an item in a list box.

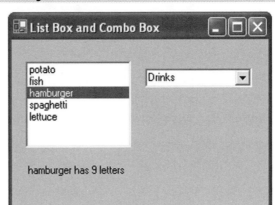

Text	Strawberries
Anchor	Top
Font	
Bold	True
(Name)	berries
display	
Text	Choose some food
AutoSize	True
Anchor	Top
(Name)	display

3.2.3   List Boxes

The ListBox control lets us display items that the user can select by clicking. Until we cover more C#, we will select just a single item, leaving the selection of multiple items until later. Figure 3.10 shows the form of Example3-5 containing a ListBox on the left with a Label below it and a ComboBox on the right. The list box lists foods. When the user selects a food, the label displays the number of letters in the word selected.

We change the (Name) property for these controls to choose the more meaningful names foodList, drinksCombo, and display.

We use the Properties window of Visual Studio .NET to enter the list items. Selecting the Items property in the Display section displays a button. Click-

Figure 3.11   Inserting items in a list box.

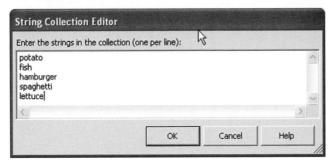

ing the button pops up the window shown in Figure 3.11 that allows us to add the list items. We add five food names. We set the Anchor property to Top to allow the list box to adjust its position during resizing. The default value of the Sorted property is False. By changing it to True we could display the list items in alphabetical order.

The default setting of BorderStyle is Fixed3D. Figure 3.10 shows the recessed implementation of the list box. The default SelectionMode value is One, meaning that the user can select only one item at a time. The SelectionMode property has four possible values:

None	No items can be selected.
One	One item can be selected.
MultiSimple	Multiple items can be selected.
MultiExtended	Multiple items can be selected, and the user can use the shift, control, and arrow keys to make the selection.

Selecting a list item generates a SelectedIndexChanged event. The index is the value by which we refer to a list item. We number the items starting with 0 at the top, so the items in listBox1 have indices 0 through 4. When the user selects an item, it changes the selected index to the index of the new selection.

To respond to the SelectedIndexChanged event, we need to write an event handler for it. Double-clicking on foodList in the Visual Studio .NET design displays the template

```
private void foodList_SelectedIndexChanged
                    (object sender, System.EventArgs e)
{
}
```

for the event-handling method.

The `SelectedItem` property of a `ListBox` refers to the selected item. To represent the item as a string we call the `ToString` method. Thus the expression

```
foodList.SelectedItem.ToString()
```

is a string representing the selected food. The `Length` property of this string represents the number of characters in the string as an integer. Again we call the `ToString` method to represent this length as a string. The expression

```
foodList.SelectedItem.ToString().Length.ToString()
```

is long, but it simply displays the number of characters in the selected word. For example, if the user selects *spaghetti*, the above expression will display 9.

Figure 3.10 displays the message *hamburger has 9 letters*. We build this expression in four parts:

hamburger   the selected item

has

9   the length of the selected word

letters

No matter which word the user selects, the second and fourth parts of the message will be the same. But parts one and three depend on what the user selects. We use C# expressions to represent the parts that change, so in C# the four parts are

```
foodList.SelectedItem.ToString()
" has "
foodList.SelectedItem.ToString().Length.ToString()
" letters "
```

Notice that we surround the words that do not change with blanks; otherwise the message would appear as *hamburgerhas9letters*, which is not what we want.

To complete the code for the event handler, we concatenate the four parts together to form the message and set the `Text` of the `display` label to this message. The + operator concatenates strings one after the other. The completed code is

```
private void foodList_SelectedIndexChanged
                (object sender, System.EventArgs e)
{
```

Figure 3.12   Choices in a combo box.

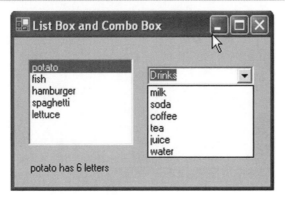

```
display.Text = foodList.SelectedItem.ToString()
             + " has "
             + foodList.SelectedItem.ToString().Length.ToString()
             + " letters";
}
```

3.2.4   Combo Boxes

Figure 3.10 shows a ComboBox on the right side of the form. Like a ListBox, the ComboBox holds choices. But in the default format shown it takes up less space than a ListBox because the choices are hidden. Clicking the button at the right of that combo box pops up the list of items shown in Figure 3.12. The user may be able to edit the text showing in the combo box.

When the user selects a drink from the combo box, the name of the drink selected appears in the combo box text and the label shows the food and drink selected. Figure 3.13 shows this result. We set the Text property of the label to *Select a food first*, because when the user selects a drink we include the selected food in the message displayed.

The DropDownStyle property determines the style of ComboBox to display. The three ComboBoxStyle values are

DropDown	The user clicks the arrow button to display the choices and can edit the text that shows.
DropDownList	The user clicks the arrow button to display the choices and cannot edit the text that shows.

Figure 3.13   Selecting milk.

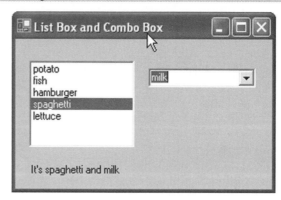

The **BIG** Picture

A PictureBox displays an image in one of four modes. Using CheckBox controls, we can make multiple selections or select nothing. We set the Appearance, Back-Color, Background-Image, CheckAlign, FlatStyle, Image, ImageAlign, and Text-Align properties to configure a CheckBox.

A ListBox conveniently holds a list of choices. A ComboBox holds a list of choices but saves space by showing only one. We use the Items, Anchor, Selec-tionMode, and Sorted properties to configure a ListBox. The Drop-DownStyle property determines the style of a ComboBox.

Simple   The choices are always visible, and the user can edit the text portion.

As with the ListBox, we entered the choices by clicking on the Items property in the Data section of the Properties window in Visual Studio .NET. We set the Text property to Drinks and the Anchor property to Top.

Test Your Understanding

6. Which PictureBoxSizeMode value changes the size of the PictureBox?

7. Explain the effect of each of the different values for the Appearance property of a CheckBox.

8. Explain the difference between the Image and the BackgroundImage properties for a CheckBox.

9. Which event will the user generate when making a selection in a ListBox?

10. Which ComboBoxStyle displays all the choices?

3.3   Keeping Track

Various controls help us keep track of dates, time, and numbers. We create a simple example to illustrate the DateTimePicker, NumericUpDown, StatusBar, and Timer controls. After covering more C# constructs in later chapters, we will be able to complete more substantial projects. Figure 3.14 shows the form of Example3-6. When the user presses the Show button, the application

Figure 3.14   The application of Example3-6.

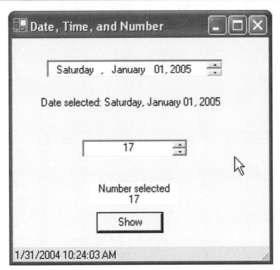

displays the date selected in one label and the number selected in another label. The current date and time appear in the status bar in the lower-left corner. Watching the application run will show that the time in the status bar updates every second. The background colors of the middle controls switch every second, giving a flashing effect.

To create Example3-6, we drag several controls from the Toolbox to the form. From the top down in Figure 3.14, these controls are: DateTimePicker, Label, NumericUpDown, Label, Button, and StatusBar. We also drag a Timer control that does not appear on the form.

3.3.1 DateTimePicker

The topmost control in Figure 3.14 is a DateTimePicker. It allows the user to select a date and time and to display it in a specific format. We choose the format by setting the Format property to one of the following four values:

Custom   Displays using a custom format.
Long   Uses the long date format set by the user's operating system.
Short   Uses the short date format set by the user's operating system.
Time   Uses the time format set by the user's operating system.

For the author's Windows XP system configured for the United States, English-speaking locale, the displays are

Long	Tuesday, January 28, 2003
Short	1/28/03
Time	10:32:56 AM

To use a custom format, we could set the `CustomFormat` property using a pattern for a custom `DateTime` string. We do not cover custom formats in this text.

By default the `MinDate` property has the value 1/1/1753 and `MaxDate` has the value 12/31/9998. Great Britain and the embryonic United States adopted the Gregorian calendar in 1752, so its first full year was 1753. The maximum date seems to allow a year to solve the Y10K problem of changing to allow five digits for a year instead of four.

The `ShowUpDown` property controls whether up-down buttons are used to modify dates rather than a drop-down calendar. In Figure 3.14, `ShowUpDown` is `True`. Clicking on January and pressing the up arrow will change the month to February. Clicking on day 28 and then the down arrow will change the day to 27. The user can similarly change the year. When one value changes, the others adjust in accordance.

When the `ShowUpDown` value is `False`, a single button shows at the right, and clicking on it pops up a calendar for that month as shown in Figure 3.15. There is also a `MonthCalendar` control that displays a calendar for the month, like the one shown in Figure 3.15. We do not use `MonthCalendar` in Example3-6.

Figure 3.15   Popping up a monthly calendar.

3.3.2   NumericUpDown

We can use a `NumericUpDown` control to specify a number. The user can change the value of the number in a `NumericUpDown` control by clicking the up or down buttons it contains. The `Minimum` value by default is 0 and the `Maximum` is 100. The default `Increment` on each button click is 1, representing the amount to increment when clicking the up button or decrement when clicking the down button.

The `DecimalPlaces` property starts with a default value of 0, representing the number of places to show following the decimal. If the `ThousandsSeparator` property is `False`, the digits will not be grouped in threes. The `Value` displayed in a `NumericUpDown` is a `Decimal` type that we will discuss later.

3.3.3   Enabling the Display

We use a `DateTimePicker` to allow the user to select a date, and a `NumericUpDown` to allow the user to select a number. For now we just display each of the selected values in a label when the user clicks the *Show* button. We need to write the event handler for the button's `Click` event. Clicking on the button in the design form displays the code template

```
private void showButton_Click
                (object sender, System.EventArgs e)
{
}
```

The event-handling code should copy the value from the `DateTimePicker` named `date` to the `Label` control under it named `dateDisplay`. The `Value` property of a `DateTimePicker` holds the date that the user selected. The `ToLongDateString` method will convert this value to a date in the `Long` format described above. The line of code we need to add is

```
dateDisplay.Text =
        "Date selected: " + date.Value.ToLongDateString();
```

The event-handling code for the `Show` button should also copy the number selected using the `NumericUpDown` control named `number` to the `Label` below it named `numberDisplay`. The `Value` property of the `NumericUpDown` control holds the number the user selected. The `ToString` method will convert that number to a string for display. Thus, the line of code we need to add to the event handler is

```
numberDisplay.Text =
   "Number selected " + number.Value.ToString();
```

The completed event-handling code for the Show button is

```
private void showButton_Click
                    (object sender, System.EventArgs e)
{
    dateDisplay.Text =
       "Date selected: " + date.Value.ToLongDateString();
    numberDisplay.Text =
       "Number selected " + number.Value.ToString();
}
```

3.3.4   StatusBar

A StatusBar displays text. By default, it is docked to the bottom of the form so that it remains there during resizing. We set the initial value of the Text property to the empty string, but the timer introduced next will copy the current time every second. Thus the status bar functions like a digital clock showing both the date and the time.

3.3.5   Timer

A Timer generates a Tick event at a set interval, say, every second. It does not have a visual representation in the form of Example3-6 shown in Figure 3.14. The Visual Studio .NET design shows it below the form as shown in Figure 3.16.

We set the Interval property to 1000 milliseconds, or one second, to specify the frequency of the Tick event. When the tick event occurs we want to show the current time in a StatusBar at the bottom of the form. We also want to change the background colors of the two Label controls and the

Figure 3.16   Adding a Timer to the form.

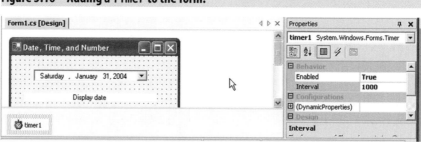

NumericUpDown to create a flashing effect. Double-clicking on the Timer control displays the event-handling template.

```
private void timer1_Tick(object sender, System.EventArgs e)
{
}
```

First we update the time in the StatusBar that we named currentDateTime.
The Now property of the DateTime type gives the current time. We call the
ToString method to get a string representation that we copy to the Text
property of the StatusBar. The first line of code we add to the event-handling method for the Timer is

```
currentDateTime.Text = DateTime.Now.ToString();
```

Next we want to use the Timer to change the background colors of three
controls every second. In Figure 3.14 we see that the dateDisplay control has
a yellow background while the number and numberDisplay controls have white
backgrounds. The code

```
number.BackColor = dateDisplay.BackColor;
dateDisplay.BackColor = numberDisplay.BackColor;
numberDisplay.BackColor = number.BackColor;
```

will change the dateDisplay to white and the number and numberDisplay controls to yellow. The next time it is executed it will revert the controls back to
their original colors. Running this code every second will flash back and
forth between these two patterns. Thus we insert this code into the event
handler for the Timer control that will be executed every second. The completed Tick event-handling code is

```
private void timer1_Tick(object sender, System.EventArgs e)
{
    currentDateTime.Text = DateTime.Now.ToString();
    number.BackColor = dateDisplay.BackColor;
    dateDisplay.BackColor = numberDisplay.BackColor;
    numberDisplay.BackColor = number.BackColor;
}
```

Test Your Understanding

11. Which control used in Example3-6 does not have a visual repre-
     sentation on the form?

12. Which property controls whether a DateTimePicker will provide a
     drop-down calendar?

The BIG Picture

A DateTimePicker
allows the user to select a
date and time and to dis-
play it in a specific format.
A NumericUpDown rep-
resents a Windows up-
down control that displays
numeric values. A Timer
generates a Tick event
at a set interval, say, every
second. A StatusBar
displays text.

13. How would you configure a NumericUpDown to allow values such as prices, which have two places after the decimal point?

14. What Interval should a Timer use to generate a Tick event four times per second?

3.4   Menus and Dialogs

Menus are a standard feature of useful software. Fortunately, the MainMenu control makes it easy to add menus to our applications. Dialogs are another friendly way to allow the user to make selections that are more involved than checking a box or clicking a list item. We illustrate the OpenFileDialog, SaveFileDialog, PrintDialog, ColorDialog, and FontDialog in this section. The RichTextBox and PrintDocument controls help us to implement Example3-7.

3.4.1   MainMenu

The MainMenu control contains the menu structure for the form. Figure 3.17 shows the start of Example3-7. Using the Toolbox, we added a MainMenu control to the form. The MainMenu does not itself appear on the form, so it is shown underneath it. A box appears in the upper-left corner of the form with the caption *Type Here*, indicating the place for us to enter our desired menu choices.

The menu structure we want will have two menus showing at the top of the form, a File menu and a Format menu. These two menus are at the upper

Figure 3.17   Adding a main menu.

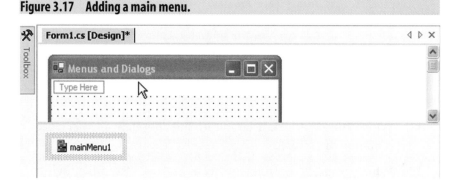

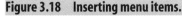

Figure 3.18   Inserting menu items.

left, as shown later in Figure 3.19. When the user clicks on the File menu we want to pop up the menu items

```
Open  Ctrl+O
Save  Ctrl+S
Print
```

The Ctrl+O indicates a keyboard shortcut. Typing the O key while holding down the Ctrl key will also activate the open file dialog. When the user clicks the Format menu, we want to pop up the choices

```
Font
Color ▶
```

The arrow indicates that Clicking on the Color menu will display additional choices, in this case,

```
Foreground
Background
```

To create this menu structure, we start by entering File as the first menu name. This brings up a box to the right of it to start a second menu on the main menu bar, and a box below to add a menu item for the File menu. Figure 3.18 shows the design at this stage.

We add Open, Save, and Print as the menu items under the File menu. To the right of the File menu item we add a Format menu. Under the Format menu we add Font and Color menu items. To the right of the Color menu we add the Foreground menu item, under which we add Background.

The Shortcut property allows us to associate a keyboard shortcut with each menu item. Clicking on Shortcut in the Properties window for the Open menu item and then clicking on the button in the field for the Shortcut value displays a list of choices for the keystrokes to operate the menu. We select CtrlO for the Open menu item and CtrlS for the Save menu item. To begin to open a file, we can either click the Open menu item or press the O key while pressing the Ctrl key. When we click on File to see its menu items, we see that the Open menu item appears as

Open   Ctrl+O

to remind the user of the shortcut.

Clicking on a menu item generates a Click event. We need to handle this Click event to make the menu item perform its intended function. Double-clicking on a menu item in the Visual Studio .NET design will display a template for the Click event handler. We will implement event handlers for the following menu items listed with their intended behavior. We will implement each event handler after describing the controls that it uses.

Open	Select a file and copy it to a rich text box.
Save	Select a file path and save the contents of the rich text box to that location.
Print	Choose print options and display a message that the printer is busy.
Font	Select a font and change the rich text box to use it for its text.
Foreground	Choose a color and make it the foreground color of the rich text box.
Background	Choose a color and make it the background color of the rich text box.

3.4.2   RichTextBox

The RichTextBox control allows the user to enter and edit text and provides advanced formatting capabilities. We use the Toolbox to select a RichTextBox control and add it to our form, stretching it to be as wide as possible and reducing the height of the form to fit. We will not add any other visible controls to the form, so we do not need any extra space. The File and Format menu items appear at the upper left of the form of Example3-7 shown in Figure 3.19.

Figure 3.19   The form of Example3-7.

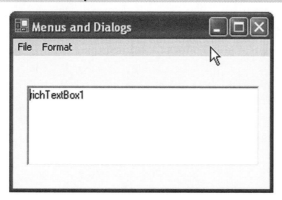

To allow richTextBox1 to expand as the user resizes the form, we set the value of the Anchor property to Top, Bottom, Left, Right. We change the value of the WordWrap property to False to avoid clumsy line breaks.

Vertical and horizontal scroll bars will automatically be added to a rich text box when necessary to view the text. The ScrollBars property enables this behavior with the default setting of Both. The choices for the Rich-TextBoxScrollBars value of the ScrollBars property are

None	No scroll bars
Horizontal	Horizontal when needed, but no vertical
Vertical	Vertical when needed, but no horizontal
Both	Both when needed
ForcedHorizontal	Always horizontal but no vertical
ForcedVertical	Always vertical but no horizontal
ForcedBoth	Always both

The RichTextBox control has a LoadFile method to load text from a file and a SaveFile method to save its text to a file. We will activate these methods from a menu via dialogs that we will introduce next. To use these methods we need to know the file name to load or save. The dialogs will allow us to choose these file names. We need to know the type of file, too. For our application we will use the PlainText type that includes simple text files without special formatting.

Figure 3.20   Selecting a file to open.

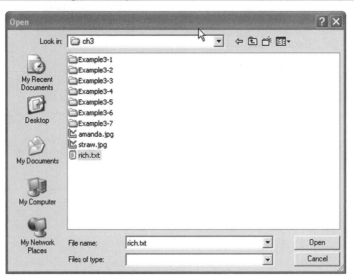

3.4.3   File Dialogs

The OpenFileDialog and SaveFileDialog controls do not visually appear in the form, so when we add them to the design they appear below it as we saw with the MainMenu control. Each has a ShowDialog method that pops up a window allowing the user to select a file to open or save to. Figure 3.20 shows that the user selected rich.txt as the file to open. Pressing the Open button will set the FileName property to the name that the user selected.

We want the event handler for the Click event, generated when the user clicks the Open menu item, to show the open file dialog and then load the selected file into richTextBox1. To write the event handler for the Click event, we first double-click the Open menu item in the Visual Studio .NET design to display the template. The code uses the meaningful names we gave the controls, openMenu for the Open menu item, openDialog for the Open-FileDialog, and displayBox for the RichTextBox. The completed event-handling template is

```
private void openMenu_Click
                (object sender, System.EventArgs e)
{
    openDialog.ShowDialog();
    displayBox.LoadFile(openDialog.FileName,
```

Figure 3.21   Displaying a file.

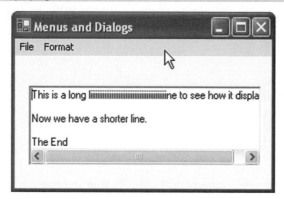

```
                RichTextBoxStreamType.PlainText);
}
```

The first line of code we wrote shows the dialog of Figure 3.20. The second line loads the file whose name the dialog saves in the FileName property. Following the LoadFile method name are the two pieces of information Load-File needs. These are called *arguments*. We will discuss methods and their arguments more fully later. We enclose method arguments in parentheses and separate them with commas. The first argument

openDialog.FileName

is the name of the file to load, and the second

RichTextBoxStreamType.PlainText

is the type of data it contains.

To illustrate loading a file, we use the simple rich.txt file shown being selected in Figure 3.20. Figure 3.21 shows how the form looks after the user clicks the Open button in Figure 3.20.

We can edit the text in displayBox. Figure 3.22 shows the form of Example3-7 after the user added a line and resized the form to make it wider.

When the user clicks on File and then on Save, it will generate a Click event, which we can handle to show a SaveFileDialog and save the edited text to the file name indicated by the user. The event handler for this Click event whose template we filled in using Visual Studio .NET is

```
private void saveMenu_Click
                (object sender, System.EventArgs e)
```

Figure 3.22   Editing the text.

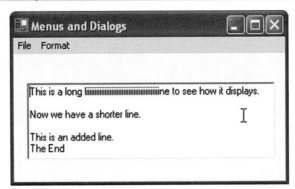

Figure 3.23   Saving a file.

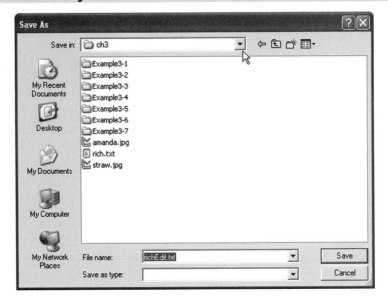

```
{
    saveDialog.ShowDialog();
    displayBox.SaveFile(saveDialog.FileName,
                RichTextBoxStreamType.PlainText);
}
```

The first line

```
saveDialog.ShowDialog();
```

shows the SaveFileDialog of Figure 3.23. In order not to overwrite the original file, the user has entered another name, richEdit.txt, under which the edited file can be saved. When the user clicks the Save button, this name will be set as the FileName property of saveDialog.

The second line

```
displayBox.SaveFile(saveDialog.FileName,
                    RichTextBoxStreamType.PlainText);
```

saves the text in displayBox using the name just chosen by the user. The first argument to the SaveFile method is the file name, and the second argument is its type, PlainText.

3.4.4   A Print Dialog

The PrintDialog control allows a user to configure a print job by selecting the printer, the number of copies, and the pages to print. Clicking on the Print menu item generates a Click event. To print, we would need to write C# code to write each line of text. We defer implementing printing until we cover more C# constructs. Even though we will defer printing, we need to add a PrintDocument control to allow for configuration of the print job later. The PrintDocument control does not appear on the form, but shows below it in the design along with the menu and dialog controls. In Example3-7, when the user clicks the Print menu item we simply display a message that the printer is busy. The event-handling method is

```
private void printMenu_Click
                    (object sender, System.EventArgs e)
{
    printDialog.Document = printDocument;
    printDialog.ShowDialog();
    displayBox.Text = "Printer busy \n Try later";
}
```

The first line of the event handler sets the Document property of printDialog to the PrintDocument, printDocument, that we will use later to configure the job. The second line shows the dialog to the user. We are not ready to use the printer selection that the user makes, so the third line will just display a message in displayBox.

3.4.5   A Color Dialog

A ColorDialog control lets the user choose a color from a palette. Figure 3.24 shows the color dialog that appears when the user clicks the Format menu, then the Color menu item, and finally the Foreground menu item. We will

Figure 3.24   A color dialog.

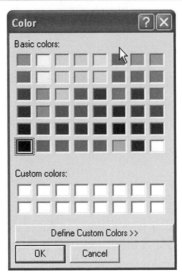

write the event handler so that when the user selects a color in the dialog, the foreground color of the text in displayBox displays in that color.

During the design we added the ColorDialog by dragging it from the Toolbox to the form. It appears below the form in the design window because this control has no visual representation on the form. Double-clicking on the Foreground menu item displays the template for the event-handling method that we complete to give

```
private void foregroundMenu_Click
                (object sender, System.EventArgs e)
{
    colorDialog.ShowDialog();
    displayBox.ForeColor =colorDialog.Color;
}
```

The first line shows the color dialog, and the second sets the ForeColor property of displayBox to the Color selected by the user.

Similarly, we can handle a click of the Background menu item to change the background color of displayBox to the color selected by the user. The event-handling code is

```
private void backgroundMenu_Click
                (object sender, System.EventArgs e)
```

Figure 3.25   A font dialog.

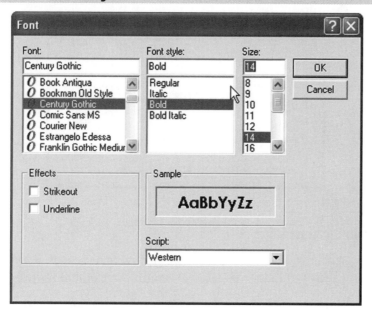

```
{
    colorDialog.ShowDialog();
    displayBox.BackColor = colorDialog.Color;
}
```

3.4.6 A Font Dialog

When the user clicks the Font menu item, we will show a font dialog to enable the user to select a font and change the font used in displayBox to that selected by the user. When building Example3-7 using Visual Studio .NET, we drag a FontDialog control from the Toolbox to the form. It appears below the form. Double-clicking on the Font menu item displays the template for the event-handling code that we complete to give the code

```
private void fontMenu_Click
                (object sender, System.EventArgs e)
{
    fontDialog.ShowDialog();
    displayBox.Font = fontDialog.Font;
}
```

Figure 3.25 shows the font dialog, and Figure 3.26 shows the result of the user's selection.

The BIG Picture

The MainMenu control represents the menu structure for the form. We can easily add menus with menu items in the Visual Studio .NET design. The RichTextBox control allows the user to enter and edit text and provides advanced formatting capabilities. An Open-FileDialog allows the user to choose a file to open, and SaveFile-Dialog lets the user save a file. Each has a Show-Dialog method. A PrintDialog allows the user to select a printer and choose which portions of the document to print. A ColorDialog control lets the user choose a color from a palette. A FontDialog lets the user choose a font.

Figure 3.26   Changing the font and colors.

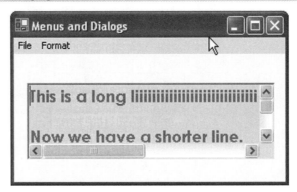

Test Your Understanding

15. Explain how to use the keyboard instead of a menu to begin saving the text in the RichTextField control of Example3-7 to a file.

16. Which controls do we use in Example3-7 that do not have a visual representation on the form?

17. Which OpenFileDialog property holds the file name selected by the user in the dialog?

18. What event does a user generate by clicking on a menu item?

19. What is the name of the C# method that pops up a dialog?

3.5   Summary

- Exactly one RadioButton of a group can be selected. By default, all RadioButton controls belong to one group. We can use a GroupBox to create another group. The BorderStyle property specifies the type of border for a Label.

- The LinkLabel control lets us add links to our form. A LinkLabel may contain more than one link. The Links property holds the collection of links. The first link is at index 0. The LinkBehavior property specifies the underline rule for the link. To start Internet Explorer, we use the Process class of the System.Diagnostics namespace.

- A `PictureBox` displays an image in one of four modes. Using `Check-Box` controls, we can make multiple selections or select nothing. We set the `Appearance`, `BackColor`, `BackgroundImage`, `CheckAlign`, `FlatStyle`, `Image`, `ImageAlign`, and `TextAlign` properties to configure a `CheckBox`.

- A `ListBox` conveniently holds a list of choices. A `ComboBox` holds a list of choices but saves space by showing only one. We use the `Items`, `Anchor`, `SelectionMode`, and `Sorted` properties to configure a `ListBox`. The `DropDownStyle` property determines the style of a `ComboBox`.

- A `DateTimePicker` allows the user to select a date and time and to display it in a specific format. A `NumericUpDown` represents a Windows up-down control that displays numeric values. A `Timer` generates a `Tick` event at a set interval, say, every second. A `StatusBar` displays text.

- The `MainMenu` control represents the menu structure for the form. We can easily add menus with menu items in the Visual Studio .NET design. The `RichTextBox` control allows the user to enter and edit text and provides advanced formatting capabilities. An `OpenFileDialog` allows the user to choose a file to open, and `SaveFileDialog` lets the user save a file. Each has a `ShowDialog` method. A `PrintDialog` allows the user to select a printer and choose which portions of the document to print. A `ColorDialog` control lets the user choose a color from a palette. A `FontDialog` lets the user choose a font.

3.6   Programming Exercises

3.1   Modify Example3-1 so the `Label` is surrounded by a black rectangle and the text is in italics.

3.2   Modify Example3-2 to choose a college. Pick three colleges to include in the choices.

3.3   Modify Example3-4 so that all four `CheckBox` controls look like buttons.

3.4   Modify Example3-5 so that the `ComboBox` shows all choices.

3.5   Modify Example3-6 so that the `DateTimePicker` works as shown in Figure 3.15.

3.6   Create a Windows application that includes two `CheckBox` and two `PictureBox` controls. Checking one box will display a photo of the author's daughter in a `PictureBox` on the left of the form. Checking the other will display a photo of the author on the right of the form.

3.7 Create a Windows application that includes radio buttons for the user to select either a small or a large size. Include a text box for the user to enter a message and two labels to display the message. Display the message in the first label if the selected size is small and in the second if it is large.

3.8 Create a Windows application that includes a `RichTextBox` and a `StatusBar`. Display the length of the text in the status bar.

3.9 Create a Windows application that includes a `DateTimePicker`, a `Label`, and a `MainMenu` including `Color` and `Font` menu items. Display the date that the user selects in the label. Display the label text in the color and font that the user selects.

3.10 Create a Windows application that includes a `Timer` and a `Label`. Display the current time in the label each second. Make the size large.

3.11 Create a Windows application that includes an *Open* button, a *Save* button, and a `RichTextBox`. When the user clicks the *Open* button, pop up an `OpenFileDialog` and display the file that the user selects in the `RichTextBox`. When the user clicks the *Save* button, pop up a `SaveFileDialog`, and save the file in the `RichTextBox` using the file name that the user selects.

CHAPTER 4

Variables and Types

We have introduced a variety of forms using Visual Studio .NET. In the next few chapters we cover some essential C# that will enable us to develop more interesting applications. In this chapter we discuss variables, types, and expressions.

Chapter Objectives:

- Learn how to construct names and expressions
- Work with useful types of data, including formatting
- Use variables and assignments

4.1   Variables and the Assignment Operator

Variables help us store data for later use in a program. The assignment operator gives a variable a value. First we need to learn the rules for naming variables and other entities.

4.1.1   Identifiers

An identifier names program elements. The identifier age names an integer variable. These identifiers can include both uppercase and lowercase characters. C# is case-sensitive, so identifiers age, Age, and AGE are all different even though they each use the same three letters of the alphabet in the same order. Good C# style starts variables with a lowercase letter.

Digits occur in identifiers but cannot be the first character. Starting an identifier with a digit would confuse it with numbers. Identifiers may also use the underscore character and even start with it. For example, _hat, hat_box, and My_____my are all valid identifiers.

We use underscores or uppercase letters to make identifiers easier to read. For example, use a_big_car or aBigCar rather than abigcar. Preferred style uses meaningful names such as age rather than arbitrary names such as xyz.

4.1.2   Keywords

Keywords are identifiers that are reserved for special uses. The event-handling templates we used in Chapter 3 started with the two keywords `private` and `void`. Because these are keywords, they cannot be user-defined names. We include the complete list of C# keywords in Appendix A.

Some valid C# identifiers are:

```
savings
textLabel
rest_stop_12
B3
_test
My____my
```

Some invalid identifiers are:

`4you`	// Starts with a number
`x<y`	// Includes an illegal character, <
`top-gun`	// Includes an illegal character, -
`int`	// Reserved keyword

4.1.3   The Character Set

The character set defines the characters that we can use in a program. The ASCII (pronounced as'-key) character set contains 128 printing and non-printing characters shown in Appendix C. The ASCII characters include uppercase and lowercase letters, digits, and punctuation. For worldwide use, a programming language must have a much bigger character set to include the many characters of the various major languages. C# uses the Unicode character set that contains thousands of characters, including all of the ASCII characters. For example, Unicode includes the Greek letter gamma, Γ. We will use only the ASCII characters in this book.

4.1.4   Variables

A variable represents a storage location. Every variable has a name and a type that determines what kind of data it holds. We must declare every variable before we use it. A variable declaration states its name and type, and may provide an initial value. For example,

```
int age;
```

declares a variable whose name is `age` and whose type is `int`. We will discuss types in the next section, where we will see that the type `int` denotes integer values.

The variable `age` represents a memory location. Figure 4.1 shows the effect of this declaration. The box signifies a location in the computer's memory. The question marks signify that we do not know the contents of that memory location. The C# compiler checks that a variable has a value before it is used.

Figure 4.1 Memory location for the age variable.

age   ???

We can initialize a variable with a value in a declaration. For example, the declaration

```
int age = 19;
```

declares the variable age and initializes it to hold 19, as Figure 4.2 shows.

Figure 4.2 A variable holding the value 19.

age   19

4.1.5 The Assignment Operator

We initialize a variable only once, in its declaration. To change the value of a variable after we have declared it, we can use the assignment operator. This, as its name suggests, assigns a value to a variable. C# uses the equal sign, `=`, for the assignment operator. An example of a simple assignment statement is

```
age = 10;
```

in which we assign the value 10 to the variable `age`. This assignment statement assumes that we have already declared the variable `age`. The compiler would report an error if we did not declare `age`.

We declare and initialize a variable only once, but we can assign it a value many times in a program. Later in the program we may wish to change the value of `age`, say, to 20, using the assignment statement

```
age = 20;
```

Remember that the variable, `age`, has one location. Each assignment replaces the old value with the newly assigned value. Figure 4.3 shows the changes taking place resulting from the above assignments to `age`.

Figure 4.3 Declaring and assigning values to a variable.

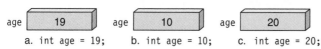

age   19   age   10   age   20

a. int age = 19;   b. int age = 10;   c. int age = 20;

Figure 4.4   The result of an assignment.

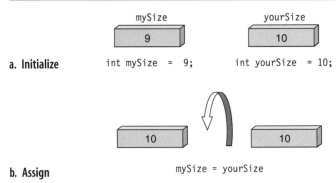

a. Initialize

b. Assign

So far we have only assigned constant values to variables, but we can also assign the value of one variable to another, as in

```
int mySize = 9;
int yourSize = 10;
mySize = yourSize;
```

The assignment takes the value of yourSize, which we initialized to 10, and assigns it to mySize. Figure 4.4 shows the locations for yourSize and mySize before and after the assignment.

We can write an arithmetic expression, such as y + 2, on the righthand side of an assignment. The computer will then evaluate the expression and assign that value to the variable on the lefthand side of the assignment. We will learn about arithmetic expressions later in this chapter. The assignment

```
mySize = yourSize + 2;
```

would give mySize a value of 12, given that yourSize still has the value of 10 that it was initialized with above.

Notice that when a variable occurs on the righthand side of an assignment, we use the value that we find in its storage location. When a variable occurs on the lefthand side of an assignment, we store a value in its memory location. Variables perform this very important function—storing values for later use—in our program.

4.1.6   Illustrating Variables

Example4-1 includes a TextBox for the user to enter a price of an item. A Label informs the user to enter a price in cents. We assume that the user will be paying with a dollar bill worth 100 cents. Pressing the *Make Change* button

Figure 4.5   Making change.

will pop up a MessageBox describing the correct amount of change in quarters, dimes, nickels, and pennies. Figure 4.5 shows the form of Example4-1.

To build Example4-1, we create the Example4-1 project and drag TextBox, Label, and Button controls from the Toolbox to the form. We click on each control to display its Properties window.[1] The properties, with their new values, that we configure are

```
Form
    Text        Change from a Dollar

TextBox
    (Name)      centsBox
    Text        "    "
    Anchor      Top

Label
    Text        Enter a price in cents
    Anchor      Top

Button
    (Name)      changeButton
    Text        Make Change
    Anchor      Top
```

The only code we need to write is the body of the event handler to respond when the user presses the *Make Change* button. We double-click on the button in the design to display the code template for the event handler, which is

```
private void changeButton_Click
                (object sender, System.EventArgs e)
{
}
```

---

[1]If the Properties window is not showing, we click the *View, Properties* menu item.

Figure 4.6
A MessageBox.

The event-handling method for the button uses local variables to hold the amount of change necessary, and the numbers of quarters, dimes, nickels, and pennies. Later in the chapter we discuss arithmetic expressions that will explain the operations used in this example. We declare local variables inside a method, and they can be used only inside the method in which they are declared. Figure 4.6 shows the pop-up MessageBox in which the event handler displays the change that results. When we learn to use control structures in the next chapter, we will be able to improve the grammar in the resulting message.

The completed event-handling code for the button is

```
private void changeButton_Click
                    (Object sender, System.EventArgs e)
{
    int price = int.Parse(centsBox.Text);   // convert string
    int change = 100 - price;               // $1 deposited
    int quarters = change / 25;      // 25 cents per quarter
    int remainder = change % 25;     // after quarters given
    int dimes = remainder / 10;      // 10 cents per dime
    remainder = remainder % 10;      // after dimes given
    int nickels = remainder / 5;     // five cents per nickel
    int pennies = remainder % 5;     // after nickels given
    MessageBox.Show("Change is \n"
                    + quarters + " quarters \n"
                    + dimes + " dimes \n"
                    + nickels + " nickels \n"
                    + pennies + " pennies");
}
```

The event-handling method declares seven local variables. The first, price, contains the price of the item that the user entered in the TextBox. Because the TextBox entry is a String, we need to convert it to an integer value using the int.Parse method. The second variable, change, represents the total amount of change we need to dispense. The user deposited one dollar, equal to 100 cents, so we subtract the price from 100 to get the amount of change. Later in the chapter we explain the C# arithmetic operator symbols used to compute the quarters, dimes, nickels, and pennies.

A MessageBox is a simple way to display a message to the user. Later we will look in more detail at String formatting techniques. Here we use the String concatenation operator, +, to join strings together. To go to the next line of the message we add the `newline` character that we represent using two keystrokes, a backslash followed by a lowercase n, `\n`.

4.1.7 Constants

We changed the value of variable `quarters` in Example4-1. We can define constants, which we cannot change. For example, the declaration

```
const int FIXED = 25;
```

declares a constant named `FIXED`. Trying to assign a value to `FIXED` would generate a compilation error.

Test Your Understanding

1. Which of the following are valid identifiers? For each nonvalid example, explain why it is not valid.

   a. `Baby` b. `_chip_eater` c. `any.time` d. `#noteThis`

   e. `&car` f. `GROUP` g. `A103` h. `76trombones`

   i. `float` j. `intNumber` k. `$$help`

2. A variable represents a _____ location.

3. We refer to a variable by its _____. The _____ of a variable determines what type of data it holds.

4. How can we improve the following declaration?

   ```
   int number;
   ```

The BIG Picture

Variables help us store data for later use in a program. The assignment operator gives a variable a value. An identifier names program elements. Keywords are identifiers that are reserved for special uses. C# uses the Unicode character set that contains thousands of characters. We can define constants, which we cannot change.

4.2 Types

C# provides a number of simple data types. We discuss `int`, `double`, `decimal`, `char`, and `bool` in this section. Figure 4.7 describes these types briefly.

The `int` type holds values ranging from −2,147,483,648 through 2,147,483,647. We can declare and initialize variables of type `double`. For example,

```
double small = 0.000345;
double large = 12345.6;
```

The type `decimal` uses a special format that allows exact representations of decimal numbers of up to 28 places. Such a representation is essential for

Figure 4.7   Some C# types.

int	Positive and negative integers of up to 9–10 digits: $-2{,}147{,}483{,}648$ to $2{,}147{,}483{,}647$
double	Positive and negative decimal numbers with 15–16-place accuracy: $\pm 5.0 \times 10^{-324}$ to $\pm 1.7 \times 10^{308}$
decimal	Positive and negative exact decimal numbers with up to 28 digits: $\pm 1.0 \times 10^{-28}$ to $\pm 7.9 \times 10^{28}$
char	Characters in various character sets
bool	Two values, True and False

financial applications where a small error in a single number could cause a large error when repeated over thousands or millions of transactions. For example, the value .10, which might represent ten cents, cannot be represented exactly in type double, but it can in type decimal. To distinguish decimal values from double, we suffix them with an m or M, as in

```
decimal tenth = .10m;
```

The char type represents characters. We use single quotes for characters, as in

```
char letter = 'a';
```

Internally C# represents each character using a numerical code. The ASCII character set includes the codes for 128 characters listed in Appendix C. The ASCII code for 'a' is 97.

Some of the ASCII characters are used to control printing and do not have a display form. For example, the character with value 10 is the newline character signifying that a new line should start. The effect is to move the cursor to the beginning of the next line. To represent special characters, C# uses an escape sequence starting with the backslash. Figure 4.8 lists some special characters.

Some examples illustrate how these special characters can help format strings. We pass a string that uses a special character to the Format method.

Figure 4.8   Some special characters.

\"	Double quote
\\	Backslash
\n	New line
\t	Horizontal tab

The result shows how the special character affects the formatting. Each use of Format is followed by the value it produces.

// Inserts a newline

```
String.Format("Use \n to go to the next line");
Use
 to go to the next line
```

// Inserts a tab

```
String.Format("***\t tab here");
***      tab here
```

// Inserts embedded quotes

```
String.Format("Do you like \"Gone With the Wind\"?");
Do you like "Gone With the Wind"?
```

// Inserts a backslash that is not an escape character

```
String.Format("The directory is c:\\newstuff");
The directory is c:\newstuff
```

4.2.1   Formatting

C# uses formatting strings to display values and text. We have several options when defining formatting strings. The simplest just inserts a value into a string. In this case, the Format method we use has two parameters, the format string and the value. For example, suppose we have an integer variable myAge. We can insert it in a string by invoking

```
String.Format("I am {0} years old.", myAge);
```

The result will be to insert the value of myAge into the string at the position marked by {0}. If myAge has the value 39, the result will be

```
I am 39 years old.
```

We can create formatting strings that include more than one value. For example, if the variables width and height have the values 15 and 12, invoking

```
String.Format
    ("The width is {0} feet and the height is {1} feet.",
      width, height);
```

results in

```
The width is 15 feet and the height is 12 feet.
```

The variable numbers used inside the braces in the format string correspond to the ordering of the arguments that follow the format string in the Format method. We start the numbering with 0.

We do not have to use the variables in the order they appear as arguments. For example, calling

```
String.Format
("The width is {1} feet and the height is {0} feet.",
  height, width);
```

would produce the same result

```
The width is 15 feet and the height is 12 feet.
```

Here the `height` variable, which appears as the second argument, occurs later in the formatting string than the variable `width`, which is the third argument to the `Format` method.

If we just want to display a value by itself as a string, we could use the `ToString` method. For example

```
myAge.ToString();
```

produces 39, and

```
String.Format("{0}", myAge);
```

gives the same result.

4.2.2   Format Specifiers

To allow more control over the format, we can use format specifiers. For example, to express a value in the local currency, dollars and cents in the United States, we would add the `C` specifier. If the `price` variable has the value `17.227`, the statement

```
String.Format
("I paid {0 : C} for that shirt including tax", price);
```

would produce the string

```
I paid $17.23 for that shirt including tax
```

We could express the price itself as a currency string using

```
price.ToString({C});
```

to produce the string $17.23.

Figure 4.9 shows some of the format types.

The `Number` format inserts commas to separate each three-digit group for easier reading. It uses a number to specify the number of places after the decimal point, so `N0` would show zero places after the point and `N2` would show two. For example,

Figure 4.9   Formatting specifiers.

Format Specifier	Name
C or c	Currency
N or n	Number
P or p	Percent
F or f	Fixed-point
G or g	General

```
123456789.ToString("N0");
```

produces 123,456,789. Using the N specifier without a number will display a default number of places after the decimal point.

The Percent format converts a number of a percent by multiplying by 100. We can add a number to indicate the number of places after the decimal point, as in

```
.0253456.ToString("P1");
```

that produces the string 2.5 %.

The Fixed-point format displays a number using a decimal point. We can specify the number of places after the decimal, as in

```
1234.56789.ToString("F3");
```

that produces the string 1234.568, obtained by rounding up because 1234.56789 is closer to 1234.568 than to 1234.567.

The General format, which is the default when we omit a format specifier, displays in fixed-point but uses scientific notation when it would be more compact. The precision specifier indicates the number of significant digits in the resulting string. Some examples are:

`1234.56789.ToString("G");`	Produces 1234.56789
`.00000123456.ToString("G");`	Produces 1.23456E-06. The number following the E indicates the number of places to move the decimal point, left if negative, right if positive.
`.00000123456.ToString("G2");`	Produces 1.2E-06

Figure 4.10   Choosing formatting parameters.

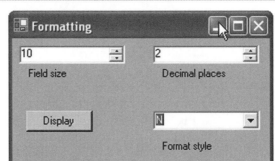

4.2.3   Field Width

We can use format specifiers to indicate the size of the field that the number will occupy. The format specifier {0, 10} indicates that the variable with index 0 should appear in a field of size 10. The field will increase in size if necessary to display the formatted value properly. A positive value for the size means that the value will be right-justified in the field, while a negative value provides for left-justification. For example,

```
String.Format("{0,10}{1,10}", 123, 45678);
String.Format("{0,-10}{1,-10}", "Jack", "Jill");
```

produces

```
       123     45678
Jack      Jill
```

We can include formatting codes when specifying the field width. For example,

```
String.Format("{0,12:C}{1,12:C}", 123, 45678);
```

produces

```
     $123.00   $45,678.00
```

Figure 4.11 Displaying a formatted value.

Example4-2 displays 9876.543 using the user's choice of formatting parameters. Pressing the Display button in Figure 4.10 shows the MessageBox of Figure 4.11 showing the string produced by

```
String.Format("{0,10:N2}", 9876.543);
```

To build Example4-2, we create a new project and drag two NumericUpDown controls, three Label controls, a Button, and a ComboBox from the Toolbox to

Figure 4.12 Entering choices for a ComboBox.

the form. We use Properties windows to configure each control. For the Form itself, we change BackColor to orange using the pop-up color dialog, and change Text to *Formatting*.

The NumericUpDown at the upper left of the form allows the user to select the field width for the number. We use its Properties window to set the Minimum property to 8 and the Maximum to 15. We set its (Name) property to selectSize and set the Text property of the Label below it to *Field size*.

The NumericUpDown at the upper right of the form allows the user to select the number of digits to display after the decimal point. We use its Properties window to set the Minimum property to 0 and the Maximum to 7. We set its (Name) property to selectPlaces and set the Text property of the Label below it to *Decimal places*.

The ComboBox in the lower-right corner of the form lets the user select a formatting style for the number. We use its Properties window to set Text to *Choose a format* and (Name) to selectFormat. To add the choices, we click on the Items property and then on the button at the right to pop up the String Collection Editor shown in Figure 4.12. We add the format choices C, N, P, F, and G, and click *OK*. We set the Text property of the Label below it to *Format*.

The Button in the lower-left corner lets the user display the number 9876.543 with a format that incorporates the selections made. We use its Properties window to change BackColor to LightBlue, (Name) to displayName, and Text to *Display*.

Constructing a formatting string from form values can be tricky. We designed Example4-2 to allow readers to experiment with formatting strings. For completeness, we show how to write the event-handling method, but do not expect readers at this stage of learning C# to create such expressions. For the example shown in Figure 4.10 and Figure 4.11, we have the form values

`numericUpDown1.Value`	field size	10
`numericUpDown2.Value`	number of digits	2
`comboBox1.Text`	format code	N

Using these values, the code we need to create the `MessageBox` of Figure 4.11 is

```
MessageBox.Show(
          String.Format("Start {0, 10:N2}", 9876.543));
```

We prefix the number with the word *Start* to show the space that the field of size 10 spans. Had the number had fewer digits, there would have been more spaces after the word *Start* in Figure 4.11 which illustrates the N format for a number using commas to group by threes and with the selected two places after the decimal point.

We need to build the string "`Start {0, 10:N2}`" using the property values determined by the user's selections. We use the `Format` method to build the formatting string. We need to distinguish between braces used to build the formatting string and those that will be part of the formatting string. We use {{ to embed a left brace, {, in the formatting string and }} to embed a right brace, }. Using this approach, we execute

```
String fString = String.Format("Start {{0,{0}:{1}{2}}}",
                  numericUpDown1.Value, comboBox1.Text,
                  numericUpDown2.Value);
```

to build the formatting string "`Start {0, 10:N2}`" that we then use to format `9876.543`.

To get the template for the button's event-handling method, we double-click on the Display button in the Visual Studio .NET design to show

```
private void displayNumber_Click
                  (object sender, System.EventArgs e)
{
}
```

Entering the code that we just devised produces the completed event-handling method for the Display button as

```
private void displayNumber_Click
                  (object sender, System.EventArgs e)
```

```
{
    String fString = String.Format
        ("Start {{0,{0}:{1}{2}}}",
        selectSize.Value, selectFormat.Text,
        selectPlaces.Value);
    MessageBox.Show(String.Format(fString, 9876.543));
}
```

The BIG Picture

C# provides a number of simple data types, including int, double, decimal, char, and bool. C# uses formatting strings to display values and text. To allow more control over the format, we can use format specifiers.

Test Your Understanding

5. The largest value that the _____ type can hold is 2,147,483,647.

6. Show the string produced from each of the following statements.

    a. String.Format("Descartes said, \"I think\ntherefore\nI am\"");

    b. String.Format("set path=c:\\C#\\bin");

    c. String.Format("12345\t678");

7. Show the string produced from each of the following statements.

    a. String.Format("I like \n\nto write C# programs.");

    b. String.Format("Ali Baba said, \"Open, Sesame!\"");

    c. String.Format("Find 3\\4 of 24");

8. Suppose that the double variable, x, has the indicated value. Show the result of x.ToString("C").

    a. 3456.789   b. .0000023456   c. .09876543

    d. 1234567890.987 e. −234567.765432

9. Suppose that the double variable, x, has the indicated value. Show the result of x.ToString("F2").

    a. 3456.789   b. .0000023456   c. .09876543

    d. 1234567890.987 e. −234567.765432

10. Suppose that the double variable, x, has the indicated value. Show the result of x.ToString("N2").

    a. 3456.789   b. .0000023456   c. .09876543

    d. 1234567890.987 e. −234567.765432

11. Suppose that the double variable, x, has the indicated value. Show the result of x.ToString("P1").

     a. 3456.789   b. .0000023456   c. .09876543

     d. 1234567890.987   e. −234567.765432

12. Show the string produced by

```
String.Format("{0,10}{0,-10}", "George", 24);
```

13. Show the string produced by

```
String.Format("{0,-10}{0,10}", "George", 24);
```

4.3   Operators and Expressions

In the process of solving problems, we perform operations on the data. Each type of data has suitable operations associated with it. Integer and decimal data have familiar arithmetic operations—addition, subtraction, multiplication, division, and negation—and a remainder operation.

A **binary** operator, such as '+,' takes two operands, as in the expression 3 + 4, where the numbers 3 and 4 are the operands. C# supports these binary arithmetic operators:

```
+    addition
-    subtraction
*    multiplication
/    division
%    remainder
```

A **unary** operator takes one operand, as in the expression -3. C# supports these unary arithmetic operators:

```
-    negation
+    (no effect)
```

If the operands are integers, then the result of an arithmetic operation will be an integer. Addition, subtraction, and multiplication behave as we expect from ordinary arithmetic. Some examples are:

Operation	Result
32 + 273	305
63 - 19	44
42 * 12	504
2.31 * 6.2	14.322

Integer division produces an integer result, truncating toward zero if necessary, meaning that it discards the fractional part, if any.

Operation	Result	
12 / 3	4	Exact.
17 / 5	3	Discards the 2/5.
-17 / 5	-3	Discards the $-2/5$.
17.0 / 5.0	2.4	Exact.

The operation x%y computes the remainder when x is divided by y.

Operation	Result	
17 % 5	2	// $3*5 + 2 = 17$
14.56 % 2.21	1.3	// $6*2.21 + 1.3 = 14.56$

Examples of the unary operations are -7, which negates the seven, and +3. In summary, Figure 4.13 shows the C# arithmetic operations for integers.

4.3.1   Precedence of Arithmetic Operators

In mathematics, we apply some common rules to decide how each operation gets its operands. For example, in the expression 3 + 4*5, we would multiply 4*5 giving 20, and then add 3+20 to get the result of 23. We say the multiplication has higher precedence than the addition, meaning that it gets its operands first. In Figure 4.14 we show that * gets its operands first by drawing a box around the expression 4*5.

Figure 4.13   C# arithmetic operations.

Operation	Math notation	C# (constants)	C# (variables)
Addition	a + b	3 + 4	score1 + score2
Subtraction	a - b	3 - 4	bats - gloves
Multiplication	ab	12 * 17	twelve * dozens
Division	a/b	7 / 3	total / quantity
Remainder	r in a=qb+r	43 % 5	cookies % people
Negation	-a	-6	-amount

Figure 4.14   Multiplication gets its operands first.

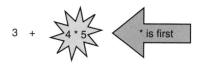

Figure 4.15   Compute within parentheses first.

If we want to do the addition first, we would need to use parentheses, as in (3+4)*5, shown in Figure 4.15. We compute everything inside parentheses first, so we would add 3+4 giving 7, and then multiply 7*5 giving 35. By remembering the rules of precedence, we can often avoid using parentheses. We could have written parentheses in the original expression, which would then be 3+(4*5), but these parentheses are not needed because we know that multiplication goes first.

Higher precedence

-, +	Unary Negation and Plus
*, /, %	Multiplication, Division, and Remainder
+, -	Binary Addition and Subtraction
=	Assignment

Lower Precedence

We evaluate x-3/y as x-(3/y) because '/' has higher precedence than '-'. We evaluate -7+10 as (-7)+10 or 3, because negation has higher precedence than addition. In the case of arithmetic operators of equal precedence, we evaluate from left to right. Thus, we compute 3+x+7 as (3+x)+7 and 10-7-5 as (10-7)-5, which is -2. We say that the *associativity* of the binary arithmetic operators is from left to right.

4.3.2   Combining Assignment and Arithmetic

Suppose we want to add 5 to a variable x. We could do that with the assignment statement

```
x = x + 5;
```

C# has an operator that combines[2] the assignment and the addition into one operator, +=. We can write the above statement more simply as

```
x += 5;
```

C# also has operators that combine assignment with the other arithmetic operators, -=, *=, /=, and %=. We must enter these two-character operators without any space between the two symbols. Some examples are:

Combined Form	Equivalent Form
y -= 7;	y = y - 7;
a *= x;	a = a * x
x /= y;	x = x / y;
w %= z;	w = w % z;
b *= z + 3;	b = b*(z + 3);

Note in the last example that we put parentheses around the entire right-hand side expression, z + 3, and multiplied that entire expression by the lefthand side variable, b.

4.3.3   Increment and Decrement Operators

C# has simple forms for the frequent operations of adding one to a variable (incrementing) or subtracting one from a variable (decrementing). To increment the variable x using the postfix form of the increment operator, we write x++. If x had a value of 5, executing x++ would give it a value of 6. The prefix form of the increment operator, ++x, also increments the variable by one. We only use the increment operator to increment a variable that is not part of a larger expression. In this case it makes no difference whether we use the prefix or the postfix form of this operator.

---

[2]Although these operators provide no new functionality, they do make it easier for the compiler to generate efficient code.

Figure 4.16   C# relational and equality operators.

Symbol	Meaning	Example	
<	less than	31 < 25	false
<=	less than or equal	464 <= 7213	true
>	greater than	-98 > -12	false
>=	greater than or equal	9 >= 99	false
==	equal	9 == 12 + 12	false
!=	not equal	292 != 377	true

TIP

The operators <=, >=, ==, and != are two-character operators that must be together, without any spaces between the two characters. The expression 3 <= 4 is fine, but 3 < = 4 will give an error. (The compiler thinks we want the '<' operator and cannot figure out why we did not give a correct righthand operand.)

C# has prefix and postfix forms of the decrement operator, --x and x--. Each decrements the value of the variable by 1.

4.3.4   Relational Operators and Expressions

Arithmetic operators take numeric operands and give numeric results. For example, the value of 3+4 is an integer, 7. By contrast, an expression such as 3 < 4, stating that 3 is less than 4, gives the value true, and the expression 7 < 2 gives the bool value, false. C# provides relational and equality operators, listed in Figure 4.16, which take two operands of a primitive type and produce a bool result.

We can use variables in relational expressions. For example, if x is an integer variable, the expression

x < 3

is true if the value of x is less than 3 and false otherwise. The expression

x == 3

evaluates to true if x equals 3, and to false otherwise.

TIP

Be careful not to confuse the equality operator, ==, with the assignment operator, =. If x has the value 12, then x == 3 evaluates to `false`, but x = 3 assigns the value 3 to x, changing it from 12.

Figure 4.17   Conditional operators.

Symbol	Meaning	Example
&&	conditional AND	(age > 20) && 35)
||	conditional OR	(height > 78.5) || (weight > 300)

TIP

The && and || operators use two-character symbols that must be typed without any space between them. Using & & instead of && would give an error.

4.3.5   The AND, OR, and NOT Operators

The C# conditional operators express the familiar **AND** and **OR** operations, which we can use to write conditions such as

John's age is greater than 20 **AND** John's age is less than 35.

John's height is greater than 78.5 **OR** John's weight is greater than 300.

Figure 4.17 shows the C# symbols for the conditional operators.

Note that the operands of the conditional operators have type `bool`. The expression age > 20 is either true or false, and so is age < 35.

4.3.6   Conditional AND

The conditional AND expression (age > 20) && (age < 35) will be true only when both of its operands are true, and false otherwise. If the variable age has the value 25, both operands are true, and the whole && expression is true. If age has the value 17, the first operand, age > 20 is false, and the whole && expression is false. Figure 4.18 shows some sample evaluations of a conditional AND expression, illustrating how the value of an && expression depends upon the values of its arguments.

Figure 4.18   Evaluating an example of a conditional AND expression.

age	age > 20	age < 35	age > 20 && age < 35
10	false	true	false
25	true	true	true
40	true	false	false

Figure 4.19   Evaluating an example of a conditional OR expression.

height	weight	height > 78.5	weight > 300	(height > 78.5) || (weight > 300)
62	125	false	false	false
80	250	true	false	true
72	310	false	true	true
80	325	true	true	true

Note that when the first operand is false, as it is when age is 17, we know that the conditional AND is false without even checking the value of the second operand.

4.3.7   Conditional OR

The conditional OR expression (height > 78.5) || (weight > 300) is true if either one of its operands is true, or if both are true. If height has the value 72 and weight has the value 310, then the first operand is false and the second operand is true, so the || expression is true. Figure 4.19 shows some sample evaluations of a conditional OR expression, illustrating how the value of an || expression depends upon the values of its arguments.

4.3.8   Logical Complement

C# uses the symbol ! for the logical complement, or NOT, operator, which has only one operand. The logical complement negates the value of its operand, as Figure 4.20 shows. If the bool variable, on, has the value true, then !on is false, but if on is false, then !on is true.

**Figure 4.20
Evaluating a logical
complement
expression.**

A	!A
true	false
false	true

Figure 4.21   Operator precedence.

Highest

NOT	!
multiplicative	* / %
additive	+ −
relational	< > <= >=
equality	== !=
conditional AND	&&
conditional OR	||
assignment	= += −= /= %=

Lowest

4.3.9   Operator Precedence

The conditional AND and conditional OR operators have lower precedence than the relational and equality operators, as shown in Figure 4.21 where we show operators of equal precedence on the same line.[3]

Remember that C# follows precedence rules in evaluating expressions, with the higher precedence operators getting their arguments first. In the expression

```
age > 20  && age < 35
```

the < and > operators have higher precedence than the && operator, so C# will evaluate it as if it had been written as

```
(age > 20)  && (age < 35)
```

4.3.10   Combining AND with OR

We can use both the && and || operators in the same expression, as in:

```
age > 50 && (height > 78.5 || height < 60)
```

---

[3]See Appendix B for the complete operator precedence table.

Figure 4.22   Converting a temperature.

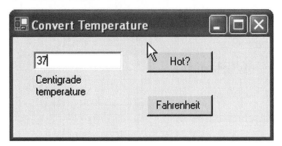

where we need the parentheses because the AND operator has higher precedence than the OR operator. Without parentheses, as in:

```
age > 50 && height > 78.5 || height < 60
```

C# will evaluate the expression as if we had written it as:

```
(age > 50 && height > 78.5) || height < 60
```

which is not what we intended.

Example4-3 allows the user to enter a temperature in degrees centigrade in the form shown in Figure 4.22. The user enters a centigrade temperature in the TextBox. Clicking the *Hot?* button pops up a MessageBox that indicates whether that temperature is hot, as shown in Figure 4.23. Clicking the *Fahrenheit* button pops up a MessageBox that shows the Fahrenheit equivalent of the Centigrade temperature that the user entered.

Figure 4.23 Checking a temperature.

To create Example4-3, we open an Example4-3 project and drag a TextBox, a Label, and two Button controls from the Toolbox to the form. We use the Properties windows to configure the controls. To change the background color of the form itself, we click on the BackColor property and then on the button that appears at the right. We selected a light green color from the grid on the Custom tab. The Text property of the Form becomes *Convert Temperature*.

We set the Text property of the TextBox to 25, so the user will have a default value entered and can try the *Hot?* or *Fahrenheit* buttons before entering a value. We set its (Name) property to enterCentigrade, and set the Text property of the Label below it to *Centigrade temperature*.

We set the BackColor property of each Button control to a medium green. The Text property of the upper Button becomes *Hot?* and its (Name) becomes isHot. The Text of the lower Button becomes *Fahrenheit* and its (Name) becomes convert.

Figure 4.24   The conversion result.

Double clicking on the *Hot?* button in the Visual Studio .NET design displays the event-handling method for this button. We add code to evaluate an expression stating that the temperature is greater than thirty degrees Centigrade. If so, we conclude that it is hot. We use the Parse method to convert the user's entry from a string to a double value. The event-handling code is

```
private void isHot_Click
                    (object sender, System.EventArgs e)
{
     double temp = double.Parse(enterCentigrade.Text);
     bool hot = temp > 30;
     MessageBox.Show(String.Format
          ("It is {0} that {1:F1} is hot", hot, temp));
}
```

Figure 4.24 shows the result of converting to Fahrenheit. To do the conversion we use the formula F = 9/5C + 32. The event-handling code is

```
private void convert_Click
                    (object sender, System.EventArgs e)
{
     double cent = double.Parse(enterCentigrade.Text);
     double fahr = 9.0*cent/5.0 + 32.0;
     MessageBox.Show(String.Format
          ("{0:F1} Centigrade is {1:F1} Fahrenheit",
          cent, fahr));
}
```

Test Your Understanding

14.   If a=4, b=23, c=-5, and d=61, evaluate

   a. b/a   b. b%a   c. a%b   d. b/c   e. c*d   f. d%b   g. c/a   h. c%a

The BIG Picture

Each type of data has suitable operations associated with it. By remembering the rules of precedence, we can often avoid using parentheses. C# includes arithmetic, relational, equality, logical, and assignment operators.

15.   Evaluate the following C# expressions, where x=2, y=3, z=-4, and w=5.

   a. x + w / 2   b. z * 4 - y   c. y + w % 2

   d. x + y - z   e. x * z / y

   f. x + z * y / w   g. y * x - z / x

   h. w * x % y - 4   i.   14 % w % y

16.   What value would C# assign each variable if, for each expression, j=7, k=11, and n=-4?

   a. j += 31;   b. k *= n;   c. k -= n + 7;

   d. k %= j   e. k /= n - 1

17.   Write a relational expression in C# for each of the following:

   a. 234 less than 52

   b. 435 not equal to 87

   c. −12 equal to −12

   d. 76 greater than or equal to 54

18.   Evaluate the following relational expressions:

   a. 23 < 45   b.   49 >= 4 + 9   c. 95 != 100 - 5

19.   Explain the difference between x = 5 and x == 5.

20.   Explain why the expression x > = 3 is not a correct C# expression to state that x is greater than or equal to 3.

21.   For each expression, find values for x and y that make it true.

   a. (x == 2) && (y > 4)   b. (x <= 5) || (y >= 5)

   c. x > 10 || y != 5   d. x > 10 && y < x + 4

4.4 Summary

- Variables help us store data for later use in a program. The assignment operator gives a variable a value. An identifier names program elements. Keywords are identifiers that are reserved for special uses. C# uses the Unicode character set that contains thousands of characters. We can define constants, which we cannot change.

- C# provides a number of simple data types, including `int`, `double`, `decimal`, `char`, and `bool`. C# uses formatting strings to display values and text. To allow more control over the format, we can use format specifiers.

- Each type of data has suitable operations associated with it. By remembering the rules of precedence, we can often avoid using parentheses. C# includes arithmetic, relational, equality, logical, and assignment operators.

4.5   Programming Exercises

4.1   Modify Example4-1 to make change without using any dimes.

4.2   Modify Example4-2 to use a `TextBox` to enter the field size rather than a `NumericUpDown`.

4.3   Modify Example4-2 to use a `ComboBox` to select the number of digits after the decimal point.

4.4   Modify Example4-3 to add a `Cold?` button that displays a `MessageBox` indicating whether the entered temperature is cold. Assume that a temperature is cold if it is below zero centigrade.

4.5   Create a Windows application that includes a `ComboBox` listing names, a `NumericUpDown` to select an age, and a `Button` to display the selected name and age in a `Label` with the name left justified and the name right justified, each in fields of size 15.

4.6   Create a Windows application that includes a `ComboBox` listing products, a `NumericUpDown` to select a price, and a `Button` to display the selected product and price in a `Label` with the name product name left justified and the price right justified, each in fields of size 15.

4.7   Create a Windows application that includes a `TextBox` to enter a numerator and another `TextBox` to enter a denominator. Allow values of type `double`. Include a `Button` to display the quotient in a `MessageBox` using each of the format specifiers N, F, C, P, and G. (Use the `double.Parse` method to convert the string in the `TextBox` to a double value.)

4.8   Create a Windows application that includes a `NumericUpDown` to select an x value and a `Button` to display the value of the polynomial $3x^2 - 7x + 2$ in a `Label`.

4.9 Create a Windows application that includes a TextBox to enter an integer number of miles. Allow the user to click a Button to convert to an equivalent number of feet and display the result in a Message-Box. (There are 5280 feet in a mile.)

4.10 Create a Windows application to convert an integer number of seconds to an equivalent number of hours, minutes, and seconds. For example, an input of 52,400 should give 14 hours, 33 minutes, and 20 seconds. (Dividing 52,400 by 3600 gives a quotient of 14 hours with a remainder of 2000 seconds. Dividing the remainder of 2000 by 60 gives a quotient of 33 minutes with a remainder of 20.) Include a TextBox for the user to enter the number of seconds, and a Button to convert and display the result in a MessageBox.

CHAPTER 5

Selection and Repetition

Our C# event-handling methods so far have been simple. All we have learned to do so far is to execute one statement after another in order. We have not had any choices. If we lived life like that, then, no matter how we felt, we would get up, get dressed, and have breakfast. In reality, we make decisions among alternatives. If we are very sick we might stay in bed and not get dressed. (If we are very lucky, someone might bring us breakfast in bed.) We might not be hungry one morning, so we would get up, get dressed, but skip breakfast. Here is a description of our morning, with decisions:

```
if (I feel ill)
    stay in bed;
else {
    get up;
    get dressed;
    if (I feel hungry)
        eat breakfast;
}
```

In this "program," what I do depends upon whether "I feel ill" is true or false. We will see in this chapter how to write C# expressions that are either true or false, and how to write C# statements that allow us to choose among alternatives based on the truth or falsity of a test expression.

Making choices gives us more flexibility, but we need even more control. For example, if I am thirsty, I might drink a glass of water, but one glass of water might not be enough. What I really want to do is to keep drinking water as long as I am still thirsty. I need to be able to repeat an action. The kind of program I want is:

```
while (I feel thirsty)
    drink a glass of water;
```

We will see in this chapter how to write C# statements that allow us to repeat steps in our program.

We think of the processor as flowing from one statement to the next as it executes our program. In this chapter we introduce C# selection statements that allow us to make choices among alternatives and repetition statements that enable us to repeat sections of code. These statements will allow us to specify how the processor should flow through our program as it executes its statements.

Chapter Objectives:

- Choose using `if`, `if-else`, and `switch` statements
- Repeat code using `while`, `for`, and `do` statements
- Use selection and repetition statements to write more powerful event-handling methods

5.1   The `if` and `if-else` Statements

We are now ready to make choices about which statements to execute. The `if` statement allows us to choose whether to execute a statement. With the `if-else` statement we can choose between two alternatives.

5.1.1   The `if` Statement

The `if` statement is essential because it allows us to make choices, and it allows us to solve more complex problems.

The `if` statement has the pattern

```
if (condition)
    if_true_statement
```

as in the example

```
if (checkBox1.Checked)
    pictureBox1.Visible = True;
```

The condition is an expression, such as `checkBox1.Checked`, that evaluates to true or false. The `if_true_statement` is a C# statement such as `picture-Box1.Visible = True`. If the condition is true, then execute the `if_true_statement`; but if the condition is false, skip the `if_true_statement` and go on to the next line of the program. In this example, if the user has checked `check-Box1`, we set the `Visible` property of `pictureBox1` to true; but if `Checked` is false, we would skip the statement `pictureBox1.Visible = True`.

The `if` statement allows us to make a choice about the control flow. A flow diagram represents the logic of an `if` statement graphically. We use a dia-

Indent all lines after the first to show that these lines are part of the if statement and to make it easier to read.

Do

```
if (checkBox1.Checked)
    pictureBox1.Visible = True;
```

Don't

```
if (checkBox1.Checked)
pictureBox1.Visible = True;
```

STYLE

Figure 5.1   Control flow for the if statement.

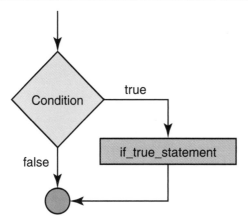

mond shape to represent a decision based on the truth or falsity of a condition. One arrow, called the true branch, shows what comes next if the condition is true. Another arrow, called the false branch, shows what comes next if the condition is false. Figure 5.1 shows the control flow for an if statement. When the condition is true, C# will execute an additional statement.

5.1.2   The if-else Statement

The if statement allows us to choose to execute a statement or not to execute it depending on the value of a test expression. With the if-else statement we can choose between two alternatives, executing one when the test condition is true and the other when the test condition is false.

Figure 5.2   Flow diagram for the if-else statement.

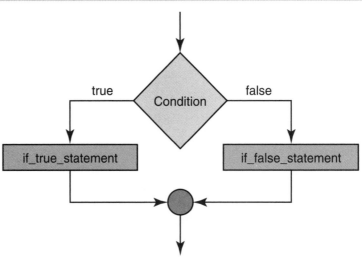

The if-else statement has the form

```
if  (condition)
      if_true_statement
else
      if_false_statement
```

For example,

```
if (checkBox1.Checked)
      pictureBox1.Visible = True;
else
      pictureBox1.Visible = False;
```

If checkBox1 is checked we make it visible, otherwise we make it invisible. The if-else statement gives us a choice between two alternatives. We choose if_true_statement if the condition is true and if_false_statement if the condition is false. Figure 5.2 shows the flow diagram for the if-else statement.

5.1.3   Blocks

We can group a sequence of statements inside curly braces to form a **block**, as in

TIP

Do not forget to enclose the statements that you want to execute if a condition is `true` within curly braces. Just indenting them, as in

```
if (y > 5)
    x = 5;
    y = -8;
    z = x * y;
```

will not group the three statements together. We indent to make the program easier to read; indenting does not affect the meaning of the program. Without the braces, C# will interpret the code as

```
if (y > 5)
    x = 5;
y = -8;
z = x * y;
```

If y is greater than five, then C# will set x to five. Whether or not y is greater than 5, C# will always set y to −8, and z to x*y. This is quite a different result than we would get if we grouped the three statements in a block, and changed the values of x, y, and z only if the condition is true.

```
{
    x = 5;
    y = -8;
    z = x * y;
}
```

We can use a block as a statement in an `if` or an `if-else` statement, as in:

```
if (y > 5) {
    x = 5;
    y = -8;
    z = x * y;
}
```

By using a block, we can perform more than one action if the test condition is `true`. In this example, if y is greater than 5, we want to set x, y, and z to new values.

Example5-1 includes two check boxes, each of which affects a picture box. Checking a box makes the picture it affects visible. Unchecking a box makes the picture it affects invisible. Figure 5.3 shows the form.

Figure 5.3   Selecting pictures.

To build Example5-1, we create a new project. Then we drag two CheckBox controls and two PictureBox controls from the Toolbox to the form. We use the Properties window for each control to configure it. We change the (Name) property of the CheckBox on the left to selectJulia and its Text property to *Julia*. We change the (Name) property of the PictureBox on the left to showJulia.

To configure the CheckBox on the right, we change its (Name) property to selectGrandpa and set its Text property to *Grandpa*. We change the TextAlign and CheckAlign properties to MiddleRight so that the two check boxes appear more symmetrically in the form. The new (Name) for the PictureBox on the right will be showGrandpa.

We write the event-handling code for each CheckBox by first double-clicking each to display its template. That code is

```
private void selectJulia_CheckedChanged
               (object sender, System.EventArgs e)
```

Use a consistent style for blocks so that it is easy to match the opening brace, {, with the closing brace, }. One choice is to put the left brace on the same line as the if or else, and to align the right brace with the if or else, as in

```
if (x < 10){
  y = 5;
  z = 8;
} else  {
  y = 9;
  z = -2;
}
```

Using this style, we can match the keyword if with the closing brace, }, to keep our code neatly organized. Another choice is to align the left brace with the if or else, as in

```
if (x < 10)
{
  y = 5;
  z = 8;
}
else
{
  y = 9;
  z = -2;
}
```

Either of these styles allows us to add or delete lines within a block without having to change the braces. The latter style makes it easier to match opening with closing braces, but uses an extra line to separate the opening brace from the code. We could make the code more compact by putting the braces on the same line as the code, but this is harder to read and modify, and not recommended.

STYLE

```
{
    if (selectJulia.Checked)
        showJulia.Visible = true;
    else
        showJulia.Visible = false;
}
private void selectGrandpa_CheckedChanged
                (object sender, System.EventArgs e)
{
```

```
if (selectGrandpa.Checked)
    showGrandpa.Visible = true;
else
    showGrandpa.Visible = false;
}
```

In each `PictureBox` we set the `SizeMode` property to `CenterImage`. Using full-size pictures with the `AutoSize` value might cause the pictures to overlap. Using the default `Normal` mode might only show the upper-left corner of the image.

The BIG Picture

The `if` statement allows us to choose whether to execute a statement. With the `if-else` statement we can choose between two alternatives.

Test Your Understanding

1. Correct the error in each of the following:

   a. `if {x == 12} y += 7;`

   b. `if (x=12) y += 7;`

   c. `if (x == 12) then y += 7;`

2. Correct the error in each of the following:

   a. `if (y > 5)`
   `    z = 7;`
   `    x = 5;`
   `else`
   `    w = 4;`

   b. `if  y > 5`
   `    z = 3;`
   `else`
   `    x = y + 2;`

   c. `if (y > 5)`
   `    z = 3;`
   `else  (`
   `    s = y + 7;`
   `    z = s - 2;`
   `);`

3. How would you improve the style in each of the following?

   a. `if (y <= 6)`
   `    z += 5;`

   b. `if (x != 0)`
   `    y+=5;`
   `else`
   `    z = y + 9;`

5.2   Nested `if`s and the `switch` Statement

With the `if-else` statement, we can choose between two alternatives. In this section we show two ways to choose between multiple alternatives, nested `if` statements and the `switch` statement.

Figure 5.4   Nested if-else statement to choose among three alternatives.

```
if (score >= 60 && score < 80)
   label1.Text = "C";
else if (score >= 80 && score < 90)
   label1.Text = "B";
else
   label1.Text = "A";
```

5.2.1   Nested if Statements

Suppose we grade test scores as 60–79 C, 80–89 B, and 90–100 A. Given a test score between 60 and 100, we can determine the grade by first checking whether the score is between 60 and 79 or higher, using the if-else statement

```
if (score >= 60 && score < 80)
   label1.Text = "C";
else
   label1.Text = "B or A";
```

This if-else statement only chooses between the two alternatives, grades C and B or better. To choose between the three alternatives, grades A, B, or C, we nest another if-else statement as the body of the else-part of our original if-else statement.

The code in Figure 5.4 has a problem. If we assume that a score is always between 60 and 100, then the code does what we expect; but let us trace the code if the score has a value of 40. Then the first test, score >=60 && score < 80, fails, so we execute the else-part, which is a nested if-else statement. Its condition, score >= 80 && score < 90, also fails, so we execute the else-part, which indicates that a score of 40 receives an A grade, not what we expect.

We can improve the code of Figure 5.4 by nesting an if statement in the last else-part to check that the score is really between 90 and 100, as shown in Figure 5.5.

We see that using nested if-else statements allows us, in this example, to choose among three alternatives:

Figure 5.5   Improved version of Figure 5.4.

```
if (score >= 60 && score < 80)
   label1.Text = "C";
else if (score >=80 && score < 90)
   label1.Text = "B";
else if (score >= 90 && score <= 100)
   label1.Text = "A";
```

Figure 5.6   Choosing from multiple alternatives.

```
if ( Is it the first alternative? ){
    First alternative code
} else if ( Is it the second alternative? ) {
    Second alternative code
}
  ...
}else if ( Is it the last alternative? ) {
    Last alternative code
}else {
    Code when none of the above alternatives is true
}
```

TIP

If you use code like Figure 5.4, having a final else with no nested if, then be sure that the code in the final else does handle everything else; that is, every case that does not come under one of the tested alternatives in the preceding if statements.

```
scores between 60 and 79
scores between 80 and 89
scores between 90 and 100
```

Figure 5.5 illustrates the style for nested if-else statements to choose from multiple alternatives. Figure 5.6 shows the general pattern.

Figure 5.7 shows the flow diagram for a nested if-else statement.

Figure 5.7   Flow diagram for the nested if-else statement.

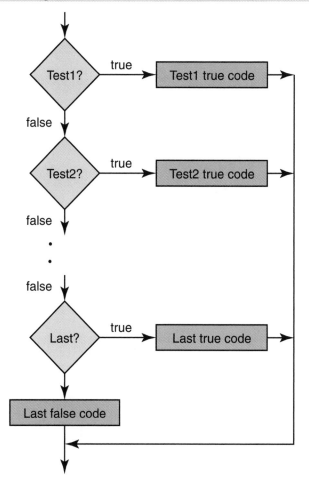

5.2.2   Pairing else with if

Without an additional rule, we cannot always determine how to read nested if statements. For example, contrast Figure 5.8 with Figure 5.9.

In Figure 5.8, we would like to pair else with the first if, but in Figure 5.9, we would like to pair the else with the second if. Unfortunately, aligning the else under the first if in Figure 5.8 will not achieve the outcome we want. As we know, C# does not consider spacing significant, so both examples will produce the same result. C# uses the rule that pairs an else with

Figure 5.8   Incorrect attempt to pair an else with an if.

```
if (score >= 60)
  if (score >= 80)
    label1.Text = "B or A";
else
  label1.Text = "D or F";           // Wrong pairing
```

Figure 5.9   Corrected pairing of an else and an if.

```
if (score >= 60)
  if (score >= 80)
    label1.Text = "B or A";
  else
    label1.Text = "C";              // Correct pairing
```

Figure 5.10   Figure 5.8 rewritten as an if-else with nested if.

```
if (score >= 60) {
 if (score >= 80)
  label1.Text = "B or A";
}else                               // Paired to first 'if'
  label1.Text = "D or F";
```

TIP

Remember the rule:

Pair an else with the nearest preceding if.

Trace each branch of nested if statements, checking carefully which values of the data will cause execution to flow to that branch.

the nearest if. Figure 5.9 is the correct version, and it would be correct even if we type the else under the first if, as in Figure 5.8.

Both Figures 5.8 and 5.9 are if statements with nested if-else statements. What we tried to do in Figure 5.8 was write an if-else statement whose if-part contained a nested if statement. To do that, we need to enclose the nested if statement in braces, as in Figure 5.10.

Figure 5.11   The form of Example5-2.

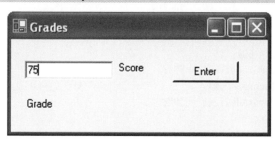

Example5-2 includes a TextBox for the user to enter a test score. Pressing the button invokes an event handler that uses a nested if statement to display the letter grade in a Label. Figure 5.11 shows the form.

To build Example5-2 we create a new project and drag a TextBox, a Label, a Button, and two more Label controls to the form. We use the Properties window for each control to configure it. To configure a control we click on it and click on the *View, Properties* menu item to show the Properties window for it. For the Form control we change the Text property to *Grades*, which will show in the title at its top. We change its BackColor property to yellow by clicking on it and selecting the yellow color from the color grid on the Custom tab.

We click on the TextBox, and using the Properties window we erase the default value, textbox1, from the Text property so that its new value will be the empty string. The form will appear without any text in the TextBox initially. We change the (Name) property of the TextBox to enterScore.

We change the Text property of the Label to the right of the TextBox to *Score*, and the Text of the Label at the lower-left of the form to *Grades*. These labels do not change and just describe other controls on the form. The third Label will display the letter grade corresponding to the numerical score that the user enters. We change its Text property to the empty string so that it will be invisible initially. We also change its (Name) property to letterGrade. The final configuration changes the Text property for the Button to *Enter* and its (Name) to showGrade.

We double-click on the button to display the template for the event handler that will be executed when the user clicks the button. We fill in the code. The event-handling code for the Button of Example5-2 is

```
private void showGrade_Click
                    (object sender, System.EventArgs e)
{
    int score = int.Parse(textBox1.Text);
    if (score < 50)
        letterGrade.Text = "F";
    else if (score < 60)
        letterGrade.Text = "D";
    else if (score < 80)
        letterGrade.Text = "C";
    else if (score < 90)
        letterGrade.Text = "B";
    else
        letterGrade.Text = "A";
}
```

We first convert the number that the user enters to an integer, and then use nested if statements to determine the letter grade. Later we will cover input validation, which will allow us to correct for invalid user input.

5.2.3   The switch Statement

Choosing among six alternatives is stretching the use of nested if statements. The efficiency of this construction declines as we add more alternatives. For example, to interpret a score of 98, Example5-2 tests five conditions, the first four of which fail. The switch statement allows us to check a large number of alternatives more efficiently.

A switch statement chooses alternatives based upon the value of a variable. In this section, we use an int variable in our switch statement. We may also use the char type, String type, or other integer types to indicate switch choices.

The switch statement has the form

```
switch (test_expression)  {
  case expression1:
                    statement1;
  case expression2:
                    statement2;
   .....
  default:
                    default_statement;
  }
```

Figure 5.12   An example of a switch statement.

```
switch(mark) {
  case 0:
  case 1:
  case 2:
  case 3:
  case 4:  label3.Text = "F";
           break;
  case 5:  label3.Text = "D";
           break;
  case 6:
  case 7:  label3.Text = "C";
           break;
  case 8:  label3.Text = "B";
           break;
  case 9:
  case 10: label3.Text = "A";
           break;
  default: label3.Text = "Incorrect score";
           break;
}
```

We can use a switch statement to replace the nested if statements of Example5-2. Computing score/10 will give a number from zero to ten because each score is between 0 and 100. For example, 87/10 is 8, and 35/10 is 3. We can assign score/10 to a variable mark as in:

```
int mark = score/10;
```

and use mark in the switch statement of Figure 5.12 to determine the grade for that score.

In Figure 5.12, C# evaluates the variable mark, jumping directly to one of twelve cases depending upon the value of mark. We specify each case with a case label such as case 5:, which is made up of the word *case* followed by the number 5, followed by a colon. The label marks the place in the code to jump to when the switch variable value matches that case label. If mark is 5, C# executes the code following the label, case 5:, which displays the grade of D; the break statement then causes a jump out of the switch statement to the code following the closing brace, }.

If mark is 10, then C# jumps to the code at the label, case 10:, which displays an A and breaks to the end of the switch. If mark is any integer other than 0 through 10, then C# jumps to the default case and displays an error message. The default case is optional. Had we omitted the default case in Figure 5.12, then C# would simply do nothing if the variable mark had any value other than 0 through 10. Note that several labels can refer to the same code, as, for example, case 6 and case 7, which both label the statement that displays a C.

We must include the break statement after each case. C# does not allow code to "fall through" to the code for the next case. However, as in Figure 5.12, several case labels may mark the same location.

The BIG Picture

Nested if statements and the switch statement allow us to choose between multiple alternatives. Pair an else with the nearest preceding if. A switch statement chooses alternatives based upon the value of a variable.

Test Your Understanding

4. A charity designates donors who give $1,000 or more as Benefactors, those who give $500–$999 as Patrons, and those who give $100–$499 as Supporters. Write a nested if-else statement that, given the amount of a contribution, assigns the correct designation for that contributor to a string variable.

5. Write a nested if-else statement that includes the categories from Question 4 and identifies donors of $1–$99 as Contributors.

6. What value will the variable x have after executing

    ```
    x = 6;
    if (k < 10)
       if (k < 5)
          x = 7;
       else
          x = 8;

    if k has the value
    ```

    a. 9   b. 3   c. 11   d. −2

7. What value will the variable x have after executing

    ```
    x = 6;
    if (k < 10)
       if (k < 5)
          x = 7;
    ```

```
else
  x = 8;
```

if k has the value

a. 9   b. 3   c. 11   d. −2

8. What value will the variable x have after executing

```
x = 6;
if (k < 10)  {
   if (k < 5)
       x = 7;
}else
      x = 8;
```

if k has the value

a. 9   b. 3   c. 11   d. −2

9. What value will the variable x have after executing

```
x = 5;
switch(k) {
   case 2:
   case 3:  x = 6;
            break;
   case 5:  x = 7;
            break;
   case 9:  x = 8;
            break;
   default: x = 9;
            break;
}
```

if k has the value

a. 1   b. 3   c. 5   d. 6

e. 9   f. −5   g. 10

10. Answer Question 9 for the code

```
x = 5;
switch(k) {
   case 2:
```

```
        case 3: x = 6;
                break;
        case 5: x = 7;
                break;
        case 9: x = 8;
                break;
    }
```

5.3   Repetition

The if, if-else, and switch statements give us the ability to make choices. In this section we will see how the while, for, and do statements enable us to repeat steps.

5.3.1   The while Statement

The while statement follows the pattern

```
while (condition)
  while_true_statement
```

where the condition evaluates to true or false, and the while_true_statement can be any C# statement including a code block. If the condition is true, C# executes the while_true_statement and goes back to check the condition again. If the condition is still true, C# executes the while_true_statement and goes back to check the condition again, and so on. This process repeats until the condition is false. Figure 5.13 shows the flow diagram for the while statement.

Figure 5.13   Flow diagram for the while loop.

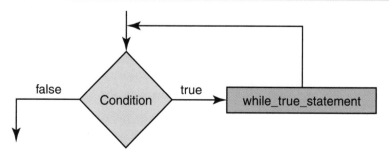

For example, suppose that the variable x has the value 7 just before C# starts to execute the while statement

```
while (x < 10)
    x += 2;
```

Because 7 < 10 is true, C# executes the statement x += 2, which changes the value of x to 9. Remember, this is a while statement, so C# again checks the condition, x < 10. Because 9 < 10 is still true, C# again executes x += 2, giving x the value 11. Now checking the condition x < 10, C# finds that 11 < 10 is false, so the execution of the while statement is finished.

The while statement is a type of loop, so-called because execution keeps looping back to check the condition after every execution of the while_true_statement, which we call the **body** of the loop. The body of the loop could be a block, in which case C# executes every statement in the block while the condition is true.

The condition in a while statement may evaluate to false on the first entry to the loop, in which case C# never executes the body of the loop. For example, if x has the value 3 before executing the loop

```
while (x >= 5)
    x -= 4;
```

then the condition, 3 >= 5, is false, and the loop body, x -= 4, is never executed.

5.3.2 Loop Termination

Each time the loop condition is true, C# executes the loop body. In order for the loop to terminate, something must change that causes the condition to fail. In the loop

```
while ( x < 10)
    x += 2;
```

we add 2 to x each time we execute the body. If x has the value 5 before the loop starts executing, eventually x will become greater than or equal to 10, so the condition x < 10 will fail and the loop will terminate.

Possibly the loop may never stop. For example, if x has the value 5, the loop

```
while (x < 10)
    x -= 2;
```

TIP

Beware of loops that never terminate. We use loops because we want repetition, but we must make sure that the repetition stops. Check each loop that you write to make sure that it will terminate.

will continue executing until the user aborts the program. (Holding the *Control* key down and pressing the *C* key will interrupt the program on Windows systems.) The value of x is 5, 3, 1, -1, -3, -5, . . ., and so on. The condition, x < 10, is always true, so the loop keeps on executing. Remember that when writing a while statement, something must eventually cause the condition to be false.

5.3.3   The for Statement

The for statement provides a powerful iteration capability. It works well when we know the number of repetitions. Technically we could use a while statement instead of a for statement in these cases, but it is much more convenient to say

```
Do this calculation 10 times.
```

than it is to write

```
Declare and initialize a count variable to zero.
while (count < 10) {
    doSomething;
    count ++;
}
```

The for statement performs the same steps but packages them more conveniently, following the pattern

```
for (initialize; test; update)
  for_body_statement
```

where for_body_statement can be a simple statement or a block. Figure 5.14 shows the flow diagram for the for statement. The code in Figure 5.15 uses a for statement to add the numbers from one to four. The initialize part declares and initializes a variable, i, called the index or counter, which will count the repetitions.

The test expression, i <= 4, checks whether we need more repetitions. C# will execute the statement sum += i, of the for loop body, if the test condition

Figure 5.14   Flow diagram for the for statement.

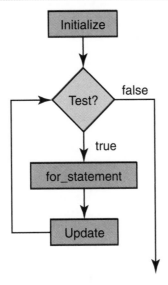

Figure 5.15   A for statement for the sum 1+2+3+4.

```
int sum = 0;
for (int i = 1; i <= 4; i++)
   sum += i;
```

is true, in this case if the count, i, is less than or equal to four. The loop ter-minates when the test condition becomes false, in this case when i is greater than four. The update expression, i++ in this example, increments the count, i, by one. C# executes the update expression, after executing the for loop body. Figure 5.16 traces the execution of the for loop of Figure 5.15.

The update expression can be more general than the increment in Figure 5.15. In Figure 5.17, we find the sum of the positive odd numbers less than 10. In each iteration, we add two to the index variable, i, which gets the values 1, 3, 5, 7, and 9, each of which is added to sum, whose final value is 25.

Normally the index variable increases at each iteration, as in the code of Figures 5.15 and 5.17. However, we can initialize the index to its highest value and decrement it at each iteration, as in Figure 5.18, which also com-putes the sum of the first four positive integers.

Figure 5.16   Trace of execution of the for loop of Figure 5.15.

```
initialize      i = 1
test            1 <= 4 is true
execute body    sum += 1                 (result:  sum = 0 + 1 = 1)
update          i++                       (result:  i = 2)
test            2 <= 4 is true
execute body    sum += 2                 (result:  sum = 1 + 2 = 3)
update          i++                       (result:  i = 3)
test            3 <= 4 is true
execute body    sum += 3                 (result:  sum = 3 + 3 = 6)
update          i++                       (result:  i = 4)
test            4 <= 4 is true
execute body    sum += 4                 (result:  sum = 6 + 4 = 10)
update          i++                       (result:  i = 5)
test            5 <= 4 is false
```

Figure 5.17   A for statement for the sum 1+3+5+7+9.

```
int sum = 0;
for (int i = 1; i < 10; i += 2)
  sum += i;
```

Figure 5.18   A for statement for the sum 4+3+2+1.

```
int sum = 0;
for (int i = 4; i >= 1; i--)
   sum += i;
```

Now that we have seen how to write a for statement, we will use it in Example5-3 to find how much our money will grow in a bank account. The account earns interest at a certain rate over a specified time, assuming that interest is compounded yearly. (At the end of the year, the interest due for that year is added to the principal.) Example5-3 uses a ComboBox for the user to select an interest rate, a TextBox to enter the initial account balance, a NumericUpDown to select the number of years, and a Button to find the accumulated amount. Three Label controls describe the purpose of the other controls. Figure 5.19 shows the form of Example5-3.

We use Properties windows to configure each control. We click on the Form in the design view and click on the *View, Properties* menu item to show the

Figure 5.19 The form of Example5-3.

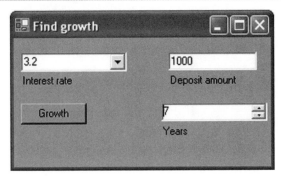

Figure 5.20 Choosing a background color.

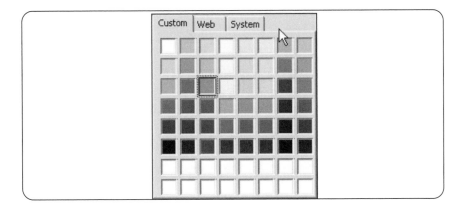

Properties window for the Form. We change the Text property to *Find growth*, which will display in the title at the top of the form. We change the BackColor to orange by choosing a color from the grid in the Custom tab that pops up when we click the button that appears at the right of the BackColor property entry. Figure 5.20 shows the color grid that appears.

We configure the ComboBox with a list of interest rates. Clicking the Items property shows a button that we click to pop up the String Collection Editor window shown in Figure 5.21, in which we enter four interest rates, 2.0, 3.2, 4.5, and 5.1. We change the (Name) of this ComboBox to selectRate and its Text property to the empty string. The Label below it will have its Text property set to *Interest rate*.

Figure 5.21   Entering the interest rate choices.

String Collection Editor

Enter the strings in the collection (one per line):

```
2.0
3.2
4.5
5.1
```

OK   Cancel   Help

We change the Text property of the TextBox to the empty string so it will be blank initially. We change its (Name) property to enterAmount. The Label below will have its Text property set to *Deposit amount*.

We set the Text of the Button to *Growth* and change its (Name) to showResult. We change the (Name) of the NumericUpDown to selectYears, and change the Text of the Label below it to *Years*.

To develop a solution, let us start with a simple case, $1000 at 5% for three years. For each year, we have to find the interest earned and add it to the account balance, as the following table shows.

Year	Interest	New Balance
1	1000 * .05 = 50	1000 + 50 = 1050
2	1050 * .05 = 52.50	1050 + 52.50 = 1102.50
3	1102.50 * .05 = 55.13	1102.50 + 55.13 = 1157.63

**Figure 5.22
Displaying the
accumulated amount.**

From this example, we see that each year we find the interest and add it to the balance to get the new balance. We will put these two steps in the body of our for statement.

The user chooses an interest rate from a ComboBox, enters an amount to deposit in a TextBox, and scrolls a NumericUpDown to specify the duration of the account. When the user clicks the *Growth* button, its event handler computes the amount of money in the account when it matures and displays it in a MessageBox as shown in Figure 5.22.

To display the template for the event handler for the Button, we double-click on it in the design view. The event-handling code is

```
private void showResult_Click
                   (object sender, System.EventArgs e)
{
    double rate = double.Parse
        (selectRate.SelectedItem.ToString())/100;
    decimal years = selectYears.Value;
    double deposit = double.Parse(enterAmount.Text);
    double result = deposit;
    for (int i = 1; i <= years; i++)
    {
        double interest = rate*result;
        result += interest;
    }
    MessageBox.Show(result.ToString("C"));
}
```

In the event handler we first place the user entries in variables. We convert the interest rate to a `double` and divide by 100 so that 3.2% becomes 0.032. The `Value` for the years in the `NumericUpDown` has type `decimal`. We convert the deposit amount to type `double` and initialize a result variable with this value.

The `for` loop computes the interest for each year and adds it to the result. A `MessageBox` displays the result in currency format.

5.3.4 The do Statement

The `while` statement lets us repeat a block of code; it checks the condition before executing the loop body. In some problems, when we know we will execute the body at least once, it is more natural to check the condition after executing the body. The `do` statement, having the syntax shown in Figure 5.23, lets us do that. C# executes the statement and then checks the

Figure 5.23 Syntax for the do statement.

```
do
   statement
while (condition) ;
```

condition. If the condition is true, C# executes the statement again, otherwise it proceeds to the next statement after the loop. The statement in the body of the do loop can be a simple statement, but most often it is a **block**, a group of statements enclosed in curly braces.

As a rule:

- Use a do statement when the loop body will always be executed at least once.

- Use a while statement when the loop body may (possibly) never be executed.

A simple example is

```
do {
    x += 5;
} while (x < 34);
```

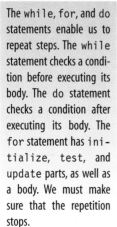

The BIG Picture

The while, for, and do statements enable us to repeat steps. The while statement checks a condition before executing its body. The do statement checks a condition after executing its body. The for statement has ini- tialize, test, and update parts, as well as a body. We must make sure that the repetition stops.

Test Your Understanding

11. Find any errors in the following while loops:

  a. while (x != 9}   b. while (x)   c. while (x =! 7)
       x +=4;   x *= 2;   x++;

12. Draw the flow diagram for the do statement.

13. Which of the following loops terminate? Assume that x has the value 12 at the start of the loop.

  a. while (x != 5)   b. while (x != 5)   c. while (x != 5)
       x++;   x--;   x = 5;

14. How many times will the body of each of following while loops be executed if x has the value 5 at the start of the loop?

  a. while (x <= 10)   b. while (x == 2)   c. while (x > 1)
       x +=3;   x -= 7;   x--;

15. Write a for statement that will sum the numbers from one through ten.

16. Write a for statement that will sum the numbers from seven through twelve.

17. Write a for statement that will sum the numbers from nine through three, in that order.

18. Write a for statement that will sum the even numbers from four through twenty.

19. What value will the variable sum have after the execution of the following code?

```
int sum = 0;
for (int i = 0; i < 8; i++)
  sum += i;
```

20. What value will the variable sum have after the execution of the following code?

```
int sum = 100;
for (int i = 2; i < 6; i++)
  sum -= i;
```

21. What value will the variable sum have after the execution of the following code?

```
int sum = 100;
for (int i = 20; i > 16 ; i--)
  sum -= i;
```

22. What value will the variable sum have after the execution of the following code?

```
int sum = 0;
for (int i = 1; i <= 20 ; i += 3)
  sum -= i;
```

23. What value will the variable sum have after the execution of the following code?

```
int sum = 100;
for (int i = 20; i > 6 ; i -= 5)
  sum -= i;
```

24. Find the value of the variable i after the execution of the following code.

```
int i = 1;
int total = 0;
```

```
do {
 total += i;
 i++ ;
} while (total < 25);
```

25. Find the value of the variable i after the execution of the following code.

```
int i = 10;
int total =100;
do {
 total -= i;
 i += 5;
} while (total > 25);
```

26. Find the value of the variable total after the execution of the following code.

```
int i = 1;
int total = 10;
do {
 total += i;
 i++ ;
} while (i < 5);
```

27. Find the value of the variable total after the execution of the following code.

```
int i = 1;
int total = 100;
do {
 total -= i;
 i++ ;
} while (i <= 7);
```

5.4 Summary

- The if statement allows us to choose whether to execute a statement. With the if-else statement we can choose between two alternatives. Nested if statements and the switch statement allow us to choose between multiple alternatives. Pair an else with the nearest preceding if. A switch statement chooses alternatives based upon the value of a variable.

- The while, for, and do statements enable us to repeat steps. The while statement checks a condition before executing its body. The do statement checks a condition after executing its body. The for statement has initialize, test, and update parts, as well as a body. We must make sure that the repetition stops.

5.5 Programming Exercises

5.1 Modify Example5-1 to use radio buttons instead of check boxes.

5.2 Modify Example5-2 to display the grade in a MessageBox rather than a Label.

5.3 Modify Example5-3 to use a ListBox instead of a ComboBox for the interest rate.

5.4 Create a Windows application that checks a grade-point average that the user inputs, and displays Congratulations, You made the honor roll if the average is 3.5 and above, but displays Sorry, You are on probation if the average is below 2.0.

5.5 Create a Windows application to convert meters to feet or inches. There are 39.37 inches in one meter and 12 inches in a foot. If the length is less than one foot, just display the number of inches. Show two digits after the decimal point. Thus 3.4 meters converts to 11.15 feet, while .2 meter converts to 7.87 inches.

5.6 Create a Windows application to determine how many months it will take to pay off a loan. The user will enter the loan amount, the annual interest rate, and the monthly payment. For example, suppose the loan amount is $1000 at 12% annual interest with monthly payments of $100. Each month you pay interest on the remaining balance. The interest rate is 1% per month, so the first month you pay $10 interest and $90 goes to reduce the balance to $910. The next month's interest is $9.10, and $90.90 is applied to reduce the balance, and so on. The last month's payment may be less than $100.

5.7 Create a Windows application that inputs the prices of a box of cereal and a quart of milk at store A and the prices of the same items at store B. The application should display the total cost of three boxes of cereal and two quarts of milk at whichever store has the lower cost. Either store is acceptable if the cost is the same at both.

5.8 Create a Windows application that includes three labels, A, B, and C, a text box, a button, and a numeric up-down. Let A, B, and C each represent a hidden number between 1 and 25. The user tries to guess the three numbers by entering a number from 1 to 25 in the text box and clicking the button to submit the guess. If the number matches one of the hidden numbers, the label representing it changes to show the number. The numeric up-down counts the number of guesses the user makes until all three numbers have been guessed. (Using random numbers, covered in the next chapter, can make this game more interesting.)

5.9 Create a Windows application that includes four groups of two radio buttons each. One radio button of each group has a Text showing the number 0, and the other shows the number 1. Create a sequence of four digits, each 0 or 1. For example 1, 0, 1, 0 is such a sequence. The user is to select one radio button from each group, either 0 or 1, and click a button to submit the four selections. The application responds by stating the number of correct selections in a label. For example, if the user chooses the sequence 0, 1, 1, 0, the response would be two correct, because the last two values, 1 and 0, match the last two positions of the 1, 0, 1, 0 sequence chosen initially. The user plays until a response of four correct is obtained. A numeric up-down displays the number of submissions that the user has made. (Using random numbers, covered in the next chapter, can make this game more interesting.)

CHAPTER 6

Reference Types

Reference types contrast with value types such as `int`. A variable of type `int` holds an integer value. A reference type such as a `String` holds a reference to a `String` object. Reference types are convenient when the values are large and of variable size. We can have several references to the same object without making unnecessary copies. In this chapter we first consider arrays and strings and then look at objects more generally.

We have written C# code for event handlers to enable controls to perform their desired functions. Arrays will enable us to be more effective. For example, if the user checks multiple check boxes, we can use an array to iterate through them to respond to the user's selections. We look more carefully at the `String` objects we have already been using to learn more about this fundamental type and compare it to `StringBuilder` for use in building strings. It will be interesting to explore some of the object types we use in the .NET Framework Class Library.

Chapter Objectives:

- Use arrays
- Study the `String` type
- Use `StringBuilder`
- Introduce objects from the .NET Framework Class Library

6.1 Arrays

An array contains a number of variables that we access through indices. For example, if a class has 30 students and each takes a test, we need 30 variables to save these scores. It would be very inconvenient to declare variables score1, score2, score3, and so on up to score30. With 300 students it would be much too much trouble.

The array declaration

```
int[] score = {65, 87, 34, 56, 98, 67, 58};
```

creates an array of seven variables, score[0], score[1], score[2], score[3], score[4], score[5], and score[6], and gives each variable an initial value. Declaring one array of seven variables is easier than declaring seven variables separately, and the advantage increases if the number of variables is larger. The type int[] denotes an array of integers. We can declare an array of any type.

The array declaration for score assigns 65 to score[0], 87 to score[1], and so on. We can use these values in expressions. For example,

```
int x = score[3] + score[4];
```

assigns the variable x a value of 154 because score[3] is 56 and score[4] is 98.

We can change array variables by assignment. For example,

```
score[6] = 85;
```

would change the value of score[6] from 58 to 85.

Often we access arrays using loops. We can use a for loop to sum the elements of the score array. Each array stores its length in the Length property, which we can use as the upper bound of the loop index. The following code computes the sum of the test scores in the score array.

```
int sum = 0;
for (int i = 0; i < score.Length; i++)
    sum += score[i];
```

This loop will sum our score array of seven scores, but it would also work without modification if the array had 300 scores. Using individual variables score1, score2, . . ., score300 would not be feasible.

In Example6-1 we use array notation in two ways, once to process multiple selections in a ListBox and again to process CheckBox selections. Figure 6.1 shows Example6-1.

On the left, a ListBox contains choices of food with three choices selected. A Label below the ListBox displays the choices the user made. This display updates immediately when the user selects or deselects a food from the list.

The four CheckBox controls on the right list subjects. The user checks or unchecks subjects and clicks the *Choose Favorites* button to show the currently selected favorite subjects in the Label at the lower left of the form.

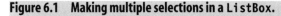

Figure 6.1 Making multiple selections in a ListBox.

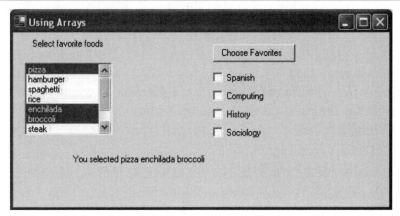

To build Example6-1, we create a new project and drag the controls we use from the Toolbox to the Form. To make the control names more meaningful, we change the default (Name) property of the following controls.

Control	New name
ListBox	foodList
Label (lower-left)	display
Button	showFavorites
CheckBox (top to bottom)	Spanish
	Computing
	History
	Sociology

6.1.1 Multiple ListBox Selections

The SelectionMode property determines the number of selections to allow in a ListBox. Its values are MultiExtended, MultiSimple, None, or One. In the Multi-Simple mode, clicking on an item with the mouse selects it, highlighting it in blue; clicking on it again deselects it. In the MultiExtended mode, the user can select a range of values. To do this, the user first clicks on an item to select it. Then, if the user holds the SHIFT key down and selects another item, the entire range between the two selections will be selected. In this mode, pressing Ctrl and clicking on an item selects or deselects it while keeping intact the remaining selections.

To enter these items into the list, we clicked on the Items entry in the Properties window of the Visual Studio .NET design. A String Collection window pops up, into which we enter the food items.

We used the Properties window in the Visual Studio .NET design to set the SelectionMode for the ListBox to MultiSimple. The user's selections appear in a Label. We would prefer to separate the selection by commas, and use "and" before the last selection. In the next section we will see how to build such strings.

To write the event handler for the ListBox selections, we first double-click on the ListBox in the Visual Studio .NET design to display the template

```
private void foodList_SelectedIndexChanged
                    (object sender, System.EventArgs e)
{
}
```

The .NET run time will call the foodList_SelectedIndexChanged method whenever the user changes a selection, either by selecting another item or deselecting one.

The SelectedItems property holds the collection of selected items. It is not an array, but it is set up to allow us to use array notation to index it. This collection has a Count property whose value is the number of selected items. Thus we can use

```
foodList.SelectedItems.Count
```

to find the number of items selected, which in Figure 6.1 is three. Because we can use array indexing, we can refer to the three items as SelectedItems[0], SelectedItems[1], and SelectedItems[2]. We write the event-handling code using a loop to add each selection item to the Text for the display label. The completed code is

```
private void foodList_SelectedIndexChanged
                    (object sender, System.EventArgs e)
{
    display.Text = "You selected ";
    for (int i = 0; i < foodList.SelectedItems.Count; i++)
        display.Text += foodList.SelectedItems[i] + " ";
}
```

6.1.2   Using the Documentation

The SelectedItems property does not appear in the Properties window in the Visual Studio .NET design because it is set at run time by the user who makes

Figure 6.2   CheckBox selections.

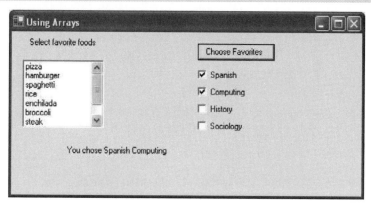

selections from the items in the ListBox. When writing the event-handling code, we can use the documentation to discover the properties of a control.

In Example6-1, while in the design mode, pressing the F1 key when the ListBox is selected displays the documentation for the ListBox members. This documentation shows many ListBox properties. The description for the SelectedItems property states that it gets a collection of the items selected by the user. Because it gets a collection, we can assume that we can use array notation to index its elements.

6.1.3   A CheckBox Array

The right section of Figure 6-2 shows four CheckBox controls. When the user selects favorite subjects and clicks the *Choose Favorites* button, the user's favorite subjects appear in the label below. Again, we will improve the display in the label after we consider strings more carefully in the next section.

The four CheckBox variables are spanish, computing, history, and sociology. We could use these names directly, but it is easier to declare an array to refer to these controls. We declare

```
CheckBox[] subject =
        {spanish, computing, history, sociology};
```

so we can refer to the controls using the subject array. For example, subject[1] refers to computing because the array indices are 0, 1, 2, and 3. The variable subject[3] refers to sociology.

When the user presses the button, we want the label to display the selected favorite subjects. In the event-handling code, we use the Checked property of

Figure 6.3   Guessing a number.

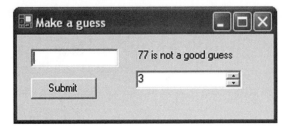

a CheckBox to determine whether it was checked, and, if so, we add it to the Text of the display label. The completed event-handling code is

```
private void showFavorites_Click
                    (object sender, System.EventArgs e)
{
    display.Text = "You chose ";
    CheckBox[] subject =
            { spanish, computing, history, and sociology };
    for (int i = 0; i < subject.Length; i++)
        if (subject[i].Checked)
            display.Text += subject[i].Text + " ";
}
```

6.1.4   A Search Game

We use an array to play a simple guessing game. Figure 6.3 shows the form of Example6-2. The user enters a number between 1 and 100 in the TextBox and clicks the *Submit* button. If the number is contained in the array of seven numbers, then the message says that the guess was good, but if not it says that the guess was bad. A NumericUpDown shows the number of guesses made so far.

We build Example6-2 by creating a project and dragging a TextBox, a Label, a Button, and a NumericUpDown from the Toolbox to the form. We give the controls more meaningful names by changing the (Name) property as follows:

Control	New name
TextBox	guessBox
Label	display
Button	submitGuess
NumericUpDown	guessCount

The event-handling code for the *Submit* button is

```
private void submitGuess_Click
                 (object sender, System.EventArgs e)
{
    int[]score = {65, 87, 34, 56, 98, 67, 58};
    int number = int.Parse(guessBox.Text);
    int i = 0;
                 // search for test in score array
    while (i < score.Length && number != score[i])
        i++;
    if (i < score.Length)               // number found
        display.Text = number + " is a good guess";
    else                                // number not found
        display.Text = number + " is not a good guess";
        guessBox.Text = "";       // remove previous entry
        guessBox.Focus();         // send key presses here
        guessCount.Value++;       // increment guesses
    }
}
```

We create the array with seven scores, and then convert the user's entry in guessBox to an integer. The while statement searches for the number in the score array. If the number is in the array at index i, the condition number != score[i] will fail and the loop will terminate. For example, if the user guesses 34, the condition 34 != score[2] is false and the loop will stop when i is 2.

If the user's guess is not one of the score elements, then i will continue to be incremented until it becomes 7 and the condition i < score.Length will fail, causing the loop to terminate. After the while loop terminates, we use an if-else statement to determine what caused the termination, finding the user's number or incrementing the index past the end of the array. We indicate the result in the label.

To make it easier for the user to enter the next number, we reset the Text in guessBox to the empty string. We call the Focus method of guessBox to direct the keystrokes to guessBox. This is helpful because when the user presses the button, it gets the focus; otherwise the user would have to click the mouse inside guessBox to direct key presses to it for the next entry.

6.1.5 Random Numbers

The guessing game of Example6-2 will not be interesting to replay because the user will soon figure out the numbers in the score array. To make it more interesting, we can generate random numbers that will change each time the program is run.

The Random class has a Next method that returns a number that appears to be randomly chosen from the integers 0 through 99. The following C# code will create an array of scores and fill it with randomly chosen numbers from 1 through 100.

```
int[] score = new score[7];
Random r = new Random();
for (int i = 0; i < score.Length; i++)
    score[i] = r.Next(100) + 1;
```

In this code, we did not initialize the array, but instead used the new operator to create seven variables, score[0], ..., score[6]. We use the new operator again to create a Random object r that we can use to generate the random numbers. In the for loop, we assign each variable a value randomly chosen from 1 through 100. The Next method returns values from 0 through 99, so we add 1 to each.

Example6-2a revises Example6-2 to fill the score array with random numbers. The easiest approach would be to modify the event-handling method for the button to fill the score array with random numbers. However, doing this would mean that each time the user made a guess the array would be recreated. We want to fill the array once and let the user keep making guesses until successfully finding a value. Thus we need to fill the score array outside of the event-handling method.

To fill the array in one place and use it in another, we need to create it so that it will be visible throughout the application. Similarly, the controls we add in the Visual Studio .NET design need to be visible throughout the application. Visual Studio initializes them inside the InitializeComponent method, and we use and change their properties inside our event-handling methods. We will declare the score array in the same location that Visual Studio .NET declares the controls. Figure 6.4 shows these declarations from Example6-2a. The private modifier indicates that only this application can use these variables directly.

Visual Studio .NET initializes the controls in the InitializeComponent method. We cannot change this method because Visual Studio automatically regenerates it when we make changes in the design and does not include any added code. Visual Studio places a comment in the code telling

Figure 6.4   Declarations of Example6-2a.

```
public class Form1 : System.Windows.Forms.Form
{

    private int[] score = new int[7];
    private System.Windows.Forms.TextBox guessBox;
    private System.Windows.Forms.Label display;
    private System.Windows.Forms.Button submitGuess;
    private
        System.Windows.Forms.NumericUpDown guessCount;
        // rest of code here
}
```

us where to add our initialization. Figure 6.5 shows the Form1 constructor. A constructor has the same name as the application class. Notice that in Figure 6.4 the class name is Form1. The constructor in Figure 6.5 has the same name, Form1, and no return value.

The .NET system calls the constructor when the application starts. The Form1 constructor calls the InitializeComponent method to initialize the controls. The TODO comment tells us to add any constructor code we need to initialize our variables, so we add the code to fill the score array with random numbers.

Figure 6.5   The Form1 constructor.

```
public Form1()
{
    //
    // Required for Windows Form Designer support
    //
    InitializeComponent();

    //
    // TODO: Add any constructor code after
    //        InitializeComponent call
    //
    Random r = new Random();
    for (int i = 0; i < score.Length; i++)
        score[i] = r.Next(100) + 1;
}
```

Figure 6.6 Primitive types hold values.

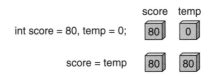

The event-handling method for the *Submit* button, submitGuess_Click, is the same as the event-handling method used in Example6-2 except that we omit the first line to initialize the score array because we have already initialized it with random numbers. Running Example6-2a will produce a form like Figure 6.3, but each time the user runs this application the score array will be different, making the game more interesting. We will elaborate on the concepts introduced in this example later in the chapter.

6.1.6   Array Variables and Values

Data, like many things, comes in different sizes. Many people have a cat that runs around their house, which they even pick up and hold from time to time. If the cat is sitting on your lap, and your sister wants to hold it, you can pass it to her. Some people have horses, but they do not give them free rein in the house, nor do they hold them on their laps—horses are too big. Both you and your sister know where to find the horses, in the stable.

Values of primitive types, such as 10, 'e', or 3.14, have fixed small sizes. Variables hold values of primitive types, and assignment copies the value from one variable to another, as Figure 6.6 shows.

Values of array types, such as {10,20,30,40,50,60,70}, can often be quite large. Variables do not hold array values, but hold references to them. A **reference** is a memory address: it tells where to find the item, in this case, an array. We indicate a reference by an arrow pointing to the location of the array. Figure 6.7 shows the memory usage for the array given by

```
int[] score = {26, 73, 92};
```

Figure 6.7   Memory usage for score.

Figure 6.8   Memory usage for an array assignment.

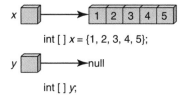

int [ ] x = {1, 2, 3, 4, 5};

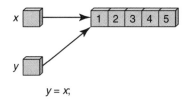

int [ ] y;

a. Before the assignment

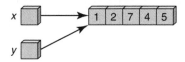

y = x;

b. After the assignment, y = x

Figure 6.9   Memory usage after the assignment y[2] = 7.

The variable score holds a reference to the array of three int elements.

Assigning one array to another copies the reference, not the array value. For example, Figure 6.8a diagrams the memory that C# uses for an array variable x initialized to refer to an array of five integers, and an uninitialized array variable y. Figure 6.8b shows the memory usage after we assign x to y.

We see that the assignment copies the reference from the variable x into the variable y. After the assignment, both variables refer to the same array. Copying a reference is more efficient than copying the whole array, which can be quite large. It takes time to copy the array values, and to create the space to hold them.

Because the variables x and y in Figure 6.8b refer to the same array, any changes made using x will affect y, and vice versa. For example, if we execute

y[2] = 7;

we will see that x[2] also has the value 7; x and y refer to the same array, so their elements must be the same. Figure 6.9 shows the effect of the assignment to y[2].

The BIG Picture

An array contains a number of variables that we access through indices. We can change array variables by assignment. Often we access arrays using loops. Each array stores its length in the Length property, which we can use as the upper bound of the loop index.

The Random class a Next method that returns a number that appears to be randomly chosen.

Test Your Understanding

1. In the array

   ```
   int[] x = {7, 8, 9};
   ```

   evaluate

   a. x[2]

   b. x.Length

2. Explain the difference between the MultiSimple and MultiExtended modes for a ListBox.

3. Which property holds the number of items in the SelectedItems collection for a ListBox?

6.2   Strings

We have used String objects often in our previous examples. For example, many controls have a Text property to display text associated with the control. For a Label, that Text is its main content.

Instances of the class String represent sequences of characters. The String class is part of the core .NET Framework library in the System namespace. Inside a String object is a sequence of characters, such as "C# is fun". The state (internal configuration) of a String object is private. Users of String objects do not need to know how the characters are represented.

6.2.1   Visualizing a String

We visualize a String as an object, such as a vending machine with a button for each service it provides. Strings have many public operations to provide their services. We show only a few in Figure 6.10, Length, IndexOf('i'), and ToUpper(). The String object, "C# is fun" in Figure 6.10 does not have a window to see inside, because strings do not show any of their state; it is all private.

When we press the Length button in Figure 6.10, we get the result of 9 because "C# is fun" has 9 characters. The result of an operation depends on the state of the object.

The IndexOf('i') button returns the first position in which the character 'i' occurs in the string, or −1 if 'i' does not occur in it. For this object the

Figure 6.10 A String object for "C# is fun".

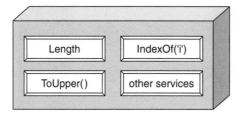

Figure 6.11 A String object for "C# IS FUN".

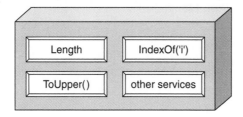

IndexOf('i') operation returns 3. The first 'i' occurs as the fourth character, but for technical reasons we start the numbering with 0, so 'i' is at index 3.

Strings objects in C# never change. The String object in Figure 6.10 will always represent "C# is fun". When we execute the ToUpper() operation, we do not change the object, but rather we get a new String object representing "C# IS FUN" shown in Figure 6.11.

Because the state is hidden, Figure 6.11 looks just like Figure 6.10, but it operates differently. Executing the IndexOf('i') operation will return −1, signifying the character 'i' does not appear in "C# IS FUN". C# is case-sensitive; a lowercase 'i' differs from an uppercase 'I'.

Visualizing a String object as a vending machine in Figures 6.10 and 6.11 really helps us to keep in mind that to use strings in C# programs, we need to create a string and ask it to execute one of its operations.

6.2.2 Creating a String

C# makes a special form of declaration available for String objects, because we use them so frequently. C# treats a literal such as "C# lets us use objects." as an instance of the String class. The declaration

```
String s = "C# lets us use objects.   ";
```

Figure 6.12   A String variable referring to a String object.

creates and initializes a String, which we refer to as s. The variable s refers to the String object, as shown schematically in Figure 6.12.

6.2.3   A String **Property**

A property is like a data field, but it does not directly represent a storage location. For example, the value of a property may be computed from other values. A property provides information about an object. For example,

```
s.Length;
```

will return the number of characters in s, 25 in this example. This string has two trailing blanks. All characters between the beginning and ending quotes are significant. We use a property like an instance variable, but internally it uses an accessor method to retrieve the length; thus we return the length using s.Length rather than s.Length(). In this text we have often used predefined properties of objects.

6.2.4   A String **Indexer**

An indexer is like a property, but it provides access by an index, like arrays. In C#, the Chars property in the String class is an indexer for the string. It returns the character at the specified index in the string. For example,

```
s[4]
```

returns 'e' because the character at index 4 is an 'e'. We use square brackets, [], to enclose an index, rather than the round parentheses, (), which we use for method arguments.

6.2.5   String **Methods**

The String class has both instance and class methods. An instance method refers to a specific String object. A class method is shared by all instances of the class. Most of the methods of the String class are instance methods.

Figure 6.13 s.ToLower() returns a new String.

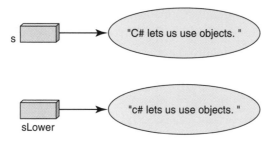

The ToLower() method returns a new String with the characters converted to lowercase. For example,

```
s.ToLower();
```

returns "c# lets us use objects.   ". To use this new String, we need to assign it to a variable, as in

```
String sLower = s.ToLower();
```

Figure 6.13 shows that we now have two String objects referred to by s and sLower.

The Trim and Substring methods also return new String objects. The Trim method removes leading and trailing **whitespace**, where whitespace includes blank spaces, newlines, and tabs. For example,

```
s.Trim();
```

returns "C# lets us use objects."

The Substring method has two parameters. The first gives the index at which the substring starts. The second indicates the number of characters in the substring. Thus

```
s.Substring(11,11);
```

returns "use objects", composed of the characters starting at position 11 in s, and including 11 characters.

6.2.6   Overloaded Methods

The String class contains overloaded methods. For example, the IndexOf method has six versions, which C# differentiates by the different parameters for each. The six methods are:

1. `public int IndexOf(char ch)`—returns the index of first occurrence of ch

2. `public int IndexOf(char ch, int from)`—returns the index of first occurrence of ch starting at index from

3. `public int IndexOf(char ch, int from, int len)`—returns the index of first occurrence of ch starting at index from—within the next len positions

4. `public int IndexOf(String str)`—returns the index of first occurrence of str

5. `public int IndexOf(String str, int from)`—returns the index of first occurrence of str starting at index from

6. `public int IndexOf(String str, int from, int len)`—returns the index of first occurrence of str starting at index from within the next len positions

To illustrate,

```
s.IndexOf('e');
```

returns 4, because the leftmost 'e' in the string occurs at index 4. The method call

```
s.IndexOf('e',8);
```

returns 13, because the first occurrence of 'e', starting from index 8, is at index 13. The method call

```
s.IndexOf('e',8,3);
```

returns -1, because there is no 'e' in the next three positions starting at index 8. The method call

```
s.IndexOf("us");
```

returns 8, because the leftmost occurrence of "us" starts at index 8. Similarly,

```
s.IndexOf("us",11);
```

returns 11 as the first occurrence of "us", starting from index 11, begins at index 11. When we try

```
s.IndexOf("us",15);
```

the result is -1, because there is no occurrence of "us" in s starting from index 15.

Programmers find it less cumbersome to use overloaded methods. For example, if the IndexOf method were not overloaded, we would have to use something like IndexOfChar, IndexOfCharFrom, IndexOfCharFromLen, IndexOf-String, IndexOfStringFrom, and IndexOfStringFromLen as the names for these six methods. Method overloading helps when we have methods that are similar except that they operate with different arguments.

When we use an overloaded method in a program, C# can determine which method to call by looking at the type of argument we pass to it. For example, in

```
String food = "potato";
int a  = food.IndexOf('a');    // passing a char
int to = food.IndexOf("to");   // passing a String
```

C# will call the IndexOf(char c) method to find the index of the first 'a' in "potato", because the argument 'a' passed in the call IndexOf('a') has type char. However, C# will call IndexOf(String s) to find the index of the first occurrence of "to", because the argument "to" has type String.

Replace is another overloaded method. One version replaces all occurrences of one character with another. The second version replaces all occurrences of a String with another. For example, in s = "C# lets us use objects. ",

```
s.Replace('e', 'o')
```

returns the String

```
"C# lots us uso objocts.  "
```

and

```
s.Replace("us", "them")
```

returns

```
"C# lets them theme objects.  "
```

Figure 6.14   The form of Example6-3.

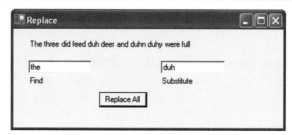

6.2.7   Class Methods

The String class has many other instance methods.[1] It also contains some class methods. Unlike an instance method, a class method does not refer to a specific object. For example,

```
double d = 3.14159265;
String w = String.Format("The price is {0:C}", d);
```

produces the String

```
"The price is $3.14"
```

Note that we prefix the Format method with the class name, String, rather than an object instance name. The Format method does not apply to a String object, in contrast to the IndexOf method and other instance methods that only make sense when applied to a String instance. Format is a class method rather than an instance method.

To illustrate the use of String methods, Example6-3 allows the user to replace every occurrence of one string with another in the string

```
"the three did feed the deer and then they were full"
```

Figure 6.14 shows the form of Example6-3. The user enters the string to find and the string to substitute for each occurrence. When the user clicks the *Replace All* button, the changed string appears in a label above the text

---

[1]The documentation for the .NET Framework Class Library is available for viewing or download from http://msdn.microsoft.com/library/default.asp?url=/library/en-us/cpref/html/cpref_start.asp. It is also available from the *Help* menu in Visual Studio .NET.

boxes. Notice that the replacement is case sensitive and does not replace the initial "The", which begins with an uppercase character.

We change the (Name) properties to give the controls the following more meaningful names:

Control	New name
Label (top)	display
TextBox (left)	find
TextBox (right)	substitute
Button	replace

We double-click on the button in the design view to display the template for its event handler. The code for the event handler for the button is

```
private void replace_Click
                   (object sender, System.EventArgs e)
{
    String oldWord = find.Text;        // word to replace
    String newWord = substitute.Text;  // replacement
    String temp = display.Text;
    int position = temp.IndexOf(oldWord);
                                       // first occurrence
    while(position != -1)
                                       // -1 indicates no match
    {
        temp = temp.Substring(0,position)
                                       // before match
            + newWord                  // replacement
            + temp.Substring(position + oldWord.Length);
                                       // after match
        position =                     // next occurrence
            temp.IndexOf(oldWord,position + newWord.Length);
    }
    display.Text = temp;
}
```

Each iteration of the while loop replaces one occurrence. We construct the new string by concatenating three parts: the substring before the occurrence, the replacement string, and the substring after the occurrence. To continue, we look for another occurrence further on in the string.

6.2.8   Using StringBuilder

The StringBuilder class represents a string-like object whose value is a sequence of characters that we can change. We can modify a StringBuilder object after it has been created by appending, removing, replacing, or inserting characters.

A C# String is immutable. It cannot be changed. The concatenation operator causes new temporary strings to be created. Creating a simple message,

```
String message = "The cow jumped over the moon";
```

presents no problem, but suppose the animal names and the thing they jump over are stored in variables. For example, suppose we have two variables, animal1 and animal2, that hold the names of animals, and a variable, thing, that holds the name of a thing. To construct a similar String, we could use the statements

```
String message = "The ";
message += animal1;
message += " and ";
message += animal2;
message += " jumped over the ";
message += thing;
```

Each concatenation would create a temporary String and change the message variable to refer to it. Figure 6.15 shows how the first step would work.

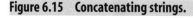
Figure 6.15   Concatenating strings.

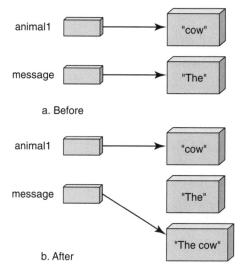

Figure 6.16   The form of Example6-4.

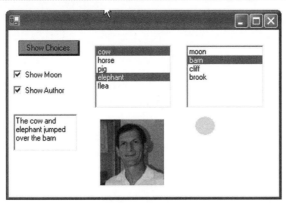

By contrast, we can change a `StringBuilder`. The `Append` method adds a string to the existing `StringBuilder` and does not need to create a new object. Using a `StringBuilder` we could create the message with the code

```
StringBuilder mess  = new StringBuilder("The ");
mess.Append(animal1);
mess.Append(" and ");
mess.Append(animal2);
mess.Append(" jumped over the ");
mess.Append(thing);
String message = mess.ToString();
```

We use a `StringBuilder` in Example6-4, where we need to make choices concerning the punctuation of the message. We leave the modification of Example6-1 to use a `StringBuilder` to improve the display to the exercises.

Figure 6.16 shows the form of Example6-4. The user can select multiple animals from a `ListBox` whose `SelectionMode` is `MultiSimple`, but must select one thing from a `ListBox` whose `SelectionMode` is `One`. When the user selects a thing, a message appears in the `TextBox` describing that choice. When the user selects animals and a thing, and then clicks the *Choose Animals* button, a message states that the animals jumped over the thing. The event handler for the button uses a `StringBuilder` to create the message. Two check boxes allow the user to display images in picture boxes.

We set the (Name) property to assign the following names to the indicated controls.

Control	New Name
Button	showChoices
ListBox (animals)	selectAnimals
ListBox (things)	selectThing
CheckBox (moon)	showMoon
CheckBox (author)	showAuthor
TextBox	display
PictureBox (author)	author
PictureBox (moon)	moon

We use the Visible property of a PictureBox to make the desired image visible when the corresponding CheckBox is checked, and not visible otherwise. The event-handling code for each CheckBox follows.

```
private void showMoon_CheckedChanged
                    (object sender, System.EventArgs e)
{
    if (showMoon.Checked)
        moon.Visible = true;
    else
        moon.Visible = false;
}

private void showAuthor_CheckedChanged
                    (object sender, System.EventArgs e)
{
    if (showAuthor.Checked)
        author.Visible = true;
    else
        author.Visible = false;
}
```

The event-handling method for selectThing, the list box containing things, just displays a message naming the selected thing. The code is

```
private void selectThing_SelectedIndexChanged
                    (object sender, System.EventArgs e)
{
    display.Text =
            "You selected " + selectThing.SelectedItem;
}
```

The event handler for the Button uses a StringBuilder to build the message combining constants such as "The " with the animals and thing, which change depending on the user's selections. When the user has not chosen a thing, we use "??" in its place. We separate the user's two choices with " and ", and use commas when the user chooses more than two animals.

```
private void showChoices_Click
                  (object sender, System.EventArgs e)
{                      // prefix with namespace
    System.Text.StringBuilder message =
        new System.Text.StringBuilder("The ");
    int length = selectAnimals.SelectedItems.Count;
    switch(length)
    {
     case 0: message.Append("??");
                 break;
     case 1: message.Append
             (selectAnimals.SelectedItems[0].ToString());
             break;
     case 2: message.Append
             (selectAnimals.SelectedItems[0].ToString());
             message.Append(" and ");
             message.Append
             (selectAnimals.SelectedItems[1].ToString());
             break;
        default:
             for(int i = 0; i < length-1; i++)
             {                  // comma after all but last
              message.Append
                  (selectAnimals.SelectedItems[i].ToString());
              message.Append(", ");
             }                      // "and" before last
             message.Append("and ");
             message.Append(selectAnimals.
                 SelectedItems[length-1].ToString());
             break;
    }
    message.Append(" jumped over the ");
    message.Append(selectThing.SelectedItem);
    display.Text = message.ToString();
}
```

The BIG Picture

Instances of the class String represent sequences of characters. The String class is part of the core .NET Framework library in the System namespace. C# makes a special form of declaration available for String objects, because we use them so frequently.

A property is like a data field, but it does not directly represent a storage location. The Length property of a String is an example. An indexer is like a property, but it provides access by an index, like arrays. For a String s, we use s[2] to represent the character at index 2 in the string.

The String class contains overloaded methods. For example, the IndexOf method has six versions, which C# differentiates by the different parameters for each.

The Format method does not apply to a String object, in contrast to the IndexOf method and other instance methods that only make sense when applied to a String instance. Format is a class method rather than an instance method.

A C# String is immutable. It cannot be changed. By contrast, we can change a StringBuilder object.

Test Your Understanding

4. Given the String object

    String s = "The three did feed the deer";

    find

    a. s.Length   b. s[5]   c. s.IndexOf('e')

    d. s.IndexOf("did") e. s.Substring(4,5) f. s.ToUpper()

5. Given the String object

    String r = "Mississippi";

    find

    a. r.IndexOf('i')   b. r.IndexOf('i',4)

    c. r.IndexOf("is",4)   d. r.IndexOf("is",9)

    e. r.IndexOf("sip")   f. r.IndexOf("sissy")

6. If String s = "Happy days are here again", find

    a. s.Replace('a', 'i')   b. s.Replace("e ", "xkd");

6.3   Library Classes

The .NET Framework Class Library provides a large number of classes, some of which we have used in our applications. These classes are grouped into namespaces.

6.3.1   Namespaces

A namespace lets us organize code and create globally unique type names. Using a name within one namespace would not preclude its being used in another, because each will have a different prefix. The namespaces we use in this text include

System	Fundamental classes
System.Data	Components that manage data
System.Data.OleDb	Database access
System.Drawing	Graphics functionality
System.Web.Services	Web services
System.Web.UI	User interfaces on a web page

System.Web.UI.WebControls	Web server controls
System.Windows.Forms	Windows user interfaces
System.Xml	XML processing
System.Xml.Schema	XML schemas
System.Xml.Xsl	Stylesheet transformations

We prefix a class with its namespace. The full declaration for a String s prefixes the System namespace that contains the String class. For example,

```
System.String s = "a big car";
```

To avoid prefixing a class with its namespace, we can add a using declaration at the top of the code file. For example, adding

```
using System;
```

allows the String to be declared as

```
String s = "a big car";
```

6.3.2   Control Objects

The classes in the .NET Framework Class Library define objects that we use in our applications. An object is an instance of a class. For example, the Button class defines the features of a button. We can create many Button instances to use in our applications. The fragment from Example6-2a shown here (see also Figure 6.4) declares five objects: a TextBox, a Label, a Button, a NumericUpDown, and an array.

```
private System.Windows.Forms.TextBox guessBox;
private System.Windows.Forms.Label display;
private System.Windows.Forms.Button submitGuess;
private
    System.Windows.Forms.NumericUpDown guessCount;
private int[] score = new int[7];
```

The declaration for the TextBox is

```
private System.Windows.Forms.TextBox guessBox;
```

The private modifier signifies that the guessBox variable is only accessible within Example6-2a in which it is defined. The prefix System.Windows.Forms represents the namespace containing the TextBox class. We chose the variable name guessBox instead of the default name textBox1. To change the variable name, we set the (Name) property of the TextBox.

The variable guessBox has a reference type, meaning that its memory location holds a reference to a TextBox, not the TextBox itself. In fact, so far there is no TextBox object. Until we assign it a TextBox, the variable guessBox has the value null, signifying an invalid reference.

Visual Studio .NET hides the creation of the user interface controls. Looking at the code for Example6-2a shows the line

```
+   Windows Form Designer generated code
```

The BIG Picture

The .NET Framework Class Library provides a large number of classes, some of which we have used in our applications. These classes are grouped into namespaces. A namespace lets us organize code and create globally unique type names. The classes in the .NET Framework Class Library define objects that we use in our applications. An object is an instance of a class. The new operator allocates memory for objects.

Clicking on the plus sign in the margin will show the code generated by Visual Studio .NET to create and position the user interface controls that we added to the form. It is hidden because we are not to modify it.

This hidden code contains the line

```
guessBox = new System.Windows.Forms.TextBox();
```

that creates a TextBox and assigns the reference to it to guessBox. The new operator allocates memory for the TextBox instance and calls the TextBox constructor, which is like an initialization method. As in Example6-2a, Visual Studio .NET creates most of the objects we need when building our applications.

Test Your Understanding

   7.   In what namespace is the String class?

   8.   In what namespace is the TextBox class?

6.4 Summary

- An array contains a number of variables that we access through indices. We can change array variables by assignment. Often we access arrays using loops. Each array stores its length in the Length property, which we can use as the upper bound of the loop index.

- The Random class has a Next method that returns an integer.

- Instances of the class String represent sequences of characters. The String class is part of the core .NET Framework library in the System namespace. C# makes a special form of declaration available for String objects because we use them so frequently.

- A property is like a data field, but it does not directly represent a storage location. The Length property of a String is an example. An indexer is like a property, but it provides access by an index, like arrays. For a String s, we use s[2] to represent the character at index 2 in the string.

- The String class contains overloaded methods. For example, the IndexOf method has six versions, which C# differentiates by the different parameters for each.

- The Format method does not apply to a String object, in contrast to the IndexOf method and other instance methods that only make sense when applied to a String instance. Format is a class method rather than an instance method.

- A C# String is immutable. It cannot be changed. By contrast, we can change a StringBuilder object.

- The .NET Framework Class Library provides a large number of classes, some of which we have used in our applications. These classes are grouped into namespaces. A namespace lets us organize code and create globally unique type names. The classes in the .NET Framework Class Library define objects that we use in our applications. An object is an instance of a class. The new operator allocates memory for objects.

6.5 Programming Exercises

6.1 Modify Example6-1 to use a CheckedListBox instead of four separate CheckBox controls.

6.2 Modify Example6-2 to use a Label instead of NumericUpDown to display the number of attempts.

6.3 Modify Example6-3 to give the user a choice of three source strings that appear in a ComboBox.

6.4 Modify Example6-1 to separate items in the display label with commas and to put an "and" before the last element. With two items, do not use a comma.

6.5 Modify Example6-4 to allow the selection of more than one thing.

6.6 Create a Windows application that changes every 'p' to a 'q' in a String entered by the user.

6.7   Create a Windows application to simulate the roll of two dice, and display the sum of the numbers on each. A die has six faces numbered 1 through 6. Each face is equally likely to occur, so we simulate a roll by generating a random number from 1 through 6.

6.8   Create a Windows application with one ListBox showing foods and another for drinks. Allow the user to make multiple selections from each, and display the user's selections in a MessageBox.

6.9   Create a Windows application that includes three labels, A, B, and C; a text box; a button; and a numeric-up-down. Let A, B, and C each represent a hidden number between 1 and 25, chosen randomly. The user tries to guess the three numbers by entering a number from 1 to 25 in the text box and clicking the button to submit the guess. If the number matches one of the hidden numbers, the label representing it changes to show the number. The numeric-up-down counts the number of guesses that the user makes until all three numbers have been guessed. You may wish to use the Tag property of a label to store the hidden number.

6.10   Create a Windows application that includes four groups of two radio buttons each. One radio button of each group has a Text showing the number 0, and the other shows the number 1. Use random numbers to create a sequence of four digits, each 0 or 1. For example, 1, 0, 1, 0 is such a sequence. The user is to select one radio button from each group, either 0 or 1, and click a button to submit the four selections. The application responds by stating the number of correct selections in a label. For example, if the user chooses the sequence 0, 1, 1, 0, the response would be two correct, because the last two values, 1 and 0, match the last two positions of the 1, 0, 1, 0 sequence chosen initially. The user plays until a response of four correct is obtained. A numeric-up-down displays the numbers of submissions that the user has made.

6.11   Create a Windows application that includes four labels, A, B, C, and D, with a ComboBox under each label. Each combo box will list the six colors: Red, Green, Blue, Yellow, White, and Orange. Choose a color for each label randomly, but do not show those colors in the form. The user will try to guess the color of each label by selecting the color for each in the combo box below it. When the user makes a selection, the label will change to the color selected. When the user presses a Button, the application will respond with a message stating how many colors are correct and how many are in the correct position. For example, if the user guesses Red, Red, Blue, Yellow, and the correct choices are Red, Blue, Yellow, and Green, the response will be 1, 2, meaning that one color matches exactly and two other colors are correct but in the wrong positions. A NumericUpDown will count the number of tries until the user guesses all four colors correctly. You may wish to use the Tag property of a label to store its color to be guessed.

6.12 Create a Windows application to play a game. The game uses six letters: a, b, c, d, e, and f. The computer chooses four letters at random, and they may be repeated, so they might be abcc or aadd, and so forth. The player enters a string of letters, say, ddec, in a TextBox and clicks the *Submit* button. The application displays two numbers, the number of letters that exactly match the pattern chosen in advance, and the number of letters that are in the pattern but that the user put in the wrong position. For example, if the pattern is abcc, some guesses and scores are:

```
adef    1, 0
deaf    0, 1
cabb    0, 3
cccc    2, 0
acbc    2, 2
```

The game continues until the user guesses all letters in the correct position (4, 0). The score is the number of guesses it takes. Naturally, lower scores are better.

CHAPTER 7

Using a Database

Visual Studio .NET tools make it easy to connect to a database to retrieve or update data. We can process data while connected to the database or we can process the data locally in our application. By processing data locally using a `DataSet`, we can free the connection to the database for others to use. Later we will develop Web applications in which the client and the server by default do not maintain a connection.

We use a .NET data provider for connecting to a database, executing commands, and retrieving results. `Connection`, `Command`, and `DataReader` objects provide these three functions. A `DataAdapter` populates a `DataSet` to process data without maintaining a connection.

The simplest and most efficient database access uses a `DataReader` to process data while connected to the database. When using multiple tiers, the user does not directly connect to the database but rather to a middle tier that provides database access. Using multiple tiers allows applications to handle many users while maintaining performance. For simplicity, we do not use multiple tiers in this chapter but do show both methods of data access: using a `DataReader` while connected and populating a `DataSet` for offline processing.

Chapter Objectives:

- Use the Northwind example database
- Use a `DataReader` while connected to a database
- Use a `DataAdapter` to load data from a data source to a `DataSet`
- Build a query to retrieve data
- Generate a `DataSet`
- Display data in a `DataGrid`
- Generate a data `Form`

7.1   The Northwind Database

The Microsoft Access database system is part of the Microsoft Office package. In this chapter we use Microsoft Access 2002. Microsoft Access comes with a Northwind database that we will use for several examples. To view it, we first open Microsoft Access. Then, clicking on *Help, SampleDatabases, Northwind Sample Database* produces the window of Figure 7.1 listing the tables in the Northwind database.[1]

7.1.1   Relational Databases

A relational database is a collection of data items organized as a set of tables from which data can be accessed in many different ways without having to reorganize the database tables. Figure 7.1 lists the eight tables of the Northwind database. The columns of a table represent categories. Each row is an entry with data in each of the categories.

Figure 7.2 shows the Shippers table. It has three columns, Shipper ID, Company Name, and Phone, and three rows containing the data for three shippers.

---

[1] If Northwind is not installed, clicking will prompt the user to install it from the Microsoft Office CD.

Figure 7.1   The Northwind database tables.

Figure 7.2 The `Shippers` table.

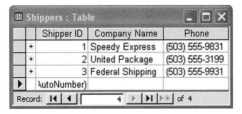

The first column, `Shipper ID`, is the key. It uniquely identifies the shipper. Even if two shippers had the same name, they would have a unique `Shipper ID` to identify them. For display purposes, the column headers have spaces, but the names in the design view are `ShipperID`, `CompanyName`, and `Phone`.

A well-designed relational database avoids duplication of information. For example, in Northwind each entry in the `Orders` table specifies the `Customer` who placed it. The `Orders` table just includes the `CustomerID`[2] and not the `Address`. If the `Orders` table included the address for each customer, then when the address changed all the entries in the `Orders` table containing that customer's address would have to change. In Northwind, the `Customers` table contains the customer's address, which only occurs once and can be updated in one place. Figure 7.3 lists the column categories for each of the Northwind tables.

The `Order Details` table has a compound key. We need both the `OrderID` and the `ProductID` to uniquely identify an `Order Details` entry. The `Order Details` table helps to avoid redundancy. Each order may include several products. Making multiple entries for each order in the `Orders` table would force repetition of the `Customer`, `Employee`, `Order Date`, and so on, which are the same for all items of the order. All the information that is the same for an entire order occurs in the `Orders` table. The information that depends on the item ordered occurs in the `Order Details` table.

7.1.2 Queries

A query retrieves information from a database. The Structured Query Language (SQL) is the standard for expressing queries, but we will not need to

---

[2]For display purposes, the `Orders` table shows the `Company Name` rather than `CustomerID`.

Figure 7.3   Columns of the Northwind tables.

```
Categories
   CategoryID (key), CategoryName, Description, Picture
Customers
   CustomerID (key), CompanyName, ContactName, ContactTitle, Address,
   City, Region, PostalCode, Country, Phone, Fax
Employees
   EmployeeID (key), LastName, FirstName, Title, TitleOfCourtesy,
   BirthDate, HireDate, Address, City, Region, PostalCode, Country,
   HomePhone, Extension, Photo, Notes, ReportsTo
Order Details
   OrderID (key), ProductID (key), UnitPrice, Quantity, Discount
Orders
   OrderID (key), CustomerID, EmployeeID, OrderDate, RequiredDate,
   ShippedDate, ShippedVia, Freight, ShipName, ShipAddress, ShipCity,
   ShipRegion, ShipPostalCode, ShipCountry
Products
   ProductID (key), ProductName, SupplierID, CategoryID, QuantityPerUnit,
   UnitPrice, UnitsInStock, UnitsOnOrder, ReorderLevel, Discontinued
Shippers
   ShipperID (key), CompanyName, Phone
Suppliers
   SupplierID (key), CompanyName, ContactName, ContactTitle, Address,
   City, Region, PostalCode, Country, Phone, Fax, HomePage
```

use it explicitly because Visual Studio .NET provides the Query Builder tool to construct queries. We will use it in the next section.

A simple query might ask for a list of all company names. We can find the company names from the Customers table. A more involved query might ask for the total sales in August 1996. This would require checking the dates in the Orders table, finding those rows of the Order Details table with Order ID corresponding to an August 1996 date, computing the sales from that item, and updating the total.

Test Your Understanding

1. Why is ProductID a better choice than ProductName as the key for the Products table in the Northwind database?

The BIG Picture

A relational database is a collection of data items organized as a set of tables from which data can be accessed in many different ways without having to reorganize the database tables. A query retrieves information from a database.

7.2   The Connected Model

In the connected model, we process data while maintaining a connection to the database. We use a data reader to read from a database for more efficient processing when we do not need a middle tier or are not sharing the dataset with many users. In Example7-1, we connect to the Northwind database. We will query Northwind to find the price for each product, and then display the products and prices in a ListBox control.

7.2.1   Connecting to a Database

We start by opening Visual Studio .NET and creating a new Windows Application project for Example7-1. In the Toolbox, we click the *Data* tab to open a list of controls useful for accessing data. A .NET data provider links our application with a data source. In this book, we use the OLE DB .NET Data Provider to communicate with the Microsoft Access Northwind database.

We drag an OleDbConnection control from the Toolbox to the form. This control represents a connection to a database. Note that in Figure 7.4 it appears below the form because it has no visible representation on the

Figure 7.4   Adding an OleDbConnection.

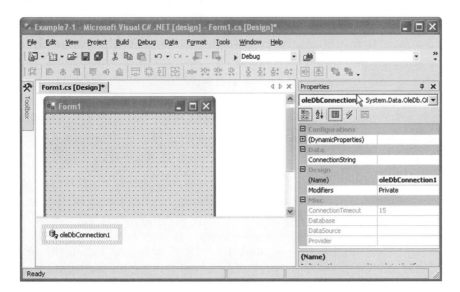

Figure 7.5   Selecting a provider.

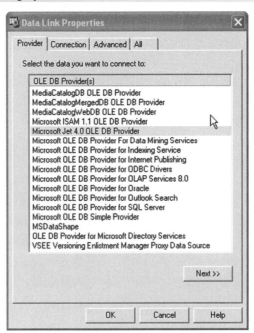

form. Its Properties window at the right allows us to configure the connection. We change the (Name) property to northwind.

To connect to the Northwind database, we need to set the ConnectionString property for the OleDbConnection. Clicking on the button at the right of the ConnectionString entry in the Properties window displays a list of connection strings previously set and a <New Connection...> choice that we select. Figure 7.5 shows the Data Link Properties window that pops up, in which we have selected the Provider tab and selected the Microsoft Jet 4.0 OLE DB Provider used to connect to a Microsoft Access database.

Clicking *Next* displays the Connection tab shown in Figure 7.6. We browse to select a database name. On the author's system, Northwind has the path

H:\Program Files\Microsoft Office\Office10\Samples\Northwind.mdb

We enter Admin as the password and check Blank Password. Clicking the *Test Connection* button should display a message saying that the test connection

Figure 7.6   Configuring a database connection.

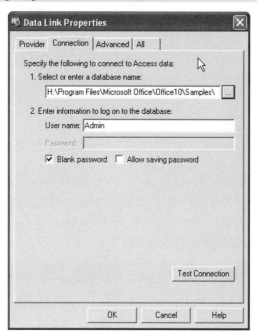

succeeded. We click *OK* to close the message box and click *OK* to close the Data Link Properties window.

7.2.2   Building a Command

We want to find the price of each Northwind product. With an OleDbCommand control, we can configure a query to the Northwind database to retrieve product information. We drag an OleDbCommand from the Toolbox to the form. It also appears below the form in the design. We change its (Name) property to productPrices.

To associate a database with the command, we set the Connection property. Clicking the button at its right displays the choices shown in Figure 7.7. Clicking the + sign to the left of *Existing* shows the existing connections. We select the northwind connection that we configured above.

The CommandText property will specify the query that we build to find the prices of Northwind products. We click on it and on the button that appears

Figure 7.7   Associating a connection with a command.

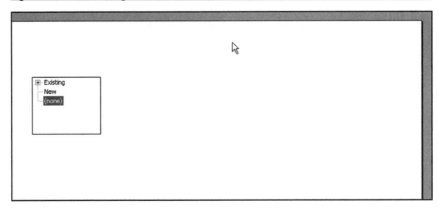

Figure 7.8   Selecting the Products table.

at the right. Figure 7.8 shows the Add Table window that appears. We will be using the Products table, so we select Products and click *Add* and *Close*. The Query Builder form appears showing the columns of the Products table. We check ProductName and UnitPrice, as shown in Figure 7.9, and click *OK*.

7.2.3   Reading and Displaying the Data

We use a data reader to read the product names and prices from the Northwind database. To display the data that we retrieve from the Northwind

Figure 7.9 Building a query.

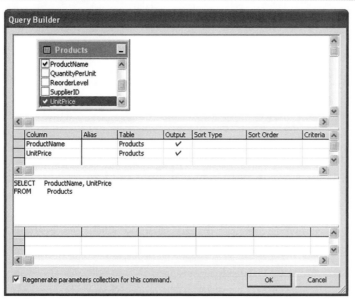

database, we need to enter it in a user interface control. We use a `ListBox` control to display the list of Northwind products with their prices. Clicking the `Windows Forms` tab in the Toolbox displays the user interface controls available. We drag a `ListBox` control to the form and change its (Name) property to `display`. We change the `Font.Name` property to `Courier New` so that the display will be evenly spaced. In the `Courier New` font, each character has the same width.

We retrieve the data from the database when the application begins execution. Double-clicking on the form displays the template

```
private void Form1_Load(object sender, System.EventArgs e)
{

}
```

for the `Form1_Load` method that executes when the application starts. We need to add the C# code to query the database and to enter the data into the `ListBox`. The completed `Form1_Load` method is

```
private void Form1_Load(object sender, System.EventArgs e)
{
```

```
        northwind.Open();
        System.Data.OleDb.OleDbDataReader reader
                        = productPrices.ExecuteReader();
        while (reader.Read())
            display.Items.Add
                (String.Format("{0,-35}{1,10:C}",
                reader.GetString(0), reader.GetDecimal(1)));
        reader.Close();
        northwind.Close();
}
```

To read the data from the database, we use an `OleDbDataReader`. First we open the connection to the database using

```
northwind.Open();
```

The `ExecuteReader` method of the `OleDbCommand` sends the command to the connection and builds an `OleDbDataReader`

```
System.Data.OleDb.OleDbDataReader reader
                    = productPrices.ExecuteReader();
```

The `Read` method reads a row of Northwind data. It returns `false` when there are no more rows. We use a `while` loop to read all the rows. We enter each row that we read into the list box. The `Items` property represents the collection of items in the list box. The `Add` method adds a string to the collection.

We built the command to get the product name and price of each Northwind product. The product name is a `String`, and the price is a `Decimal`. We use the `GetString` method to retrieve a string field and the `GetDecimal` method to return a decimal field. We refer to the fields in each row by indices, starting with 0. Thus

```
reader.GetString(0)
```

returns the product name and

```
reader.GetDecimal(1)
```

returns the price. The `Format` method

```
String.Format("{0,-35}{1,10:C}",
            reader.GetString(0), reader.GetDecimal(1))
```

left-justifies each product name in a field of width 35 and right-justifies the price as a currency in a field of size 10. Finally, we close the reader and the connection to release the resources that they are using back to the system.

Figure 7.10 Northwind product names and prices.

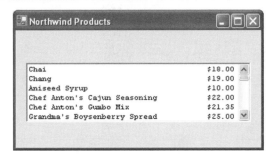

```
reader.Close();
northwind.Close();
```

Figure 7.10 shows the application of Example7-1 displaying the Northwind products and prices.

Test Your Understanding

2. List the controls in Example7-1 that do not have visual representations on the form.

3. Which OLE DB Provider class contains the Read method to read from a database while maintaining a connection?

7.3 The Disconnected Model

A data adapter serves as a bridge between a data source and a data set in memory. A data set is an in-memory cache of data retrieved from a database. We use a data set because we do not want to maintain a connection to the database or because we are accessing the data via a middle tier and cannot maintain a connection. Too many users connecting to a database will degrade performance. By using a data set, we can offload processing to our local computer and leave the database available for other users.

A data adapter can fill the data set with data from the data source and can update the data source. It uses a data connection to connect to a database only for the purpose of filling the data set, and then it disconnects from the database, allowing the user to process the data locally. A data command specifies a query or an update to the database. In Example7-2, we redo Example7-1 to illustrate the disconnected model. We will use a data adapter to fill a data set that we bind to a DataGrid control. The user will

The BIG Picture

In the connected model, we process data while maintaining a connection to the database. We use an `OleDbConnection` to connect, an `OleDbCommand` to query, and an `OleDbDataReader` to read from the database.

Figure 7.11   Selecting a data connection.

work with the data grid. We will not make any changes, but if we did, the data adapter could update the database to reflect the changes made while processing locally.

7.3.1   The Data Adapter Configuration Wizard

We start by opening Visual Studio .NET and creating a new Windows Application project for Example7-2. In the Toolbox, we click the *Data* tab to open a list of controls useful for accessing data. There are two data adapters in the first .NET version, SqlDataAdapter and OleDbDataAdapter, and additional adapters in later versions. The SqlDataAdapter can be applied to the Microsoft SQL Server database. We use the OleDbDataAdapter to connect to the Microsoft Access database. Dragging an OleDbDataAdapter from the Toolbox to the form of Example7-2 displays the Data Adapter Configuration Wizard. Clicking *Next* on the welcome screen displays the Choose Your Data Connection window shown in Figure 7.11. We select the connection we configured in Example7-1. Clicking *Next* displays the Choose a Query Type screen shown in Figure 7.12. We check the *Use SQL statements* radio button and click *Next*.

Figure 7.12 Choosing a query type.

7.3.2 A Query Builder

In the `Generate the SQL statements` window, click the *Query Builder* button at the lower right. The Query Builder tool builds a query to extract information from the database. Figure 7.8 shows the `Add Table` window that appears. We will be using the `Products` table, so we select `Products` and click *Add* and *Close*. The `Query Builder` form appears showing the columns of the `Products` table. We check `ProductName` and `UnitPrice` as shown in Figure 7.9 and click *OK*.

We are only going to read the data and do not need the capability to insert, delete, or update data. By default, the data adapter configuration wizard will generate commands to insert, delete, and update. To change the default, we click the *Advanced Options...* button in the `Generate the SQL statements` screen shown in Figure 7.13. We remove the check from the *Generate Insert, Update, and Delete statements* box and click *OK*.

We click *Next* in the `Generate the SQL statements` screen and then click *Finish*. We have configured the data adapter with a data connection and a query to extract information. As in Example7-1, these controls appear

Figure 7.13   Generating SQL statements.

below the form in the design. We change the (Name) property of the Ole-DbAdapter to northwindAdapter and that of the OleDbConnection to northwind-Connection. Now that we have built the query, we need to generate a DataSet to hold the data in our application.

7.3.3   A Data Set

A DataSet holds data in memory that has been received from a database. We use a DataSet in our program to receive the Northwind data. We start by clicking the *Data, Generate Dataset* menu item that displays the Generate Dataset form of Figure 7.14. We click *OK* to accept the default setting showing that the Products table will be part of the data set. The data set control also appears below the form in the design. We change its (Name) property to productPrices.

To display the data, we can use a DataGrid control. We drag a DataGrid control from the Windows Forms tab of the Toolbox to the form in the Visual Studio .NET design. We click on the DataSource property in the Properties window and choose productPrices.Products. This will enter the ProductName, Unit-

Figure 7.14 Generating a data set.

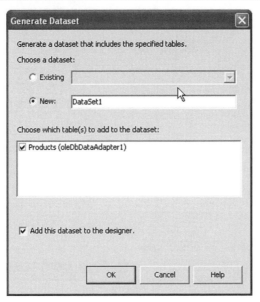

Price, and ProductID in the DataGrid control. Notice that the ProductID key was automatically added. We need to widen the DataGrid to show all the fields.

To fill the DataGrid with the desired information, we use the Fill method of the OleDbDataAdapter. We double-click on the form (not the DataGrid control) in the Visual Studio .NET design to display the Form1_Load template and enter the code to fill the data set, giving

```
private void Form1_Load(object sender, System.EventArgs e)
{
    northwindAdapter.Fill(productPrices);
}
```

Figure 7.15 shows the resulting data from the Products table.

7.3.4 Using the Data Form Wizard

With the Data Form Wizard, we can display information from a dataset using a Windows Form, either in a DataGrid or in individual controls. Example7-3 uses the Data Form Wizard to create a Form to present the Products table from the Northwind database.

Figure 7.15   The Northwind product prices.

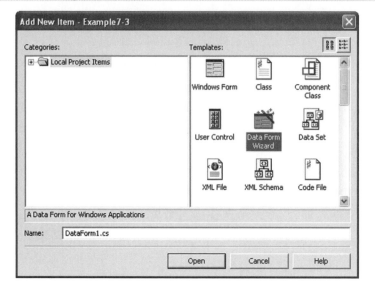

Figure 7.16   Adding a data form.

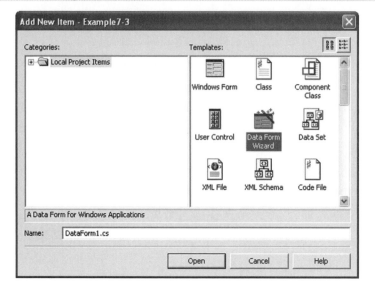

We start by creating a new Windows Application project, Example7-3, in Visual Studio .NET. Clicking *File, Add New Item* displays the screen of Figure 7.16. We choose Data Form Wizard and click *Open* to display the welcome screen. Clicking *Next* displays the *Choose the dataset you want to use* screen. We check the *Create a new dataset* radio button, enter the name products, and click *Next*.

In the *Choose a data connection* screen, we select the Northwind database and click *Next*. In the *Choose tables or views* screen of Figure 7.17, we select

Figure 7.17 Selecting the Products table.

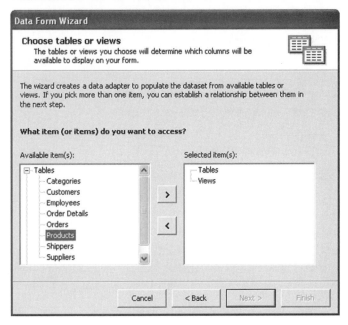

the Products table, click the right arrow to transfer it to the *Selected items* area, and click *Next*.

By default, the *Choose tables and columns to display on the form* screen shown in Figure 7.18 has all columns of the Products table selected. Clicking *Next* displays the *Choose the display style* screen of Figure 7.19. We select the *Single record in individual controls* radio button to display each field in its own control. We uncheck the Add, Delete, and Cancel check boxes because we do not want to make any changes to the Northwind database, but we check the Navigation controls check box to inspect the data from the Products table.

Clicking the *Finish* button produces the DataForm1 form, which we need to make the start-up form so that it will appear when we execute this application. We right-click on Form1 in the Visual Studio .NET design and click *View Code*. We scroll down to the Main method and change Form1 to DataForm1 so that the Main method reads

```
static void Main()
{
    Application.Run(new DataForm1());
}
```

Figure 7.18   Choose tables and columns to display on the form.

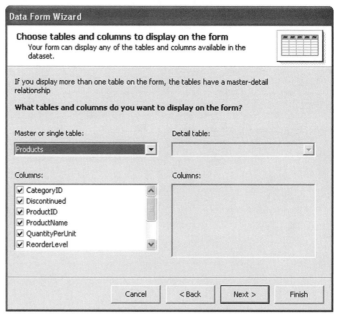

Figure 7.19   Choose the display style.

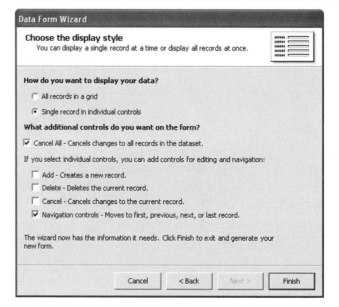

Figure 7.20   The data form showing Northwind products.

Northwind Products

| Load | | | | Update |

CategoryID	1		ReorderLevel	10
Discontinued	☐		SupplierID	1
ProductID	1		UnitPrice	18
ProductName	Chai		UnitsInStock	39
QuantityPerUnit	10 boxes x 20 bags		UnitsOnOrder	0

| << | < | 1 of 77 | > | >> |

We execute Example7-3 and press the Load button to fill the form with the data from the Northwind Products table as shown in Figure 7.20.

Test Your Understanding

4. Which control represents data from the database in memory?

5. Which control displays data in a scrollable grid?

6. What does SQL stand for?

7.4   Using Multiple Tables

The most interesting uses of databases require data to be gathered from multiple tables. When using a relational database, the database system processes the query to make it access the data efficiently. In Example7-4, we will display the names of all the products from the Seafood category. The Products table does not directly show the category name for each product. It lists the CategoryID.

If we use the Categories table, we can match the CategoryID for a product with the CategoryID in the Categories table and find the corresponding CategoryName for that CategoryID. For example, the first product, Chai, has a CategoryID of 1. Looking at entry 1 in the Categories table shows that its CategoryName is Beverages, so Chai is not part of the result. However, the tenth product, Ikura, has a CategoryID of 8. From the Categories table we find that the corresponding CategoryName is Seafood, so it is one of the results. This is the kind of processing performed by the database system,

The BIG Picture

In the disconnected model, we use a data set to process data locally. A data adapter serves as a bridge between a data source and a data set for retrieving and storing data. The Data Adapter Configuration Wizard adds a data connection configured to a particular database. Its query builder tool constructs a query to get the desired information from the database.

A DataSet holds data in memory that has been received from a database. It allows us to process data without maintaining a connection to the database. The DataGrid control displays data on a form. We fill the Data-Grid when the form loads.

With the Data Form Wizard, we can display information from a data set using a Windows Form, either in a Data-Grid or in individual controls. It adds another form to the project, which can be started by modifying the Main method of the original form.

Figure 7.21   Selecting multiple tables.

Microsoft Access in our example. We use Visual Studio .NET tools to set up our query.

7.4.1   Building the Query

We start by creating Example7-4 as a new Windows Application. Dragging an OleDbDataAdapter onto the form brings up the Data Adapter Configuration Wizard. Clicking *Next* displays the Choose Your Data Connection screen. We select the Northwind database and click *Next*. In the *Choose a Query Type* screen, we select *Use SQL statements* and click *Next*. In the *Generate the SQL statements* screen, we click the *Query Builder* button. In the *Add Table* screen shown in Figure 7.21, we select the Categories table and hold the *Ctrl* key down while selecting the Products table. Holding the *Ctrl* key down allows us to make multiple selections.

Clicking *Add* and *Close* shows the Query Builder form with the columns of the Categories and Products tables displayed. We check ProductName in the Products table because that is the result we want to show in our application. Figure 7.22 shows the Query Builder form.

The Query Builder shown in Figure 7.22 has four panes. From top to bottom they are the Diagram, Grid, SQL, and Results panes. The Diagram pane displays the tables we are using. A bar joins the CategoryID field in the Categories table with the CategoryID field in the Products table. This identifies the search process described above where we matched the CategoryID of a prod-

Figure 7.22   Selecting ProductName in the Query Builder.

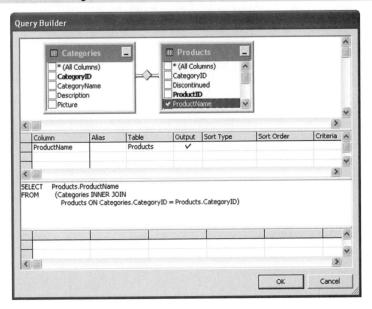

uct in the Products table with the same CategoryID in the Categories table to find the corresponding CategoryName for that product. The boldface type in the Categories table indicates that CategoryID is the primary key of that table. The CategoryID field appears as a foreign key in the Products table.

The Grid pane allows us to specify options about the data to be selected. Checking the ProductName column in the Products table in the Diagram pane makes an entry in the Grid pane showing, by default, that ProductName will be part of the output. We want to include a condition restricting the output to products in the Seafood category. The restriction we want is that the CategoryName in the Categories table be Seafood.

To add this restriction, we first check the CategoryName column in the Categories table in the Diagram pane. This will add it to the Grid pane. We then uncheck the Output column in the Grid pane for the CategoryName row. This will also uncheck the CategoryName box in the Categories table in the Diagram pane. In the Criteria column for the CategoryName row in the Grid pane, we add the constraint " = 'Seafood' ". Figure 7.23 shows the Query Builder window after these steps.

The SQL pane shows the SQL statement for this query that was constructed using the Query Builder tool. We click *OK* to return to the *Generate the SQL*

Figure 7.23   The configured query.

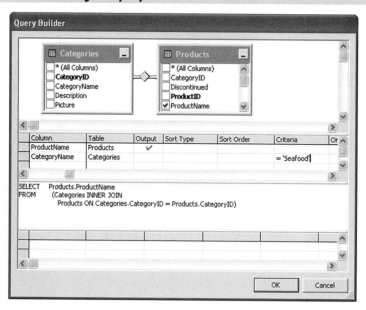

statements screen. We click *Advanced Options* and uncheck the *Generate Insert, Update, and Delete statements* box, because we will not be using these statements. We click *OK* to return to the *Generate the SQL statements* screen and then click *Next*. Finally, we click *Finish* in the *View Wizard Results* screen.

7.4.2   Displaying the Query Results

We first add a DataSet to hold the results of the query. Clicking on the *Data, Generate dataset* menu item displays the Generate Dataset form of Figure 7.24. We enter seafoodProducts as the name of the new data set and click *OK*.

To display the results, we drag a DataGrid control from the Toolbox to the form. We choose seafoodProducts1.Products as the DataSource in the Properties window for the DataGrid. We expand the DataGrid to show the fields fully.

To fill the DataGrid with the desired information, we double-click on the form (not the DataGrid control) in the Visual Studio .NET design and fill in the Form1_Load template as shown:

```
private void Form1_Load(object sender, System.EventArgs e)
{
    oleDbDataAdapter1.Fill(seafoodProducts1);
}
```

Figure 7.24   Generating a data set.

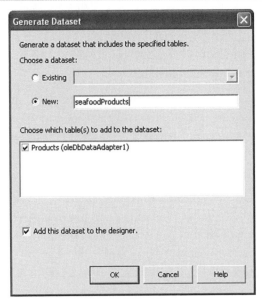

Figure 7.25   The seafood products from the Northwind database.

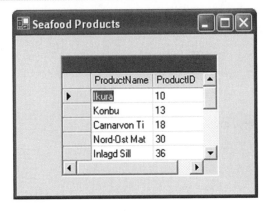

Figure 7.25 shows the seafood products in the DataGrid on the form of Example7-4.

Test Your Understanding

7.   Name the four sections of the Query Builder screen.

The BIG Picture

The most interesting uses of databases require data to be gathered from multiple tables. We use Query Builder to construct a query that uses multiple tables.

7.5   Summary

- A relational database is a collection of data items organized as a set of tables from which data can be accessed in many different ways without having to reorganize the database tables. A query retrieves information from a database.

- In the connected model, we process data while maintaining a connection to the database. We use an OleDbConnection to connect, an OleDbCommand to query, and an OleDbDataReader to read from the database.

- In the disconnected model, we use a data set to process data locally. A data adapter serves as a bridge between a data source and a data set for retrieving and storing data. The Data Adapter Configuration Wizard adds a data connection configured to a particular database. Its query builder tool constructs a query to get the desired information from the database. A DataSet holds data in memory that has been received from a database. The DataGrid control displays data on a form. We fill the DataGrid when the form loads.

- With the Data Form Wizard, we can display information from a data set using a Windows Form, either in a DataGrid or in individual controls. It adds another form to the project, which can be started by modifying the Main method of the original form.

- The most interesting uses of databases require data to be gathered from multiple tables. We use Query Builder to construct a query that uses multiple tables.

7.6   Programming Exercises

7.1   Modify Example7-1 to add the quantity of each product in stock to the display.

7.2   Modify Example7-3 to use a DataGrid rather than individual controls. Continue to use the Data Form Wizard.

7.3   Modify Example7-4 to show the beverages rather than the seafood products.

7.4   Create a Windows application to display the names and titles of all Northwind employees.

7.5   Create a Windows application to display the order date of each order from the Orders table.

7.6 Use the Data Form Wizard to display the CompanyName, ContactName, Address, and City from the Northwind Customers table in individual controls.

7.7 Create a Windows application to display the CompanyName of all Northwind customers who ordered beverages.

7.8 Create a Windows application to list the CompanyName of all Northwind customers whose orders were shipped by Speedy Express.

CHAPTER 8

Web Applications

The browser provides access to Web sites all over the world. It is the primary mode of computing for many users. Static World Wide Web pages return the same content to every user, but very often users submit information and receive responses based on that information. The Web server uses programs running on the server to provide a response tailored to the client. Microsoft includes ASP.NET in the .NET Framework to support dynamic Web pages. ASP (Active Server Pages), the previous Web technology from Microsoft, in its new form uses the .NET Framework Class Library.

Browsers display HTML documents. HTML (Hypertext Markup Language) is the language used to write Web pages, adding markup tags to indicate how the browser should present the document. A Web form can pass information to a C# program running on the server, called the **code behind**, which processes it and sends results back to the client. This approach separates the presentation in the Web form seen by the client using the browser from the content in the code behind run on the server. A Web page designer can focus on the presentation while a C# developer prepares the code behind.

With a three-tiered architecture, the client communicates with the code behind on the middle-tier, which in turn connects with a database server on the third tier. In this way, clients do not have to connect directly to a database.

HTTP connections are stateless, meaning that when a client connects again there is no record of previous connections. Session-tracking allows servers to maintain client information from one connection to the next, an essential feature needed for many Web applications including Web commerce.

Chapter Objectives:

- Introduce HTML
- Use Web forms and code behind to provide dynamic Web pages
- Add database connectivity in a three-tiered architecture
- Use multiple Web forms in a single application

8.1   HTML

The Internet includes many applications, of which the most used is e-mail. The rapidly growing World Wide Web (WWW) allows computers all over the world to explore the enormous web of links from one site to another for educational, commercial, and recreational purposes. We introduce the HTML notation used to write Web pages.

8.1.1   Some HTML Tags

Web page files often have the `.html` extension. We use **HTML** to create the hypertext files found on the Web. This mark-up language adds tags to specify the formatting of the text. For example, the tag `<br>` causes a break to a new line. A browser, such as Internet Explorer, interprets these tags, formatting the page for the client. Using tags allows browsers of different capabilities to interpret the tags differently. For example, the tag `<em>`, requesting emphasis for the text that follows, might cause one browser to display the text in italics, but another browser, without the capability to use italics, might underline that text for emphasis.

The World Wide Web must adapt itself to many computers with differing capabilities. By using HTML tags, Web documents can be displayed by a variety of browsers including those on terminals without graphics capabilities.

Although HTML is not hard to learn to use, we need only an introduction to experiment with Web forms. To get the flavor of HTML, we list a few tags in Figure 8.1 and use them to write a rudimentary Web page.

We can insert an empty tag such as `<br>` anywhere to cause a line break. Non-empty tags such as `<em>` have a closing form using the forward slash that marks the end of the text covered by that tag. Thus

```
<em> .NET is fun. </em>
```

would emphasize the text, *.NET is fun.* The six levels of header tags specify the importance of the header, with `<h1>` being the most important, and `<h6>` the least. Browsers will try to make the more important headers larger and more impressive. An unordered list `<ul>` includes, between its starting and ending tags, various list elements with tags `<li>`.

Figure 8.1 Some HTML tags.

` `	Break to the next line
`<p>`	New paragraph (after a blank line)
`<em>...</em>`	Emphasize the text
`<strong>...</strong>`	Strongly emphasize the text
`<title>...</title>`	Title, displayed separately from the text
`<h1>...</h1>`	Top-level header
`<h3>...</h3>`	Third-level header (lowest is sixth)
`<ul>...</ul>`	An unordered list
`<li>`	Element of a list
`<a>...</a>`	An anchor, a hypertext link
`<img>`	An image

Some tags use attributes embedded in the tag to provide information needed to interpret that tag. The anchor tag uses the `href` attribute to specify the URL of a hypertext link. For example, to link to Microsoft's .NET home page we can use the anchor

```
<a href = "http://www.microsoft.com/net/"> Microsoft's .NET home page. </a>
```

The `href` attribute gives the URL for Microsoft's .NET home page. The text, *Microsoft's .NET home page*, will usually appear underlined and in blue, indicating that a mouse click will cause the browser to request, using HTTP, the Microsoft server to serve up its .NET home page HTML file, which the browser then interprets, displaying Microsoft's .NET home page.

The client must be connected to the Internet to link to other computers. Anchors can also link to files on the same machine using a relative URL. For example, to link to a file `funStuff.html` in the same directory, we could use the anchor

```
<a href = "funStuff.html"> some fun stuff </a>
```

We use the `<img>` tag to display an image, with an `src` attribute that gives the URL of the source of the picture. For example, to display a picture of the author of the text, found in the same directory as the Web page itself, use

```
<img src="gittleman.gif">
```

Figure 8.2   A WebPage.html.

```
<!- Illustrates some html tags in
 - a simple Web page.
  ->

<title> Let's try HTML </title>

<h1> .NET is fun </h1>
<p>
<h3> With <em>C# and .NET</em> we can </h3>
<ul> <li> Do object-oriented programming
    <li> Create nifty graphics
    <li> Display dynamic Web pages
    <li> Network to remote computers
    <li> Deploy Web services
</ul><p>

<strong>Download the .NET Framework SDK from</strong>
 <a href =
  "http://msdn.microsoft.com/netframework/downloads/">
  Downloads for the .NET Framework </a>
<br>

<h2> Get ready - Here comes the prof
<img src=gittleman.gif><br>
    who wrote this Web page </h2><br>
```

A browser that cannot display graphics will fill the space with text such as [IMAGE]. The image file uses a GIF, a graphics format.

Comments in HTML documents start with <!-- and end with -->. The <title> displays at the top of the frame, not in the document itself. Web search engines use the title in their searches.

Figure 8.2 shows an HTML file for a very simple Web page, displayed in Figure 8.3, which uses some of the tags from Figure 8.1.

Use a browser to see this page. In Netscape Navigator, click on *File*, click on *Open File*, and browse to locate a Web page file. In Microsoft Internet Explorer, click on *File*, click on *Open*, and click on *Browse* to locate a Web

Figure 8.3 Displaying WebPage.html in a browser.

page. The URL is a file URL, using the file protocol. The domain name of the server is just the local host, which can be omitted, so the URL looks like

file:///path/AWebPage.html

where path is the path on the local machine to the AWebPage.html file.

Figure 8.3 shows us browsing a local file, but this is just for testing purposes during development. We deploy Web pages on a Web site, making them available to anyone who has a browser and is connected to the Internet. Browsing the author's Web site at

http://www.cecs.csulb.edu/~artg/AWebPage.html

will download this Web page.

The Web site runs a Web server that expects Web pages to be in a default directory, often named *htdocs*. On the author's Web site, the files A Web-Page.html and gittleman.gif are in the htdocs folder.

The BIG Picture

Using a browser, we can connect to sites anywhere in the World Wide Web to display Web pages, written using HTML, the Hypertext Markup Language. HTML uses tags enclosed in angle brackets to indicate formatting.

Test Your Understanding

1. Which protocol does the browser use to download Web pages?

2. Given the URL

   `http://www.cecs.csulb.edu/~artg/AWebPage.html`

   a. What is the protocol?

   b. What is the domain name of the server?

   c. What is the path to the resource?

3. What language do we use to write Web pages?

4. Which header tag, h2 or h5, will most likely cause a more prominent display of the text to which it applies?

5. For what purpose is an HTML anchor tag used?

8.2   Web Server Controls and Code Behind

Web server controls provide much richer Web pages. Using Visual Studio .NET, we can drag these controls from the Toolbox to a Web form, creating the desired user interface. Visual Studio .NET creates an HTML file with special tags for these controls that the server translates into HTML for the particular client. When the user interacts with the control, our event-handling code will be called. We put the event-handling code in a separate code-behind file to separate the C# code from the HTML.

8.2.1   Hosting a Web Page

We need a .NET Web server to host our Web pages. With Microsoft Windows 2000 or XP Professional operating systems, we can install IIS (Internet Information Server) to host our Web pages. If IIS is not available in this way, another option is to download Web Matrix from `http://www.asp.net/webmatrix`. Web Matrix provides a free web server that runs locally. The README file available after installation shows how to use it.

To create a Web application, we open a new project in Visual Studio .NET choosing `Visual C# Projects` and the `ASP .NET Web Application` templates. In the `Location` field, we change the default name `WebApplication1` to a name of our choice. In this case we use Example8-1. This will create an Example8-1 folder in a special folder in which IIS keeps the Web pages it hosts. On the author's machine that folder is `C:\Inetpub\wwwroot`, so this is where the

Figure 8.4   An ASP.NET Web Application project.

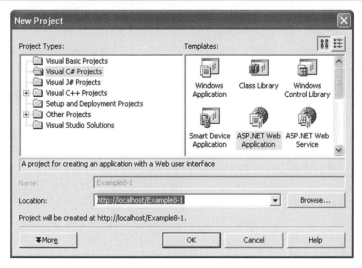

Example8-1 folder will be created.[1] Figure 8.4 shows the Visual Studio .NET New Project screen.

Web forms use the .aspx extension. The Example8-1 project opens with a Web form whose default name is WebForm1.aspx. We have a choice of two layout styles for our Web forms, GridLayout or FlowLayout. These layout modes determine how we can position elements in a Web page. Using Grid-Layout, the default, positions elements at fixed coordinate values that do not change. FlowLayout positions elements from top to bottom, allowing resizing by different browsers. It is the more flexible layout. To change to FlowLayout, we would set the pageLayout property in the Properties window to FlowLayout.

---

[1]Rather than placing our code in the special directory used by IIS, we can create a virtual directory to refer to another folder containing our Web page and code. To create a virtual directory, we click on *Start, Control Panel, Administrative Tools, Internet Information Services* to open the Microsoft Management Console. Right-clicking on *Default Web Site, New, Virtual Directory* opens the Virtual Directory Creation Wizard. We click *Next*, enter ch8 as the alias for our virtual directory, and click *Next*. We browse to find the directory that contains the Web pages we want to host in this virtual directory. We click *Next*, and *Next* again in the Permissions screen, and then click *Finish*. The name of the virtual directory appears in the URL referring to the Web page.

Example8-1 is a simple Web application with a `Label`, a `TextBox`, a `Button`, and another `Label`. We enter an item in the `TextBox`. Pressing the button sends that item name to the server. In a fully developed application, the server might check that item for availability or provide more information. To illustrate how a Web application works, we simply have the server tell the user that the submission was received.

8.2.2   Server Controls

When creating a Web application, we could use various HTML input tags to enable the user to submit data to the server, but the .NET Framework provides server controls that handle the details of the HTML. They execute on the server using a code-behind file that we will introduce soon. Visual Studio .NET shows both the `Design` and the `HTML` views. Unless we want to add HTML code to that generated by Visual Studio .NET, we can concentrate on the `Design` view.

To set up Example8-1, we drag a `Label`, a `TextBox`, a `Button`, and another `Label` from the Web Forms tab in the Toolbox onto the Web form in the Visual Studio .NET design. Figure 8.5 shows some of the Web Forms controls in the Toolbox.

**Figure 8.5
Some Web Forms
controls.**

We select the first `Label` in the `Design` view and change its `Text` property to *Enter an item name*. We change the `Text` property of the button to *Submit* and the `Text` property of the second `Label` to the empty string. We change the (ID) property of a control to give it a more meaningful name. In Example8-1 we set the following new names. Visual Studio .NET uses uppercase letters to start names in Web applications.

```
TextBox        EnterItem
Button         SubmitItem
Label (lower)  DisplayItem
```

Figure 8.6 shows the Visual Studio .NET design for Example8-1.

8.2.3   Code Behind

The code-behind file contains the C# code that initializes the page and the event-handler methods. We double-click on the `Button` to create the event-handler template that will be called when the user clicks the button. Visual Studio .NET displays a C# file, WebForm1.aspx.cs, which contains the event-handling template.

Figure 8.6   Designing Example8-1.

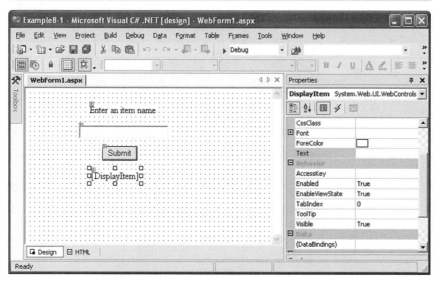

```
private void SubmitItem_Click
                (object sender, System.EventArgs e)
{
}
```

We want the second label to show the text that the user entered in the TextBox, so we add

```
DisplayItem.Text = "You ordered " + EnterItem.Text;
```

to the template, giving

```
private void SubmitItem_Click
                (object sender, System.EventArgs e)
{
    DisplayItem.Text = "You ordered " + EnterItem.Text;
}
```

To view the Web page, WebForm1.aspx, of Example 8-1, we enter the URL

```
http://localhost/Example8-1/WebForm1.aspx
```

in the address field of the Internet Explorer browser. Figure 8.7 shows this simple Web application.

Figure 8.7   The Web application of Example8-1.

8.2.4   More Web Controls

In Example8-2 we illustrate the TextBox, ListBox, CheckBoxList, RadioButton-List, Button, and Label Web server controls. The user creates an order for an ice cream sundae. The server sends a message acknowledging receipt of the order. After opening a new ASP .NET Web Application project, we drag Web controls in six rows to create the application of Figure 8.8. The first row contains a Label and a TextBox to enter the user's name, while the second row contains a Label and a TextBox to enter the user's password. The TextMode property of a TextBox has three possible values: SingleLine, Multi-Line, and Password. We accept the SingleLine default for the first TextBox, but set the TextMode of the second to Password.

Next, we add a ListBox to the Web form to hold the ice cream flavors. We accept the default SelectionMode of Single rather than change it to Multiple because we only allow one flavor of ice cream to be selected. To add the flavors, we click on the value of the Items property of the ListBox to display a ListItem Collection Editor. We add the flavors Vanilla, Chocolate, and Straw-berry. To add a flavor, we click the *Add* button and fill in the Text property of the item we want to add, as shown in Figure 8.9 for Vanilla.

We will allow several choices of toppings and will use a CheckBoxList control to display the choices. We click on the value of the Items property to display the ListItem Collection Editor and add the toppings, Hot Fudge, But-terscotch, Nuts, and Whipped Cream.

Figure 8.8   The Web form of Example8-2.

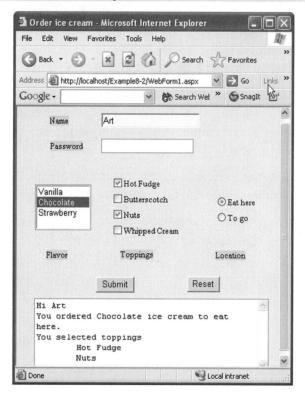

Figure 8.9   Adding an item to the ListBox.

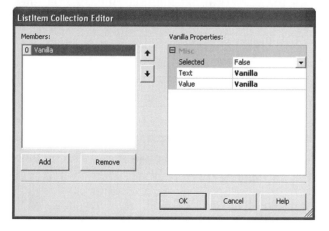

We add a `RadioButtonList` to allow the user to select whether to eat at the facility or to take it out. The choices, again added using the `ListItem Collection Editor`, are *Eat here* and *Take out*. We next add a `Label` under each of the three list controls to label the lists *Flavor*, *Toppings*, and *Location*.

We add two buttons, one to submit the user's entries and another to reset them. We set the `Text` property of the first to *Submit* and the second to *Reset*. To finish the form, we add a `TextBox` to hold the message that the server returns, set its `Text` property to the empty string, and set its `TextMode` property to `MultiLine`.

We use the Properties window to set the (`ID`) property of the following controls to give them more meaningful names.

```
TextBox (at top)      Name
TextBox               Password
ListBox               Flavor
CheckBoxList          Toppings
RadioButtonList       Location
Button (left)         Submit
Button (right)        Reset
TextBox (bottom)      Display
```

The `Submit` button should send the data to the server and place the server's response in the bottom `TextBox`. We double-click on the `Submit` button to display the template for its event-handling method in the code-behind file. We first check the password that the user entered. In a fully developed application, we would check the password in a database. Here we just check that it is "1234" using the code

```
if (Password.Text == "1234") {
  // respond to user's selections
}
```

When the server responds to the user's selections, it first sends a greeting including the user's name, taken from the first `TextBox`, and adds a `newline` at the end so that the next part of the message will start on the second line.

```
Display.Text = "Hi " + Name.Text + "\n";
```

Next, the event-handling code will add the user's choice of flavor to the message.

```
Display.Text += "You ordered "
            + Flavor.SelectedItem.Text + " ice cream";
```

The next addition to the code concatenates the location to the message.

```
if (Location.SelectedItem.Value == "Eat here")
    Display.Text += " to eat here.";
else
    Display.Text += " to go.";
```

The event-handling code needs a loop to add each of the selected toppings to the response message.

```
    // If checkbox selected, add its item to the toppings
Display.Text += "\nYou selected toppings";
    // The Count property gives the number of checkboxes
for (int i = 0; i < Toppings.Items.Count; i++)
    if (Toppings.Items[i].Selected)
        Display.Text
            += "\n\t" + Toppings.Items[i].Text;
```

Figure 8.10 shows the complete event-handling code for the Submit button.

To handle the click of the Reset button, we set the Text in the three TextBox controls to the empty string, and set the SelectedIndex of the ListBox, Check-BoxList, and RadioButtonList controls to −1. Setting the SelectedIndex to −1 causes all items to be unchecked. Figure 8.11 shows this event handler.

Figure 8.10   The Submit button click event handler.

```
private void Submit_Click
                   (object sender, System.EventArgs e)
{
    if (Password.Text == "1234")
    {
        Display.Text = "Hi " + Name.Text + "\n";
        Display.Text += "You ordered "
            + Flavor.SelectedItem.Text + " ice cream";
        if (Location.SelectedItem.Value == "Eat here")
            Display.Text += " to eat here.";
        else
            Display.Text += " to go.";
    // If checkbox selected, add its item to the toppings
        Display.Text += "\nYou selected toppings";
    // The Count property gives the number of checkboxes
        for (int i = 0; i < Toppings.Items.Count; i++)
        if (Toppings.Items[i].Selected)
        Display.Text += "\n\t" + Toppings.Items[i].Text;
    }
}
```

The BIG Picture

Web server controls provide much richer Web pages. Using Visual Studio .NET, we can drag these controls from the Toolbox to a Web form, creating the desired user interface. Visual Studio .NET creates an HTML file with special tags for these controls that the server translates into HTML for the particular client. When the user interacts with the control, our event-handling code will be called. We put the event-handling code in a separate code-behind file to separate the C# code from the HTML. Web server controls include `TextBox`, `ListBox`, `CheckBoxList`, `RadioButtonList`, `Button`, and `Label`.

Figure 8.11   The Reset button click event handler.

```
private void Reset_Click(object sender, System.EventArgs e)
{
    Name.Text = "";
    Password.Text = "";
    Display.Text = "";
    Flavor.SelectedIndex = -1;
    Toppings.SelectedIndex = -1;
    Location.SelectedIndex = -1;
}
```

Test Your Understanding

6. Name the two layout styles for a Web form and describe how each works.

7. What does a code-behind file include?

8. Which property of a `ListBox` determines whether the user can select more than one item?

9. Which property of a `TextBox` determines whether it can hold more than one line?

10. Which property of a `CheckBoxList` contains the collection of check box choices?

11. What value should the `SelectedIndex` property of a `RadioButtonList` be assigned to uncheck all of its radio buttons?

8.3   Accessing a Database

Using a browser, we can get information from a database using the Web. We develop a Web application that displays the names and addresses of the suppliers in the Northwind database. The client Web application connects to the Web server, which in turn connects to the Northwind database to execute a query and presents the results in a `DataGrid` control.

In this example, we do not use a `DataSet` to save the data locally. This means that we do not need a data adapter to fill the dataset from the database. Because we only execute one query, we use a data reader to obtain the data while connected and bind it directly to the `DataGrid`. The data reader is a read-only forward-only reader optimized for fast access. We do not want to update the database, so we will not have to make another connection.

8.3.1   Adding a Connection

We create Example8-3 in Visual Studio .NET as a C# ASP .NET Web Application project. We set the title property of the document to *Display Northwind Suppliers*. From the Data tab on the Toolbox, we add an OleDbConnection to the design. We click on the value of its ConnectionString property in the Properties window and select the path to the Northwind database. It should be already available from creating the Chapter 7 examples, but if not, we can repeat the steps we used there. We set the (Name) property to northwind.

8.3.2   Configuring a Command

We add an OleDbCommand from the Toolbox. This command will express the query that we want to make of the Northwind database. We need to associate it with the connection to Northwind that we just configured. Clicking on its Connection property pops up a choice of Existing or New. Clicking Existing displays the northwind connection that we added to the form. We select this connection. We set the (Name) property to suppliers.

We need to create the specific command that we wish to execute. Clicking on the value of the CommandText property of the OleDbCommand that we added displays a small button at the right. Clicking it displays the Query Builder with the Add Table window open and showing the list of the Northwind tables. We select Suppliers and click the *Add* button and then the *Close* button. The Query Builder shows a list of all the pieces of information available for each supplier listed in the Northwind database. We do not want to show all this information, so we select the Address, City, and CompanyName fields and click *OK*.

8.3.3   Displaying in a DataGrid

We will display the supplier data in a DataGrid control. We open the Web Forms tab in the Toolbox, drag a DataGrid control onto the form, and set its (ID) property to Display. We click on the AutoFormat link at the bottom of the Properties window for the DataGrid to choose a format for the data. We choose Colorful1 from the Auto Format screen shown in Figure 8.12 and click *OK*.

Figure 8.12   The AutoFormat screen.

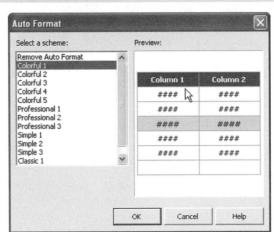

8.3.4   Writing the Event Handler

The Page_Load method executes when the page that we are creating is loaded. Double-clicking on the form will display the template for it in the code-behind file. We will put the code here that will read the data from the database and bind it to the DataGrid for viewing. To read the data from the database we use an OleDbDataReader. First, we open the connection to the database using

```
northwind.Open();
```

The ExecuteReader method of the OleDbCommand sends the command to the connection and builds an OleDbDataReader

```
System.Data.OleDb.OleDbDataReader Reader
                  = suppliers.ExecuteReader();
```

We set this Reader as the DataSource property of the DataGrid and execute the DataBind method of the DataGrid so that as the reader reads from the database it will display the data in the data grid.

```
Display.DataSource = Reader;
Display.DataBind();
```

Finally, we close the reader and the connection to release the resources they are using back to the system.

Figure 8.13   Initializing a Web form with data.

```
private void Page_Load(object sender, System.EventArgs e)
{
    northwind.Open();
    System.Data.OleDb.OleDbDataReader Reader
                = suppliers.ExecuteReader();
    Display.DataSource = Reader;
    Display.DataBind();
    Reader.Close();
    northwind.Close();
}
```

```
Reader.Close();
northwind.Close();
```

Figure 8.13 shows the complete Page_Load method.

Running the application produces Figure 8.14.[2]

8.3.5   Choosing Data to Display

Example8-4 creates a simple Web form, shown in Figure 8.15, that gives the user a choice of displaying the Northwind supplier data as we did in Example8-3 or displaying information about Northwind products. For this form, we set the pageLayout property in the Properties window to FlowLayout. The FlowLayout lets us type on the form. We can use the space bar to position Web controls. We set the title property of the Web form to *Suppliers or Products.*

We start by adding two RadioButton controls to the Web page. They appear at the upper left of the page with empty Text property values. We set the Text property of the first RadioButton to Suppliers and that of the second to Products. We change the (ID) properties to selectSuppliers and selectProperties. Figure 8.16 shows the page so far.

---

[2]The default ConnectionString for northwind may cause a database access error. In this case, click on the value of the ConnectionString property and remove everything after Northwind.mdb.

Figure 8.14   Displaying Northwind suppliers.

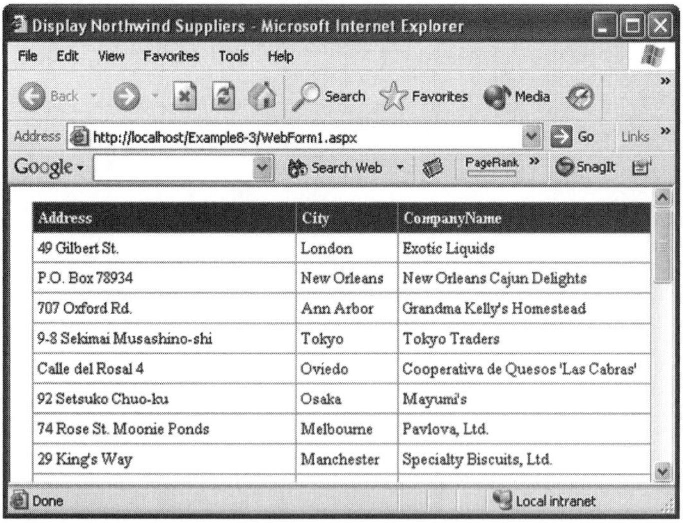

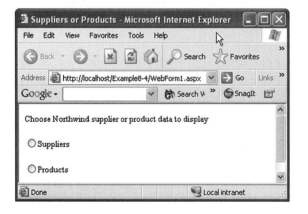

Figure 8.15   The initial Web page of Example8-4.

To enter a message in the Web page, we position the cursor in the Visual
Studio .NET design just before the first RadioButton and press the *Enter* key
to open a blank line above. We enter the message *Choose Northwind supplier or product data to display*. To display each RadioButton on a separate
line, we position the cursor between the two RadioButton controls and hit
the *Enter* key.

Figure 8.16   Adding RadioButton controls using FlowLayout.

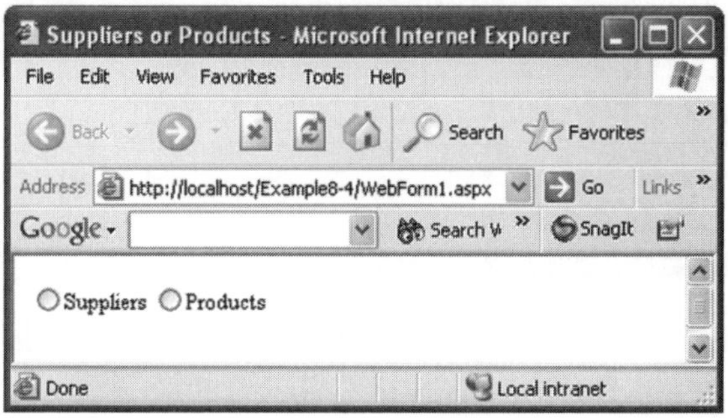

We need to change the AutoPostBack property of each RadioButton from False to True.[3] Remember that the user checks a RadioButton on the client. We use the AutoPostBack property to indicate whether the state of the check box for the radio button is posted back to the server when an event such as checking or unchecking a RadioButton occurs. We want to post back to the server so that it will respond by getting and displaying the data corresponding to the RadioButton checked.

The RadioButton controls need to be part of a group, so exactly one of the group will be checked. We will display the Supplier data or the Product data, but not both, so the user should only be able to select one or the other RadioButton. To put both radio buttons in the same group, we set the Group-Name property of each to Group1.

We position the cursor below the second RadioButton and drag a DataGrid to the Web page. It does not show in the initial page of Figure 8.15 because we have not entered any data yet. We set its (ID) property to Display. We select the DataGrid and click the AutoFormat link at the bottom of the Properties window. After choosing Colorful1 in the AutoFormat screen, we click *OK*.

From the Data tab in the Toolbox we add an OleDbConnection and two OleDb-Command controls. We set the (Name) property of the OleDbConnection to north-wind and the (Name) property of the OleDbCommand controls to suppliers and products. We will use a command to acquire the data requested by a RadioButton.

---

[3]The AutoPostBack property is false by default for a RadioButton because we often use a Button to submit data to the server. The AutoPostBack property for a Button has a default of true.

Figure 8.17   Configuring the products command.

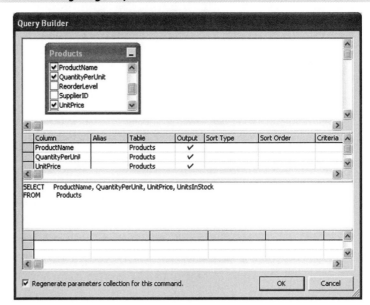

To set the ConnectionString property of the northwind connection, we click on it in the Properties window and select the connection string that we configured in earlier examples. On the author's system, this string is

```
Provider=Microsoft.Jet.OLEDB.4.0;Password="";User ID=Admin;
Data Source="C:\Program Files\Microsoft Office\Office10\
Samples\Northwind.mdb"
```

The Data Source file may differ somewhat on other systems.

For each OleDbCommand, we set the Connection property by choosing northwind from the Existing connections shown in the Connection property box. Both commands will use the same connection. For the suppliers command, we use the QueryBuilder as in Example8-3 to set the CommandText property, again including the Address, City, and CompanyName fields of the Suppliers table in the display.

For the products command, we click on the value of the CommandText property to display the Add Table screen, click *Products*, and then *Add* and *Close*.

Figure 8.18   The event handler for suppliers.

```
private void selectSuppliers_CheckedChanged
                     (object sender, System.EventArgs e)
{
    northwind.Open();
    System.Data.OleDb.OleDbDataReader Reader
                         = suppliers.ExecuteReader();
    Display.DataSource = Reader;
    Display.DataBind();
    Reader.Close();
    northwind.Close();
}
```

Figure 8.19   The event handler for products.

```
private void selectProducts_CheckedChanged
                     (object sender, System.EventArgs e)
{
    northwind.Open();
    System.Data.OleDb.OleDbDataReader Reader
                         = products.ExecuteReader();
    Display.DataSource = Reader;
    Display.DataBind();
    Reader.Close();
    northwind.Close();
}
```

From the Products list in the QueryBuilder, we select ProductName, Quantity-PerUnit, UnitPrice, and UnitsInStock, as shown in Figure 8.17, and click *OK*.

When the user selects a RadioButton, we want to connect to the database, create an OleDbDataReader to read the data, and bind the OleDbDataReader to the DataGrid for display. The code is like that of Example8-3, but we need to do it twice, once in each of the RadioButton event handlers. We click on each RadioButton to display the template. Figure 8.18 shows the code to display the supplier data while Figure 8.19 shows the analogous code to display the Product data.

Figure 8.20 shows the Web form of Example8-4 when the user requests the Products display.

Figure 8.20   Displaying the Northwind Product data.

Suppliers or Products - Microsoft Internet Explorer

File   Edit   View   Favorites   Tools   Help

Back ·   · |x| |2| |△| Search   Favorites   Media »

Address   http://localhost/Example8-4/WebForm1.aspx   ▼   → Go   Links »

Google ·   www.runraceresults.com   ▼   Search Web   ▼   » SnagIt

Choose Northwind supplier or product data to display

○ Suppliers

◉ Products

ProductName	QuantityPerUnit	UnitPrice	UnitsInStock
Chai	10 boxes x 20 bags	18	39
Chang	24 - 12 oz bottles	19	17
Aniseed Syrup	12 - 550 ml bottles	10	13
Chef Anton's Cajun Seasoning	48 - 6 oz jars	22	53
Chef Anton's Gumbo Mix	36 boxes	21.35	0
Grandma's Boysenberry Spread	12 - 8 oz jars	25	120

Done   Local intranet

The BIG Picture

Using a browser, we can get information from a database using the Web. The client Web application connects to the Web server, which in turn connects to the database to execute a query and presents the results in a Web form control. We use a data reader to obtain the data while connected to the database. When using a data reader, we need to add a data connection to connect to the database and a data command to specify a query.

Test Your Understanding

12.   Which control can we use to read data from a database while connected to it?

13.   Which control can we use to express the query that we want to execute?

14.   Which C# method executes when a Web page is loaded and initialized?

15.   Which property of a control determines whether its state is sent to the server when an event occurs?

8.4   Using Multiple Web Forms

Often a Web application uses several forms. Our example will use three forms.

8.4.1   Redirecting a Response

The Response property of a Page allows us to access the HttpResponse that the server sends to the client's request. We will use it to redirect the response to

Figure 8.21 The initial Web form of Example8-5.

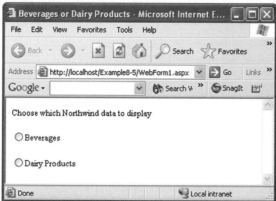

another Web page. The initial Web form of Example8-5 will ask the user to choose whether to see the list of Northwind beverages or dairy products. Whichever the user chooses will display in another Web form, allowing the user to select items from the list. Figure 8.21 shows the initial Web form.

After creating the Example8-5 ASP .NET Web application project, we set the pageLayout property to FlowLayout to allow us to type on the form. We ask the user to choose which Northwind data to display and add two radio buttons, one for each choice. We set the Text property of the upper radio button to *Beverages* and its (ID) property to selectBeverages. We set the Text property of the lower radio button to *Dairy Products* and its (ID) property to selectDairy. We set the GroupName property for each RadioButton to Group1, because we want the user to select one or the other but not both.

8.4.2 The AutoPostBack Property

When the user makes a selection, we want to redirect the response to come from another page. Each time the user interacts with a form, the application makes a roundtrip to the server sending the request and receiving the response to it. The AutoPostBack property of a control determines whether the state of that control is sent to the server during a post back. By default, the AutoPostBack property of a RadioButton is set to false, because we often depend on Button controls instead to submit the request to the server. In this form, we would like to send the state of the radio buttons to the server when the user makes a selection, so we set the AutoPostBack property of each to true.

When the user checks a RadioButton, we want to redirect the response to another Web form. We click on each RadioButton in the Visual Studio .NET design to display the event-handling templates and fill in the code to give

```
private void selectBeverages_CheckedChanged
                    (object sender, System.EventArgs e)
{
    Response.Redirect("WebForm2.aspx");
}

private void selectDairy_CheckedChanged
                    (object sender, System.EventArgs e)
{
    Response.Redirect("WebForm3.aspx");
}
```

8.4.3   Adding a Web Form to a Project

To add the second Web form, we click *Project, Add Web Form,* and click *Open* in the Add New Item screen that appears. The form's default name will be WebForm2.aspx. We want this form to display Northwind data, so we add an OleDbDataConnection and an OleDbDataCommand. We set the (Name) property of the data connection to northwind and the ConnectionString property to

```
Provider=Microsoft.Jet.OLEDB.4.0;Password="";User ID= Admin;Data
Source="C:\Program Files\Microsoft Office \Office10\Samples\Northwind.mdb"
```

The Data Source path may vary on other systems.

For the OleDbCommand, we select northwind as the Connection property and set its (Name) property to beverages. We use Query Builder to set the CommandText property to show Northwind beverages. In the Add Tables screen, we add Categories and Products, clicking *Add* twice and then *Close.* In the Query Builder, we select ProductName from Products and CategoryName from Categories. In the CategoryName row, we add

```
= 'Beverages'
```

in the Criteria column, uncheck the box in the Output column as shown in Figure 8.22, and click *OK.*

We add a CheckBoxList to the form to hold the data and allow the user to select beverages. By default, when the user checks a box it is not posted to the server. The AutoPostBack property of a CheckBoxList is false. This reflects the common usage that lets a user complete making selections and then

Figure 8.22 Building a query for beverages.

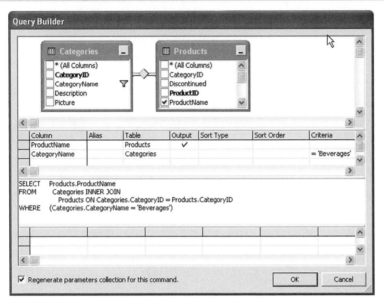

submit them using a button. We set the (ID) property to BeveragesList. We set the DataTextField property to ProductName to display the product name for each beverage.

We add a Button Web server control to submit the selections, and change its (ID) property to SubmitChoices and its Text property to *Select*. We add a second button to restart the selection process, changing its (ID) property to Back and its Text property to *Restart*. We add a Label to display the user's selections and change its (ID) property to Display.

8.4.4 Initializing the Page

When the user makes a selection of beverages in the original Web forms, the Page_Load method of the second Web page will be called. To display the template for this event handler, we double-click on the second Web form. We insert the code to connect to the database, create a data reader for the command that we configured, and bind the data reader to the check box so that each box will represent a beverage from the Northwind database. The code is

```
private void Page_Load(object sender, System.EventArgs e)
{
    if (!IsPostBack)
```

```
        {
            northwind.Open();
            System.Data.OleDb.OleDbDataReader Reader
                            = beverages.ExecuteReader();
            BeveragesList.DataSource = Reader;
            BeveragesList.DataBind();
            Reader.Close();
            northwind.Close();
        }
}
```

Whenever the user interacts with the form, it generates a post back to the server, which recreates the form to submit the response back to the user. The server will execute the Page_Load method once to create the form the first time, and then again every time that the user generates an event by interacting with a control. Because we only need to connect to the database once, we only do it when IsPostBack is false, which occurs once when the form is first created before the user interacts with any controls.

Each Button has its AutoPostBack property set to true by default, so pressing a button will submit the request to the server. In the event handler for the Select button, we add the text of each selected checkbox to the label.

```
private void SubmitChoices_Click
                    (object sender, System.EventArgs e)
{
    Display.Text = "Selections: ";
    for (int i = 0; i < BeveragesList.Items.Count; i++)

            // Add each selected item to the label
        if (BeveragesList.Items[i].Selected)
            Display.Text +=
                BeveragesList.Items[i].Text + ", ";
            // Remove the trailing comma and space
    Display.Text =
      Display.Text.Substring(0, Display.Text.Length -2);
}
```

8.4.5   Hidden State

Each time the user makes a selection or clicks a button, it generates a round trip to the server. When using standard HTML controls, the information sent in one trip is not preserved in the next unless special effort is made to save the state between posts. Web server controls hide action by the server

Figure 8.23   Selecting beverages.

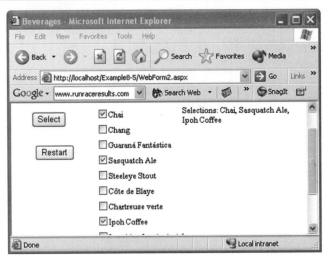

to save the state between round trips automatically. Thus, when the user submits a selection of beverages to the server, the response comes back with the selections still checked, ready for the user to make changes if desired.

The Restart button sends the user back to the original form to choose again between beverages and dairy products. The beverage data selected will now be lost. The code for this event handler is

```
private void Back_Click
                (object sender, System.EventArgs e
{
    Response.Redirect("WebForm1.aspx");
}
```

Figure 8.23 shows the Web form for selecting beverages.

Creating the Web form for selecting dairy products is very similar. The difference is that in the Query Builder, we add the criteria

```
= 'Dairy Products'
```

To add the third Web form, we click *Project, Add Web Form,* and click *Open* in the Add New Item screen that appears. The form's default name will be Web-Form3.aspx. We want this form to display Northwind data, so we add an OleDbDataConnection and an OleDbDataCommand. We set the (Name) property of the data connection to northwind and the ConnectionString property to

Figure 8.24   Building a query for dairy products.

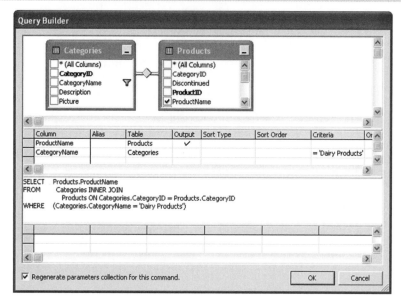

```
Provider=Microsoft.Jet.OLEDB.4.0;Password="";User ID= Admin;Data
Source="C:\Program Files\Microsoft Office \Office10\Samples\Northwind.mdb"
```

The Data Source path may vary on other systems.

For the OleDbCommand, we select northwind as the Connection property and set its (Name) property to dairy. We use Query Builder to set the CommandText property to show Northwind dairy products. In the Add Tables screen, we add Categories and Products, clicking *Add* twice and then *Close*. In the Query Builder, we select ProductName from Products and CategoryName from Categories. In the CategoryName row, we add

```
= 'Dairy Products'
```

in the Criteria column, uncheck the box in the Output column as shown in Figure 8.24, and click *OK*.

We add a CheckBoxList to the form to hold the data and allow the user to select dairy products. We set the (ID) property to DairyList. We set the DataTextField property to ProductName to display the product name for each beverage.

We add a Button Web server control to submit the selections, and change its (ID) property to SubmitChoices and its Text property to *Select*. We add a second button to restart the selection process, changing its (ID) property to

Back and its Text property to *Restart*. We add a Label to display the user's selections and change its (ID) property to Display.

8.4.6 Initializing the Page

When the user makes a selection of dairy products in the original Web forms, the Page_Load method of the third Web page will be called. To display the template for this event handler, we double-click on the third Web form. We insert the code to connect to the database, create a data reader for the command we configured, and bind the data reader to the check box so that each box will represent a beverage from the Northwind database. The code is

```
private void Page_Load(object sender, System.EventArgs e)
{
    if (!IsPostBack)
    {
        northwind.Open();
        System.Data.OleDb.OleDbDataReader Reader
                    = beverages.ExecuteReader();
        DairyList.DataSource = Reader;
        DairyList.DataBind();
        Reader.Close();
        northwind.Close();
    }
}
```

Each Button has its AutoPostBack property set to true by default, so pressing a button will submit the request to the server. In the event handler for the Select button, we add the text of each selected checkbox to the label.

```
private void SubmitChoices_Click
                (object sender, System.EventArgs e)
{
    Display.Text = "Selections: ";
    for (int i = 0; i < DairyList.Items.Count; i++)

            // Add each selected item to the label
        if (DairyList.Items[i].Selected)
            Display.Text +=
                DairyList.Items[i].Text + ", ";

            // Remove the trailing comma and space
    Display.Text =
        Display.Text.Substring(0, Display.Text.Length -2);
}
```

Figure 8.25   Selecting dairy products.

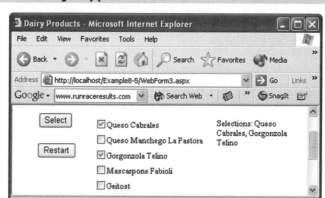

The BIG Picture

Often a Web application uses several forms. We use the Response property to redirect the response to another Web page. A page is recreated every time an event occurs that causes a post back to the server. To perform initialization only once, we do it only when IsPostBack is false. Web server controls hide action by the server to save the state between round trips automatically.

The Restart button sends the user back to the original form to choose again between beverages and dairy products. The beverage data selected will now be lost. The code for this event handler is

```
private void Back_Click
                      (object sender, System.EventArgs e
{
    Response.Redirect("WebForm1.aspx");
}
```

Figure 8.25 shows the form for selecting dairy products.

Test Your Understanding

16. Which property of a Web page holds the HttpResponse that we can use to redirect a response to another page?

17. Which property is false when a page is first loaded but true whenever the page contacts the server after that?

8.5   Summary

- Using a browser, we can connect to sites anywhere in the World Wide Web to display Web pages, written using HTML, the Hypertext Markup Language. HTML uses tags enclosed in angle brackets to indicate formatting.

- Web server controls provide much richer Web pages. Using Visual Studio .NET, we can drag these controls from the Toolbox to a Web form, creating the desired user interface. Visual Studio .NET creates an HTML file with special tags for these controls that the server translates into HTML for the particular client. When the user interacts with the control, our event-handling code will be called. We put the event-handling code in a separate code-behind file to separate the C# code from the HTML. Web server controls include `TextBox`, `ListBox`, `CheckBoxList`, `RadioButtonList`, `Button`, and `Label`.

- Using a browser, we can get information from a database using the Web. The client Web application connects to the Web server, which in turn connects to the database to execute a query and presents the results in a Web form control. We use a data reader to obtain the data while connected to the database. When using a data reader, we need to add a data connection to connect to the database and a data command to specify a query.

- Often a Web application uses several forms. We use the `Response` property to redirect the response to another Web page. A page is recreated every time an event occurs that causes a post back to the server. To perform initialization only once, we do it only when `IsPostBack` is false. Web server controls hide action by the server to save the state between round trips automatically.

8.6   Programming Exercises

8.1 Modify Example8-1 to display the result message in a larger size and in red.

8.2 Modify Example8-2 to accept three passwords: 1234, 5678, and 9999.

8.3 Modify Example8-3 to add the contact name to the display.

8.4 Modify Example8-4 to add a third choice, `Shippers`, which will display the `Shippers` data.

8.5 Modify Example8-5 to add a third choice, `Confections`.

8.6 Create a Web application in which the user orders a pizza, selecting the size and the toppings. The server should send a message verifying the order.

8.7 Write a Web application that will give the user a choice of which Northwind table to list. List all the data for all fields of the table the user selects.

8.8   Create a Web application that lets the user choose whether to order pizza or ice cream. If the user chooses pizza, another form will appear that allows the user to choose the size and the toppings. If the user chooses ice cream, a form will appear that allows the user to choose the flavor and the toppings. In each case the application displays the user's choices.

8.9   Create a Web application that allows the user to choose various items of clothing. The choices will show the items with the price for each. When the user makes a selection, a `RadioButtonList` will display a list of available sizes. When the user clicks the *Submit* button, the application will describe the order, including the total price.

8.10   Create a Web application that provides a list of Northwind employees. When the user chooses an employee, the application will list orders by that employee, the cost of each order, and the total cost of all the orders by that employee.

CHAPTER 9

Validation Controls

Users may forget to enter data in a field or may enter it in an incorrect format. Before the .NET Framework became available, validation often involved writing extra client-side code, usually in a separate scripting language. Validation controls enable the server to check the user's entry and return the form for corrections before processing.

Chapter Objectives:

- Check that required fields are not empty
- Check that values are entered in the correct range
- Compare field values
- Validate an expression
- Summarize validation messages

9.1   Checking Required Fields

Forms often have many entries, and users may try to submit a form with insufficient information. To make sure that the user completes a field, we can associate a `RequiredFieldValidator` Web control with the original control. It will display a message if the user leaves that field empty. In Example9-1, we ask the user to enter a name and an address and validate that the user does in fact change the default entry.

We create a new ASP .NET Web Application project named Example9-1. Figure 9.1 shows the validation controls available in the Toolbox.

We drag a `TextBox` to the form, and to the right of it we drag a `Required-FieldValidator` control. To the left we drag a `Label`. We change the (`ID`) property of the `TextBox` to `EnterName`, and the `Text` property of the `Label` to *Last*

Figure 9.1 Validation controls.

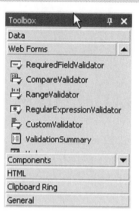

Name. Figure 9.2 shows the Visual Studio .NET design. The `Properties` window at the right, for the `RequiredFieldValidator` control, contains the `InitialValue` property with a default value of the empty string. After we associate the `RequiredFieldValidator` with the `TextBox`, the `InitialValue` property will determine what the user must enter in that text box to avoid a validation error.

We want to make sure that the user makes an entry. To associate a `RequiredFieldValidator` with the `EnterName` text box, we click the `RequiredFieldValidator` control in the Visual Studio .NET design and set its `ControlToValidate` property to `EnterName` in the `Properties` window. We set its `ErrorMessage` property to *A last name is required*. This error message will display if the user does not make any entry in the `EnterName` text box. Figure 9.3 shows these property entries.

Figure 9.2 Adding a `RequiredFieldValidator` control.

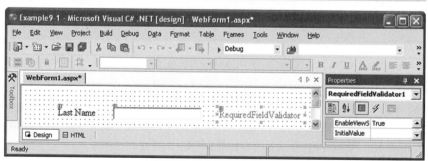

Figure 9.3   Configuring a RequiredFieldValidator control.

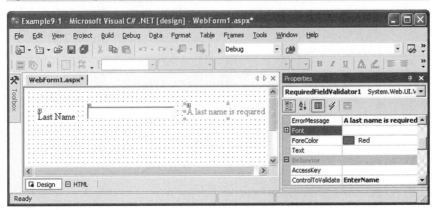

The InitialValue property of the RequiredFieldValidator determines what the user must enter to make the entry valid. The user must make an entry that differs from the InitialValue. The RequiredFieldValidator control used to validate the EnterName entry has its InitialValue property set to the empty string by default, so the user must enter a non-empty string in TextBox1 to avoid receiving an error message from the validator.

To show another way to use a RequiredFieldValidator, we add another Label, TextBox, and RequiredFieldValidator in a second row below the first three controls that we already added. We set the Text property of the Label to *Address* and the (ID) property of the second TextBox to EnterAddress. We left the EnterName text box blank initially, but we set the Text property of the EnterAddress text box to *Enter your address*. The easiest response from the user would be to leave this message and not replace it with an address. To check that this does not happen, we use the second RequiredFieldValidator, setting the following properties:

ControlToValidate   EnterAddress

ErrorMessage   *An address is required*

InitialValue   *Enter your address*

The InitialValue property is the same as the initial Text in the EnterAddress text box. Its associated RequiredFieldValidator will display an error message unless the user changes the initial entry in the EnterAddress text box, in which case it will differ from InitialValue.

Figure 9.4   Validation errors.

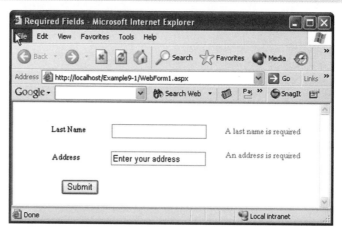

The Web form of Example9-1 includes a Button to submit the user's entries. We change the Text property of the Button to *Submit* and the (ID) property to SubmitInfo. Figure 9.4 shows the response when the user does not make any changes to the initial form and receives two error messages.

Had we left the InitialValue property as the empty string, the second error message would not be displayed because the default entry in the EnterAddress text box would differ from the InitialValue property of the associated RequiredFieldValidator control.

The Web form of Example9-1 has a third Label used to display the last name and address that the user enters. We change its (ID) property to Display. We set the Text of this Label in the event-handling method for the Submit button. Clicking on this button in the Visual Studio .NET design displays the event-handling template to which we add code to display the last name with the address below it. We are making an entry on a Web page, so we use the <br> tag to go to the next line. The event-handling method is

```
private void SubmitInfo_Click
                (object sender, System.EventArgs e)
{
    Display.Text = "Name: " + EnterName.Text + "<br>"
                + "Address: " + EnterAddress.Text;
}
```

Figure 9.5   Valid entries.

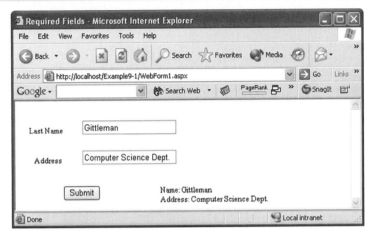

The Display label does not show in Figure 9.4 because when validation fails the server sends the error messages to display rather than responding as it would to valid input. Figure 9.5 shows the response to valid user entries.

Test Your Understanding

1. Which RequiredFieldValidator property specifies the control that it is validating?

2. How does the RequiredFieldValidator indicate the string that the user must change in order to make an entry valid?

9.2   Range Checking

Using a RangeValidator Web control, we can require that the user enter values in a specified range. Figure 9.6 shows the data types for which we can validate ranges.

Example9-2 illustrates validating String, Integer, Date, and Currency values. We add four TextBox Web server controls and pair each with a RangeValidator control. We precede each TextBox with a label describing its contents. A Button at the bottom submits the data to the server. Figure 9.7 shows the design view of Example9-2.

From top to bottom, we change the (ID) properties of the four text boxes to EnterString, EnterInt, EnterDate, and EnterPrice. We also change the (ID) property of the Button to SubmitInfo and that of the Label to its right to Display.

The BIG Picture

Forms often have many entries, and users may try to submit a form with insufficient information. To make sure that the user completes a field, we can associate a Required-FieldValidator Web control with the original control. It will display a message if the user does not change the field entry from the Initial-Value specified in the validator.

Figure 9.6   Validation data types.

Type	Description
String	A character string, compared alphabetically
Integer	An integer value
Double	A double value
Date	A date expressed numerically
Currency	A value in dollars and cents (in the US)

Figure 9.7   Adding the controls for Example9-2.

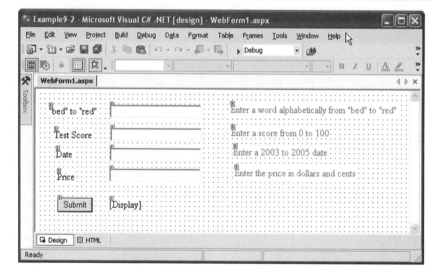

9.2.1   String Values

In the topmost text box, we ask the user to enter a word between "bed" and "red", and add a RangeValidator to validate the entry. We set the following properties for the topmost RangeValidator:

ControlToValidate	EnterString
ErrorMessage	*Enter a word alphabetically from "bed" to "red"*
MaximumValue	red
MinimumValue	bed

The default `Type` is `String`, so we do not need to set it. A valid entry, such as `potato`, will be submitted to the server. An entry that is out of the specified range, such as `trip`, will cause the display of the error message. Entries are case sensitive, so `Potato` will generate an error because the ASCII value of 'P' is less than the value of 'b', the smallest possible start of a valid word in this example.

9.2.2 Integer Values

The second `EnterInt` text box will hold a test score, which we require to be between 0 and 100. The properties we set for the `RangeValidator` to its right are:

ControlToValidate	EnterInt
ErrorMessage	*Enter a score from 0 to 100*
MaximumValue	100
MinimumValue	0
Type	Integer

Entering anything except an integer between 0 and 100 will cause display of the error message. The value 64 will be valid, but 102 will cause an error, as will 59.5 or "red". An empty string will not cause an error. To rule this out, we could add a `RequiredFieldValidator` as we did in Example9-1.

9.2.3 Dates

The third text box, `EnterDate`, holds a date that we require to be within the years 2003, 2004, and 2005. The properties we set for the `RangeValidator` to its right are:

ControlToValidate	EnterDate
ErrorMessage	*Enter a 2003 to 2005 date*
MaximumValue	12/31/2005
MinimumValue	1/1/2003
Type	Date

Dates must be formatted numerically. We can use four-digit or two-digit years, as in 5/28/2003 or 5/28/03. We can use one- or two-digit days or months, as in 5/28/03 or 05/28/03. The forward slash or the dash can separate the month, day, and year, as in 5/28/03 or 5-28-03. However, we cannot write out the months, as in May 28, 2003.

9.2.4   Currency

We can restrict entries to a range of currency values. In the United States, we use the period as a decimal point and the comma to separate groups of three digits. We can use these symbols in our currency values. In Example9-2, we will restrict the entries in the `EnterPrice` text box to the range of zero to one hundred thousand dollars. The property settings for the `RangeValidator` to its right are:

ControlToValidate	EnterPrice
ErrorMessage	*Enter the price in dollars and cents*
MaximumValue	100,000
MinimumValue	0
Type	Currency

Values 32.35, 12,567.22, and 12 are valid, but the value 1,000,000 is invalid because it is too large, and the value 123.456 is invalid because it has three decimal places rather than two. Unfortunately, a value such as 12,34.56 is deemed valid, because the validator does not require grouping by threes when using the comma separator. Figure 9.8 shows the Web form of Example 9-2 with all values valid, while Figure 9.9 shows invalid entries.

Figure 9.8   Entries in the specified range.

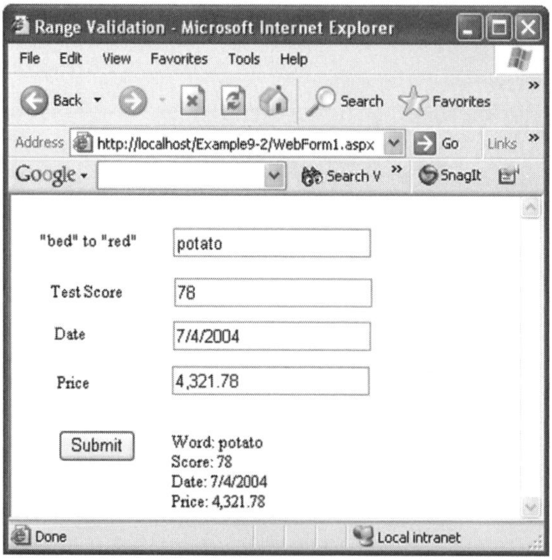

Figure 9.9   Invalid entries in Example9-2.

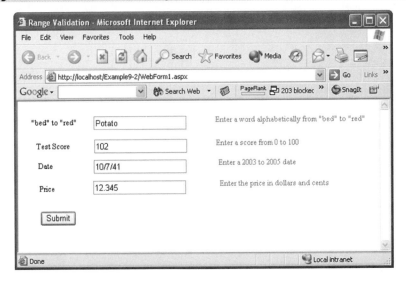

Test Your Understanding

3. Which properties do we need to set to specify the allowable values for a RangeValidator to verify?

4. What is the default value of the Type property for a RangeValidator control?

5. Is either 05/31/2003 or 3/31/03 a valid date between the beginning of 2003 and the end of 2005?

6. Is either 56.780 or 5,6.78 a valid currency format?

The BIG Picture

Using a RangeValidator Web control, we can require that the user enter values in a specified range. We can do range checking on string, integer, double, date, and currency data.

9.3   Comparing Values

Many situations require a comparison of the value in one control with the value in another. In Example9-3, we add a TextBox to enter a password and another to have the user confirm the first entry. The second entry must equal the first to verify the user's entry. We can use a CompareValidator Web control to compare values from two controls. Its Operator property can have the values

```
Equal
NotEqual
GreaterThan
GreaterThanEqual
```

```
LessThan
LessThanEqual
DataTypeCheck
```

The `GreaterThanEqual` value requires that the value in the `ControlToValidate` be greater than or equal to the value in the `ControlToCompare`. The `DataTypeCheck` operator does not compare the value to the value in another control. It requires that the value of the `ControlToValidate` be of a type specified by the `Type` property. Type choices are `String`, `Integer`, `Double`, `Date`, and `Currency`.

In Example9-3, we add a `TextBox` for the user to enter a password, setting its (ID) property to `EnterPassword`. We set its `TextMode` property to `Password`, so the password will not show when the user enters it. A `Label` added at its left has its `Text` property set to *Password* to indicate the desired entry in the `EnterPassword` text box.

We add another `TextBox` for the user to confirm the password, setting its (ID) property to `ConfirmPassword` and its `TextMode` property to `Password`. To the left of this text box we add a `Label` with the `Text` property changed to *Confirm*. On the right of this text box we add a `CompareValidator`. The properties we set are:

```
ErrorMessage          Entry does not match password field
ControlToCompare      EnterPassword
ControlToValidate     ConfirmPassword
```

If the `EnterPassword` text box entry does not match the `ConfirmPassword` entry, this `CompareValidator` will display the error message.

To illustrate type checking, we add a third `TextBox` labeled `Code`, and set the (ID) of this text box to `EnterCode`. We want to require that the user enters an integer value for the code, so we add another `CompareValidator` and set the following properties for it:

```
ErrorMessage          Code must be an integer
ControlToValidate     EnterCode
Operator              DataTypeCheck
Type                  Integer
```

Figure 9.10   Valid entries in Example9-3.

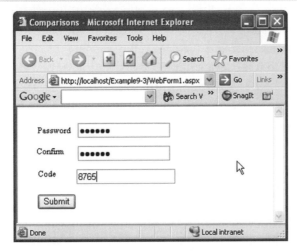

Figure 9.11   Comparison errors.

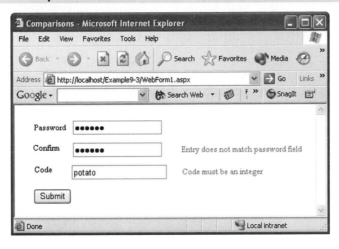

Figure 9.10 shows all valid entries and no error messages, before clicking the *Submit* button. Figure 9.11 shows the failure to confirm a password and the failure to enter an integer value.

9.3.1   Client-Side Versus Server-Side Validation

Notice that when entering values using Internet Explorer, the messages appear before the click of the *Submit* button. This indicates that the browser client is performing validation before submitting the data to the server. Validating on the client side improves efficiency, saving round trips to the server of bad data with error messages coming back. With client-side validation, the user corrects the data before sending it to the server. Before .NET, one had to write JavaScript or other client-side code to perform such validation. The .NET validation controls generate this JavaScript automatically. We can view it by clicking *View, Source* in Internet Explorer when running the application.

When the user confirms the password correctly and enters a valid integer code, clicking the *Submit* button sends the data to the server for processing. In Example9-3 we display the message "No data entry errors" in another label. We need to write the event-handling code for the *Submit* button. In the design, we double-click on the button to display the template for the event handler and fill it in, to give

```
private void SubmitInfo_Click
                   (object sender, System.EventArgs e)
{
    Display.Text = "No data entry errors";
}
```

where Display is the (ID) property of the label to the right of the button. Figure 9.12 shows the form after the user has confirmed a valid password

Figure 9.12   Submitting valid entries.

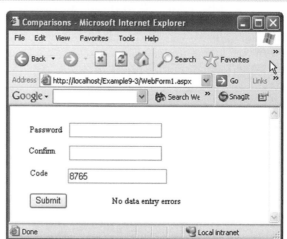

and entered a valid integer code. The application displays the message and empties the password fields after they have been submitted to the server.

Test Your Understanding

7. Which CompareValidator properties do we set to specify the two controls whose values it will compare?

8. What is the advantage of validating controls on the client instead of on the server?

9. How can we configure a CompareValidator to check that a value has type double?

9.4   Validating Expressions and Summarizing

Often, a field requires that data fit a certain pattern. For example, a U.S. phone number has 10 digits including the area code. One common format is (ddd)ddd-dddd, where d stands for some digit. A format such as ddd*ddd*dddd is not used. A phone number pattern such as (dd)dd-ddd would not match U.S. phone numbers.

9.4.1   Validating Expressions

The RegularExpressionValidator Web control lets us validate that user entries match a particular pattern. The regular expression syntax is a way of expressing patterns. Writing regular expressions is beyond the scope of this text, but we do not need to, as the RegularExpressionValidator control provides patterns for the following expression types:

```
French Phone Number
French Postal Code
German Phone Number
German Postal Code
Japanese Phone Number
Japanese Postal Code
P.R.C. Phone Number
P.R.C. Postal Code
P.R.C. Social Security Number (ID Number)
U.S. Phone Number
U.S. Zip Code
```

The BIG Picture

Many situations require a comparison of the value in one control with the value in another. We can use a CompareValidator Web control to compare values from two controls. It uses an operator to compare the two values. The DataTypeCheck operator does not compare the value to the value in another control. It requires that the value of the ControlToValidate be of a type specified by the Type property.

```
Internet E-mail Address
Internet URL
U.S. Social Security Number
```

In Example9-4, we illustrate the validation of a URL, an e-mail address, a phone number, a social security number, and a zip code. For each field we add a Label to identify the data, a TextBox for the user to enter it, and a RegularExpressionValidator to validate it. There will be five rows of these three controls, one for each type of field. Below these five rows we include a Button to submit the validated data and a Label to indicate that the user entered all the fields correctly. Figure 9.13 shows the design. From top to bottom, we set the (ID) properties of the five TextBox controls to EnterURL, EnterEmail, EnterPhone, EnterSSN, and EnterZip. We set the (ID) property of the Button to SubmitInfo and that of the Label to its right to Display.

The EnterURL text box will hold a URL, so we configure the RegularExpressionValidator to its right by setting the following properties:

ErrorMessage	Format: *http://www.cecs.csulb.edu/index.html*
ControlToValidate	EnterURL
ValidationExpression	Internet URL

Figure 9.13   Validating expressions.

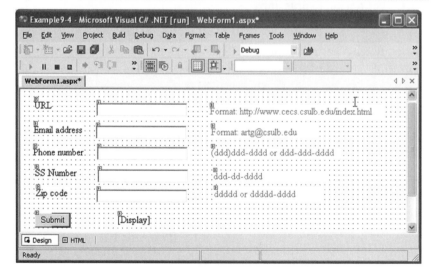

The regular expression pattern for an Internet URL requires starting with `http://` and requires at least one period in the address part. Thus `http://localhost` would not fit the default pattern, although one could write a custom regular expression that would include it.

The `EnterEmail` text box requires a correctly formatted e-mail address. It requires at least two words separated by a period after the `@` character. Thus it accepts `artg@csulb.edu` but not `artg@csulb`. It also accepts `g.art@csulb.edu`, `g-art@csulb.edu`, and `g+art@csulb.edu`. We set the properties for the `Regular-ExpressionValidator` to its right as follows:

```
ErrorMessage          Format: artg@csulb.edu
ControlToValidate     EnterEmail
ValidationExpression  Internet E-mail Address
```

The regular expression for validating a phone number that we use to validate the `EnterPhone` text box accepts two formats, `(ddd)ddd-dddd` or `ddd-ddd-dddd`, where `d` stands for a digit from 0 through 9. Thus it would accept `(123)456-7890` and `123-456-7890` but not `123 456 7890`. We set the following properties for the `RegularExpressionValidator` to its right:

```
ErrorMessage          (ddd)ddd-dddd or ddd-ddd-dddd
ControlToValidate     EnterPhone
ValidationExpression  U.S. Phone Number
```

The social security number format requires the pattern `ddd-dd-dddd`. Thus `222-22-2222` is valid but `222222222` is not. The properties we set for the `RegularExpressionValidator` to the right of the `EnterSSN` text box that validates the social security number field are

```
ErrorMessage          ddd-dd-dddd
ControlToValidate     EnterSSN
ValidationExpression  U.S. Social Security Number
```

A zip code may either have five or nine digits. Acceptable formats are `ddddd` or `ddddd-dddd`. For `RegularExpressionValidator`, to the right of the EnterZip text box we set the following properties:

```
ErrorMessage          ddddd or ddddd-dddd
ControlToValidate     EnterZip
ValidationExpression  U.S. Zip code
```

Figure 9.14 shows valid data entry for every field, while Figure 9.15 shows invalid values.

Figure 9.14   Valid entries.

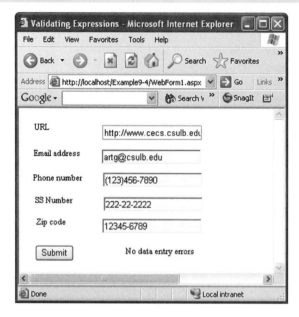

Figure 9.15   Invalid entries.

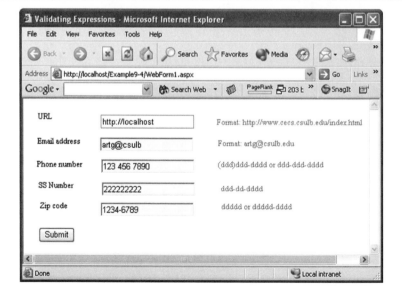

Figure 9.16   Using a validation summary.

9.4.2   Summarizing Validation Errors

Instead of displaying error messages next to each control, we can summarize all of the error messages at the bottom of the form. This might allow an improved layout of controls. With this approach, we add a ValidationSummary at the bottom of the form. It does not need any configuration. We do need to specify the Text property for each of the other validation controls to be the text we want to display next to the control that it validates.

We can use a ValidationSummary with any of the validation controls. We illustrate by modifying Example9-4, adding a ValidationSummary control and setting the Text property of each of the five RegularExpressionValidator controls to *, so that a * will display to the right of the invalid entry with the summary of all error messages at the bottom, as shown in Figure 9.16.

Test Your Understanding

10.   Which of the following would a RegularExpressionValidator recognize as a valid e-mail format: csulb@g.art or g.art@csulb?

The BIG Picture

Often a field requires that data fit a certain pattern. The RegularExpressionValidator Web control lets us validate that user entries match a particular pattern. This control comes with predefined patterns for the validation of a URL, an e-mail address, a phone number, a social security number, and a zip code. Instead of displaying error messages next to each control, we can summarize all the error messages at the bottom of the form.

11. Show two U.S. phone number formats that a `RegularExpressionVa-lidator` would accept using the digits 1, 2, 3, 4, 5, 6, 7, 8, 9, and 0, in that order.

12. Using a `ValidationSummary`, where do the error messages appear?

9.5   Summary

- Validation controls enable the server to check the user's entry and return the form for corrections before processing. Forms often have many entries, and users may try to submit a form with insufficient information. To make sure that the user completes a field, we can associate a `RequiredFieldValidator` Web control with the original control. It will display a message if the user leaves that field empty.

- Using a `RangeValidator` Web control, we can require that the user enter values in a specified range. We can do range checking on string, integer, double, date, and currency data.

- Many situations require a comparison of the value in one control with the value in another. We can use a `CompareValidator` Web control to compare values from two controls. It uses an operator to compare the two values. The `DataTypeCheck` operator does not compare the value to the value in another control. It requires that the value of the `ControlToValidate` be of a type specified by the `Type` property.

- Often a field requires that data fit a certain pattern. The `RegularExpressionValidator` Web control lets us validate that user entries match a particular pattern. This control comes with predefined patterns for the validation of a URL, an e-mail address, a phone number, a social security number, and a zip code. Instead of displaying error messages next to each control, we can summarize all the error messages at the bottom of the form.

9.6   Programming Exercises

9.1   Modify Example9-1 to include an initial message in the First Name box.

9.2   Modify Example9-2 to include a `TextBox` that checks that a double value is between -4.5 and 4.5.

9.3 Modify Example9-2 to use a `ValidationSummary` control.

9.4 Modify Example9-2 to add `RequiredFieldValidator` controls for each field.

9.5 Modify Example9-3 to include a `TextBox` that requires a value of type `double`.

9.6 Modify Example8-2 to use a `RadioButtonList` for the radio buttons, and validate that the user has selected one by using a `RequiredFieldValidator`.

9.7 Modify Example8-2 to use a `RequiredFieldValidator` to check that the user has selected a flavor from the `ListBox`.

9.8 Create a Web application in which the user orders a pizza, selecting the size and the toppings. The user enters a phone number. Use a `RegularExpressionValidator` to check that it has the correct format. If the phone number has a valid format, the server should send a message verifying the order.

9.9 Write a Web application that will give the user a choice of which Northwind table to list. Use a `RequiredFieldValidator` to require the user to enter a password, so the password field may not be left blank. If the user enters "1234", list all the data for all fields of the table that the user selects.

9.10 Create a Web application that lets the user sign up to receive a free magazine. The user must enter a name, address, city, state, zip code, and phone number. Require that each field has an entry and that the zip code and phone numbers have correct formats. If so, display a message that the magazine will be sent.

9.11 Create a Web application that allows the user to choose various items of clothing. The choices show the items with the price for each. Include a `TextBox` for each item in which the user enters the quantity to order. Add a validation control to check that the value is correctly formatted as an integer and that its value is within reasonable bounds. When the user clicks the *Submit* button, the application describes the order, including the total price.

CHAPTER 10

XML

Web pages use HTML to indicate formatting to a browser. The Web has become very popular in part because HTML is relatively simple and easy to use. But HTML focuses on presentation, making it hard to determine the information on a page. XML (Extensible Mark-up Language) lets us devise our own tags to reflect the information content. We can pass these standard XML files among various applications to transfer information from one program to another. Web services, which we cover in the next chapter, use XML to allow programs to communicate even though they may be written in different languages and may run on different hardware.

Chapter Objectives:

- Learn XML syntax
- Use a schema to specify a valid XML type
- Try DOM (Document Object Model) for processing XML files
- Use XSLT to transform XML to other representations

10.1 XML and Its Syntax

We first touch upon the limitations of HTML for representing content before introducing XML.

10.1.1 The Limitations of HTML

With HTML we can easily format data for display, but the content is not easy to retrieve. Figure 10.1 shows the Web page displayed by the Internet Explorer browser given the HTML file of Figure 10.2.

Figure 10.1   Listing an author's books.

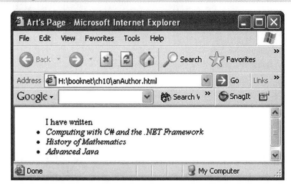

Figure 10.2   The `anAuthor.html` file for the Web page of Figure 10.1.

```
<html>
<title>Art's Page</title>
<ul>I have written
  <li> <em>Computing with C# and the .NET Framework</em>
  <li> <em>History of Mathematics</em>
  <li> <em>Advanced Java</em>
</html>
```

Most of the tags in Figure 10.2 refer to the display of the file. `<ul>` indicates an unordered list, while `<li>` specifies a list item. A human reader might deduce quickly that a person named Art is listing books he has written, but the word "`books`" is never used. A program processing this file would find it very difficult to determine its content.

Moreover browsers accept many variations in HTML syntax. In Figure 10.2, the end tag `</ul>` for the unordered list does not appear, and none of the list items have end tags `</li>`. We could have omitted the `<html>` and `</html>` tags. Permitting such variations in syntax makes it hard for programs to extract information from HTML files.

10.1.2   XML Syntax

We can define our own XML tags to indicate the content.[1] For example, we might rewrite (and expand) the HTML file of Figure 10.2 as the XML file of Figure 10.3.

---

[1]See `http://www.w3.org/XML` for the XML specification.

Figure 10.3   The anAuthor.xml file.

```
<?xml version="1.0" encoding="utf-8" ?>
<author xmlns="http://tempuri.org/XSDSchema1.xsd">
  <name>
    <first>Art</first>
    <last>Gittleman</last>
  </name>
  <age>39+</age>
  <books>
    <book kind="text">
      <title>
        Computing with C# and the .NET Framework
      </title>
      <edition> first </edition>
      <copyright> 2003 </copyright>
      <isbn> 0-7637-2339-8 </isbn>
    </book>
    <book kind="text">
      <title>History of Mathematics</title>
      <edition> first </edition>
      <copyright> 1975 </copyright>
      <isbn> 0-675-08784-8 </isbn>
    </book>
    <book kind="text">
      <title>Advanced Java</title>
      <edition> second </edition>
      <copyright> 2002 </copyright>
      <isbn> 1-57676-096-0 </isbn>
    </book>
  </books>
</author>
```

Notice that the anAuthor.xml file of Figure 10.3 has content tags such as <author> and <book>, rather than formatting tags such as <li> and <em>. The human reader finds it easy to read, and understandable. More importantly, programs can easily find relevant information such as the copyright date or the ISBN number.

Each XML file starts with an optional prolog, which in Figure 10.3 is

```
<?xml version="1.0"?>
```

XML comments use the same HTML syntax, as in

```
<!-- Comments go here. -->
```

Tags may have attributes. For example the `<book>` tag in Figure 10.3 has the `kind` attribute with value "text". Attributes may be optional. For example, the `<title>` tag has a `full` attribute that appears in one title, but not in others.

For programs to easily process XML, the syntax rules are precise. They are:

- Each tag must have an end tag.

  For example, the `<book>` tag must have a `</book>` tag to mark the end of the `<book>` element. We place the content between the start and the end tags. A tag may be empty, meaning it has no content. For example, in Figure 10.3 we might have used a `<softcover>` tag to indicate that a book has a soft cover. The correct form would be

  ```
  <softcover></softcover>
  ```

  which may be abbreviated as

  ```
  <softcover/>
  ```

- Tags must be nested.

  For example, if the start tag `<title>` occurs between `<book>` and `</book>`, then its end tag `</title>` must occur before `</book>`.

  Correct: `<book> ... <title> ... </title> ... </book>`

  Incorrect: `<book> ... <title> ... </book> ... </title>`

- Attribute values must be enclosed in quotes.

  Correct: `kind = "text"`

  Incorrect: `kind = text`

An XML document is well-formed if it follows all the rules of XML syntax, but we still need a way to define the intended usage of the tags we have created. For example, is it OK to omit the `<age>` tag? Can a `<first>` tag appear more than once? We introduce schemas in the next section that allow us to define the intended structure of an XML document.

Test Your Understanding

1. Which of the following are well-formed XML documents?

   a. `<author>`

The BIG Picture

XML allows us to define a language to represent data. We define tags and their structure. Well-formed XML follows precise rules to make it easier to transfer XML documents between programs.

```
        <name>
          <first> Art </first>
          <last> Gittleman </last>
        </name>
      </author>
```

b.
```
   <author>
       <name/>
         <first> Art </first>
         <last> Gittleman </last>
     </author>
```

c. `<author/>`

2. Write an XML document for a record collection.

10.2 Schemas

A well-formed XML document uses correct XML syntax. A document that had an `<author>` tag without an `</author>` tag would not be well-formed. However, a well-formed document may not make sense. For example, the fragment

```
<name>
   <first> George </first>
   <first> John </first>
   <first> Mary </first>
</name>
```

uses correct syntax, but does not look appropriate. A name has three `first` entries and no `last` entry.

We can use an XML schema to specify the form of a valid type of XML document. Before we create a schema, we show the tree structure of the author type in Figure 10.4. Because XML tags must nest, we can always diagram XML document structure in tree form.

The schema for the `<author>` XML document type will specify the structure shown in Figure 10.4. It will specify the types of each tag. For example, the `<first>` and `<last>` tags have no nested tags. They just contain the string data for the first and last names of the author. By contrast, the `<name>` tag is not simple. It contains two nested tags, a `<first>` tag followed by a `<last>` tag. We want the schema to show this structure for the `<author>` type.

Figure 10.4   The tree structure of the author document type.

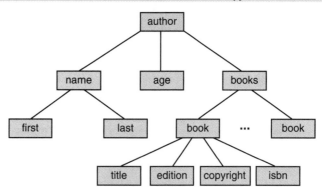

We can also specify how many times a tag may occur. By default, a tag occurs exactly once, but we can specify its `minOccurs` and `maxOccurs` properties to allow it to be optional or to have multiple occurrences. For example, in the schema for the `<author>` type we will want to specify that the `<age>` tag is optional and that the `<book>` tag must occur at least once but may occur more than once. After all, an author may not want to reveal his age and he may have written more than one book.

10.2.1   Building a Schema in Visual Studio .NET

We can create a schema in Visual Studio .NET. If we create the schema first, we can use it as guide when creating XML documents that follow that schema. The schema will define the structure of the author document type as shown in Figure 10.4. It will include the type of data present in each tag. It will indicate optional tags or tags that may occur more than once.

We start by creating Example10-1 as an ASP .NET Web Application. Clicking on *File, Add New Item,* we choose the XML Schema template and click *Open* in the Add New Item window. This will create a tab for XSDSchema1.xsd on which we can develop a schema for the XML document for the `<author>` tag. The Toolbox in Figure 10.5 now shows an XML Schema tab containing the various components we use to define an XML document type.

We can drag Toolbox entries to create the schema. First, we drag an `element` tag onto the form and enter `author` as its name. The box in Figure 10.6 has an E in the upper-left corner signifying that it represents an XML element. The `<author>` tag, as we see from the structure of Figure 10.4, has nested `<name>`, `<age>`, and `<books>` tags. We want the schema to specify this struc-

Figure 10.5 The XML Schema tab.

ture, so we enter each of these tags in three rows of the <author> tag box. Figure 10.6 initially shows one empty row. As we enter each row, another blank row appears below it for the next entry.

We add name in the first row and hit the *Enter* key. This will enter the default type of string. We see from Figure 10.4 that <name> is not a simple type. It is composed of a <first> tag and a <last> tag. If we click on the string entry, we get a choice of types. Choosing Unnamed complex type will replace string by the placeholder (name) for the type and add a child box to enter the fields

Figure 10.6 Starting to create a schema.

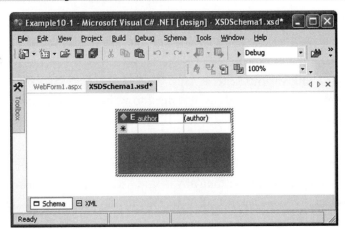

Figure 10.7   Describing the `<author>` tag.

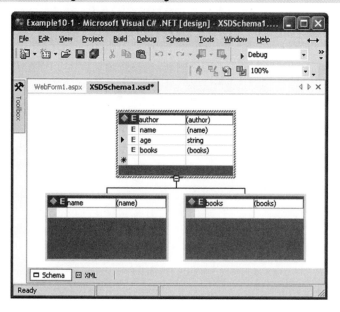

for the `<name>` element. In this way, we can continue to create the structure shown in Figure 10.4.

In the second row, we add `age` and accept the default `string` type. We want the `<age>` tag to be optional, so we click on the `age` entry and open the `Properties` window. We set the `minOccurs` property to `0` and the `maxOccurs` to `1`. In the third row, we add `books` and again choose `Unnamed complex type` from the pop-up box. Figure 10.7 shows the schema so far.

Notice that there are two tabs, `Schema` and `XML`, at the bottom of the screen. We are using the graphical view on the `Schema` tab. The schema is an XML document using various schema tags. We can see the XML version of the schema on the XML tab, but do not need to write XML ourselves because Visual Studio .NET is creating the XML schema as we add to the diagram.

In the `name` box, we enter the rows `first` and `last` and accept the default `string` type for each because the `<first>` and `<last>` tags contain the first and last name strings rather than any nested XML tags. In the `books` box, we enter `book` and choose `Unnamed complex type` to add a `book` box to define the book entries.

The book entry has some interesting features. An author may have written several books, so we allow the <book> tag to appear one or more times. To specify this, we click on the book box, open the Properties window, and set the minOccurs property to 1 and the maxOccurs property to unbounded.

The <book> tag contains <title>, <edition>, <copyright>, and <isbn> tags, and a kind attribute indicating if the book is a textbook primarily for student use or a trade book for the general reader. We add entries for title, edition, copyright, and isbn in the book box. We want the <edition>, <copyright>, and <isbn> tags to be optional, so we set the minOccurs property for each to 0, and the maxOccurs property to 1.

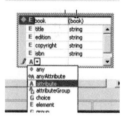

Figure 10.8
Adding an attribute.

We see the kind attribute used in the XML document of Figure 10.3. Each of the <book kind="text"> tags includes the kind attribute with the value "text". The other choice of attribute would be "trade", but this author has not written any trade books. To add the kind attribute, we click the small box at the left of the bottom row in the book box and choose attribute from the box that pops up, as shown in Figure 10.8. This will place an A at the left of this row, indicating that it represents an attribute. We enter kind as its name.

To define the type for the kind attribute, we drag a simpleType from the Toolbox and name it bookType. We want this type to have two values, text and trade. Clicking on the left of the first row allows us to choose facet, a constraint on a type, which places an F at the left of the row. The facets will constrain the string type to have two values. We choose enumeration as the kind of facet and text as its value. We do the same in the next row to create a trade facet for this type.

Once we define bookType we can use it in the rest of the schema. If we click on the type entry for the kind attribute in the book box, bookType will show as one of the entries and we select it. Figure 10.8 shows the kind attribute with the bookType type. We want to require that this attribute always be included in the <book> tag, so we select it and set its use property in the Properties window to required. Figure 10.9 shows additions to the schema descending from the author box of Figure 10.7.

10.2.2   Valid Documents

A valid XML document follows the rules given in its schema. A document can be well-formed without being valid. For example, the fragment

Figure 10.9   Completing a schema for the `<author>` type.

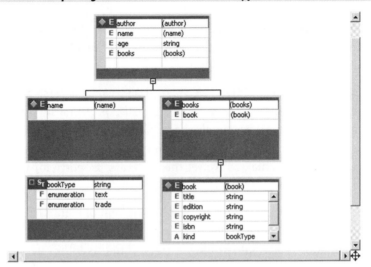

```
<name>
    <first> George </first>
    <first> John </first>
    <first> Mary </first>
</name>
```

is not valid. The rule for `<name>` specifies a single `<first>` followed by a single `<last>`.

10.2.3   Using a Schema to Create an XML Document

The schema we created defines a pattern that a valid XML document has to follow. If we add an XML file to our project and associate this schema with it, the IntelliSense feature of Visual Studio .NET will prompt us for the correct tags to enter as we create the XML document.

We click *File, Add New Item* and choose XML File. In its Properties window we select http://tempuri/XSDSchema1 as the targetSource. This is the URL created for the schema we just developed. Each schema is associated with a URL. Because we did not define our own name, Visual Studio .NET uses the name tempuri. The XMLFile1.xml tab that we added to our project now shows

```
<?xml version="1.0" encoding="utf-8" ?>
<author xmlns="http://tempuri.org/XSDSchema1.xsd">

</author>
```

This template allows space for us to fill in the tags nested inside the author tag. Typing the left bracket, <, to start a nested tag brings up the IntelliSense choice of age, books, or name. We select name and add the right bracket, >. IntelliSense adds the closing tag </name> and we start another tag and select <first>.

At any time we can click the *XML, Validate XML Data* menu item to check that the document we are creating is following the schema pattern. Any deviation will be reported in a window below the XML file. For example, the file

```
<?xml version="1.0" encoding="utf-8" ?>
<author xmlns="http://tempuri.org/XSDSchema1.xsd">
  <stuff></stuff>
</author>
```

would generate a validation error even though it is well-formed. There is no <stuff> tag in the schema associated with this file.

As we continue to create an XML document, we get to the book tag that has an attribute. The document so far is

```
<?xml version="1.0" encoding="utf-8" ?>
<author xmlns="http://tempuri.org/XSDSchema1.xsd">
    <name>
        <first>Art</first>
        <last>Gittleman</last>
    </name>
    <age>39+</age>
    <books>
    <book
</author>
```

If we space after we enter <book, IntelliSense will provide the attribute name, kind, so we choose it to add that attribute. Continuing to use the IntelliSense guide, we create the XML file shown in Figure 10.3.

Now that we can use XML Designer to create a schema and can create an XML document that we validate with respect to the schema, we will see some XML applications in the next sections.

Test Your Understanding

3. Which of the following are valid XML documents with respect to the schema of Figures 10.7 and 10.9?

    a. `<author>`

        `<name>`

The BIG Picture

We can use an XML schema to specify the form of a valid type of XML document. We can create a schema in Visual Studio .NET. If we create the schema first, we can use it as a guide when creating XML documents that follow that schema. A valid XML document follows the rules given in its schema. A document can be well-formed without being valid.

The schema we created defines a pattern that a valid XML document has to follow. If we add an XML file to our project and associate this schema with it, the IntelliSense feature of Visual Studio .NET will prompt us for the correct tags to enter as we create the XML document.

```
            <first> Art </first>
            <last> Gittleman </last>
          </name>
          <books>
            <book>
              <title>Objects to Components with the C#
                     Platform
              </title>
            </book>
          </books>
        </author>
```

b.

```
      <author>
        <name>
          <last> Gittleman </last>
        </name>
        <age> 39+ </age>
        <books>
          <book>
            <title>Objects to Components with the
                   C# Platform</title>
          </book>
        </books>
      </author>
```

4.   When creating a schema, how can we designate that a tag is optional?

10.3   From Data to XML

Each database vendor uses special formats and methods for storing data. With the connectivity of the Internet, it becomes increasingly important to be able to share data among diverse applications. XML provides a standard format for data. If we take data from the database and put it in an XML file, we can transmit that file to other applications, which can then transform the XML to whatever internal formats they need.

10.3.1   Northwind Data to XML

Example10-2 will put the data from the `Customers` table into an XML file. We create a `Windows Application` project and drag an `OleDbDataAdapter` from

the Toolbox to the form. We set its (Name) property to northwind. When the
Data Adapter Configuration Wizard appears, we select the Northwind database that we used in examples in previous chapters.

In the Generate the SQL statements screen, we click the *Query Builder* button, choose Customers from the Add Tables window, and click *Add* and then
Close. In the Customers box in Query Builder, we check the *All Columns* box
and click *OK*. We click *Next* when the Generate the SQL statements window
returns, and click *Finish* in the View SQL Results screen.

We begin creating a data set to hold the Northwind customer data by clicking the *Data, Generate Dataset* menu item. We accept the default selection
of a New data set with the Customers table added, enter customerTable as the
data set name, and click *OK*.

To display the data, we drag a DataGrid control from the Windows Forms tab of
the Toolbox. We open the Properties window for the DataGrid and select
customerTable.Customers as its DataSource property. We expand the size of
the DataGrid control in the Visual Studio .NET design so that it will be easier to view the data.

In Example 10-2, we will display the Customer data in a DataGrid and save it
as an XML file that we can send to other applications. To perform these
operations we add code to the Form1_Load method, which we display by
double-clicking on the form itself, not the data grid control. We fill in the
code in the Form1_Load method as follows:

```
private void Form1_Load(object sender, System.EventArgs e)
{
        // fill the data set from the database
    northwind.Fill(customerTable, "Customers");

        // make an XML document from the data
    System.Xml.XmlDocument customers
        = new System.Xml.XmlDataDocument(customerTable);

        // store the XML document
    customers.Save("customers.xml");
}
```

The Fill method fills the data set with the Northwind data. We create an
XmlDocument from the data set and use its Save method to save the XML document containing the Northwind customer data. Figure 10.10 shows the

Figure 10.10   Displaying the Northwind customers.

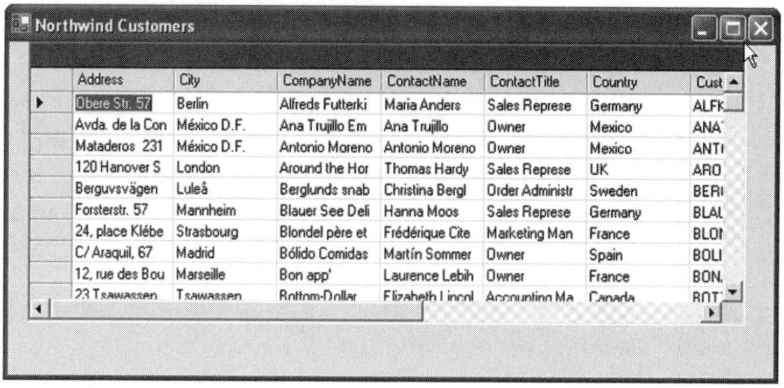

Figure 10.11   The customers.xml file.

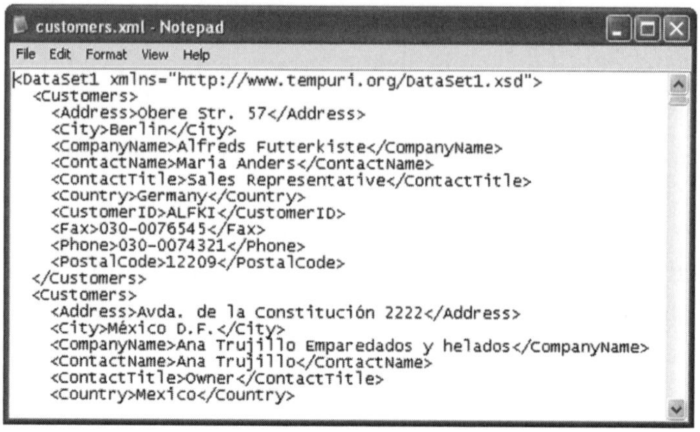

windows form displaying the customers, and Figure 10.11 shows the XML file we created.

10.3.2   The Document Object Mode (DOM)

The DOM (Document Object Model) API supports the reading of the entire document to make a tree model of it in memory. We can access nodes of the tree to locate information contained in the XML document. We use the following classes from the System.XML namespace.

Figure 10.12   Extracting titles from an XML document.

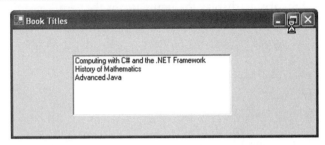

Class	Description
XmlDocument	Represents the entire XML document
XmlDataDocument	Allows data to be manipulated through a DataSet
XmlElement	Represents an element in an XML document
XmlNode	Represents a single node in an XML document
XmlNodeList	A collection of nodes
XmlText	The text of an element or attribute

10.3.3   Processing an XML Document

If we receive an XML document, we can create an XmlDocument object and use its features to extract information from the document. In Example10-3, we process the anAuthor.xml file that we created in Example10-1. We also use the schema that we developed, but rename it anAuthor.xsd.[2] We will build an XmlDocument and find all the <title> tags so that we can display the book titles in a ListBox as shown in Figure 10.12. We leave for the exercises the making of a user interface to allow users to choose what information from the XML file to display.

We create Example10-3 as a Windows Application project. We click on *File*, *Add Existing Item* to add anAuthor.xml and anAuthor.xsd to the project. To create a DataSet for the schema, we click on the anAuthor.xsd tab to show the schema, and then click *Schema, Generate Dataset*. This creates a DataSet named anAuthor. We drag a DataSet control from the Toolbox to the form and click *OK* in the Add Dataset dialog that appears. We change the name of the data set to anAuthor.

---

[2] We also change the URL so that the author tag becomes <author xmlns = "http://tempuri. org/anAuthor.xsd">.

We will create the XMLDocument and process it when the form loads. We double-click on the form to display the template for the Form1_Load method and
complete the code as follows:

```csharp
private void Form1_Load(object sender, System.EventArgs e)
{
        // read XML file into data set
    anAuthor.ReadXml
                ("c:\\booknet\\ch10\\anAuthor.xml");

        // represent XML document in memory
    System.Xml.XmlDocument author
        = new System.Xml.XmlDataDocument(anAuthor);

        // get the root element
    System.Xml.XmlElement root = author.DocumentElement;

        // get all the <title> tags
    System.Xml.XmlNodeList titles
                = root.GetElementsByTagName("title");

        // process each <title>
    for (int i=0; i < titles.Count; i++)
    {
            // get the text from each <title>
        System.Xml.XmlNode text = titles[i].FirstChild;

            // add title to the list box
        listBox1.Items.Add(text.Value);
    }
}
```

The ReadXml method reads the XML file into the DataSet. The XmlDataDocument constructor takes the DataSet and builds the XmlDocument representing it
in memory using the Document Object Model. Its DocumentElement property holds the XmlElement that is the root tag of the document. All other tags
are nested in this root. We use its GetElementsByTag method to find all
<title> tags. These are an XmlNodeList.

The Count property tells us the number of <title> tags. We use a for loop to
process each <title> tag. The FirstChild property of the <title> tag holds
an XmlNode containing the text of the <title> tag. The Value of this node is
the book title. We add each title to the ListBox.

Test Your Understanding

5. What type of argument did we pass to the `XmlDataDocument` constructor in Example10-2?

6. In Example10-3, we start with an XML file and a schema. How did we use Visual Studio .NET to get a `DataSet` to represent the schema? What method did we use to add data from the XML file to the data set?

7. Which property of an `XmlDocument` represents the root element of the document?

10.4   Transforming XML

XML provides a platform-independent representation for data. We can pass XML data from system to system. Often, receivers of XML data will need to transform it to a format suited to their needs. Moreover, XML focuses on content rather than presentation. We can transform an XML document to HTML for presentation.

10.4.1   XSLT (Extensible Stylesheet Language for Transformations)

XSL (Extensible Stylesheet Language) has two parts, one for formatting and the other for transformations. The transformation part, XSLT (Extensible Stylesheet Language for Transformations), has been developed first. It allows us to transform one document to another. We can transform an XML document to another XML document or to HTML for display in a browser.

Stylesheets

We specify the transformations in a stylesheet. The stylesheet follows XML syntax. The transformations use templates that a processor matches against the tags in an XML file. Example10-4 applies a stylesheet to an XML document to produce an HTML file. Figure 10.13 shows the Web page produced using the stylesheet of Figure 10.14 for the `anAuthorStyle.xml`, a slight modification of the XML file of Figure 10.3, which changes the first two lines to

```
<?xml version="1.0" encoding="utf-8" ?>
<?xml:stylesheet type="text/xsl" href="author.xslt" ?>
<author>
```

The BIG Picture

XML provides a standard format for data. If we take data from the database and put it in an XML file, we can transmit that file to other applications, which can then transform the XML to whatever internal formats they need.

If we receive an XML document, we can create an `XmlDocument` object and use its features to extract information from the document. The DOM (Document Object Model) API supports the reading of the entire document to make a tree model in memory. We can access nodes of the tree to locate information contained in the XML document.

Figure 10.13   Transforming an XML document to HTML.

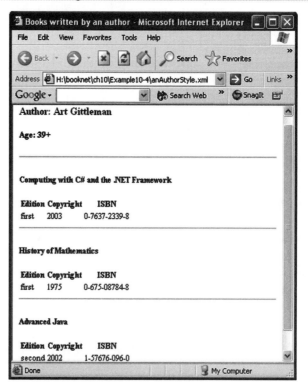

The new second line indicates that we wish to apply an XML stylesheet found in the file author.xslt. The third line, the <author> tag, omits the reference to the schema. To view the transformed XML document locally, we enter the path to the document in the browser address fields. Figure 10.13 shows that on the author's system that path is

```
H:\booknet\ch10\Example10-4\anAuthorStyle.xml
```

As with other XML files, we start the stylesheet with the processing instruction

```
<?xml version="1.0"?>
```

Processing instructions occur between <? and ?>. XSLT stylesheets use the XSLT namespace to provide a context for the XSLT commands. Each command uses a tag with the xsl prefix, as in xsl:template. The xsl:stylesheet tag

```
<xsl:stylesheet version="1.0"
  xmlns:xsl="http://www.w3.org/1999/XSL/Transform">
```

indicates the version, 1.0. The `xmlns:xsl` attribute states that the namespace name is `xsl` and gives the URL where that namespace is defined. As with all XML tags, the `xsl:stylesheet` tag has a closing tag at the end of the stylesheet.

The top-level structure of the stylesheet of Figure 10.14 uses five `xsl:template` tags:

```
<xsl:template match="author">
<xsl:template match="name">
<xsl:template match="age">
<xsl:template match="books">
<xsl:template match="book">
```

Each template applies to tags whose names match the value of the `match` attribute. The first template applies to `<author>` tags, the second to `<name>` tags, and so on. When transforming an XML document using a stylesheet, the processor outputs the body of the template when it finds a match.

When the XSLT processor applies the first template to `anAuthorStyle.xml`, it finds a match with the author template from Figure 10.14, copied here as

```
<xsl:template match="author">
   <html>
     <head>
       <title> Books written by an author </title>
     </head>
     <body>
       <xsl:apply-templates />
     </body>
   </html>
</xsl:template>
```

and the `<author>` tag, and outputs the template body

```
<html>
  <head>
    <title> Books written by an author </title>
  </head>
  <body>
    <xsl:apply-templates />
  </body>
</html>
```

Figure 10.14   An XSLT stylesheet, author.xslt.

```
<?xml version="1.0"?>
<xsl:stylesheet version="1.0"
    xmlns:xsl="http://www.w3.org/1999/XSL/Transform">

   <xsl:template match="author">
      <html>
        <head>
          <title> Books written by an author </title>
        </head>
        <body>
          <xsl:apply-templates />
        </body>
      </html>
   </xsl:template>

   <xsl:template match="name">
      <h3>
         Author: <xsl:value-of select="first"/>
                 <xsl:text> </xsl:text>
                 <xsl:value-of select="last"/><br/>
      </h3>
   </xsl:template>
   <xsl:template match="age">
      <h4>
         Age: <xsl:value-of select="." />
      </h4>
      <hr/>
   </xsl:template>
   <xsl:template match="books">
      <xsl:apply-templates />
   </xsl:template>
   <xsl:template match="book">
      <h4><strong><xsl:value-of select="title"/>
      </strong></h4>
      <table>
        <th>Edition</th>
        <th>Copyright</th>
        <th>ISBN</th>
        <tr>
          <td><xsl:value-of select="edition"/></td>
          <td><xsl:value-of select="copyright"/></td>
          <td><xsl:value-of select="isbn"/></td>
        </tr>
      </table>
      <hr/>
   </xsl:template>
</xsl:stylesheet>
```

The `<xsl:apply-templates />` tag applies the templates of the stylesheet to tags nested within the `<author>` tag. Because it is an empty tag, we use the short form, closing it with a forward slash.

Next the XSLT processor finds a match with the `<xsl:template match="name">` template and the `<name>` tag, so it adds the template body

```
<h3>
   Author: <xsl:value-of select="first"/>
           <xsl:text> </xsl:text>
           <xsl:value-of select="last"/><br/>
</h3>
```

to the HTML file produced so far, giving

```
<html>
  <head>
    <title> Books written by an author </title>
  </head>
  <body>
    <h3>
      Author: <xsl:value-of select="first"/>
              <xsl:text> </xsl:text>
              <xsl:value-of select="last"/><br/>
    </h3>
  </body>
</html>
```

The `<xsl:value-of select="first"/>` tag returns the text body of the `<first>` tag as a `String`. We use the `<xsl:text>` tag to include text in the output. Here we include one space between the first and last names. The `<xsl:value-of select="last"/>` tag returns the last name.

The `author.xsl` stylesheet uses the `<xsl:value-of select="." />` tag inside the age match. The "." in the `select` attribute refers to the tag of the match containing the `value-of` command, which in this case is the age tag. Thus this `value-of` template returns the text of the age tag, which is 39+.

The match for the `<books>` tag does not directly add any new HTML code, but it specifies the `<xsl:apply-templates />` template, which causes the XSLT processor to apply the templates to the tags nested within `<books>`. When matching `<book>`, we display the title followed by a table containing the book information. The `<th>` tag indicates a table header, while `<tr>` specifies a table row, and `<td>` represents the table data in one cell. We follow each table with the empty `<hr/>` tag to insert a horizontal rule.

Figure 10.15   The transformed file of `anAuthorStyle.xml` using `author.xslt`.

```
<html>
  <head> <title>Book written by an author</title> </head>
  <body>
    <h3> Author:  Art  Gittleman <br /> </h3>
    <h4> Age:  39+   </h4><hr />
    <h4><strong> Computing with C# and the .NET Framework
    </strong></h4>
    <table><th>Edition</th><th>Copyright</th><th>ISBN</th>
     <tr>
       <td> first </td><td> 2003 </td><td> xxxxxxxxxx </td>
     </tr>
    </table><hr />
    <h4><strong> History of Mathematics </strong></h4>
    <table><th>Edition</th><th>Copyright</th><th>ISBN</th>
     <tr>
      <td>first</td><td>1975</td><td> 0-675-08784-8 </td>
     </tr>
    </table><hr />
    <h4><strong> Advanced Java </strong></h4>
    <table><th>Edition</th><th>Copyright</th><th>ISBN</th>
     <tr>
      <td>second</td><td>2002</td><td>1-57676-096-0</td>
     </tr>
    </table><hr /></body></html>
```

Figure 10.15 shows the HTML file produced by applying the stylesheet of Figure 10.14 to `anAuthorStyle.xml`. Internet Explorer applies the stylesheet and displays the transformed file in Figure 10.13.

Using a Stylesheet

Example10-3 created a DOM tree from an XML file and then processed it to find the book titles. Example10-5 uses a stylesheet to transform the XML file `anAuthorTitles.xml` to an HTML file to display the book titles on a Web page. The `anAuthorTitles.xml` document changes the line

```
<author xmlns="http://tempuri.org/XSDSchema1.xsd">
```

of `anAuthor.xml` to

```
<?xml:stylesheet type="text/xsl" href="titles.xslt" ?>
  <author>
```

We use a stylesheet and remove the reference to the schema. Figure 10.16 shows the stylesheet, `titles.xslt`.

We use templates to match each of the `<author>`, `<age>`, `<name>`, `<books>`, `<book>`, and `<title>` tags. The template for `<author>` will match first because `<author>` is the root of the document. The HTML output will then contain the body of the template:

```
<html>
  <head>
    <title> Book titles </title>
  </head>
  <body>
    <xsl:apply-templates />
  </body>
</html>
```

The `<xsl:apply-templates>` tag will insert the output of matches with nested tags.

We do not want to include any age or name information in the HTML output. The `<xsl:apply-templates />` command in the root template will apply to all of the nested tags including `<age>` and `<name>`. If we omit an "age" match, the default will be to include the text of the `<age>` tag. To prevent this, we include an "age" match with an empty body, so no code will be added to the HTML output. For the same reason, we include a "name" match with an empty body.

When we match the `<books>` tag, the template body

```
<xsl:apply-templates />
```

just continues searching for matches with nested tags. When matching a `<book>` tag, the template body

```
<xsl:apply-templates select="title"/>
```

will only apply templates to the `<title>` tag, and will ignore the `<edition>`, `<copyright>`, and `<isbn>` tags.

Matching a `<title>` tag will add

```
<h4><strong>
  <xsl:value-of select="."/>
</strong></h4>
<hr/>
```

Figure 10.16   The `titles.xsl` stylesheet.

```
<?xml version="1.0"?>
<xsl:stylesheet version="1.0"
    xmlns:xsl="http://www.w3.org/1999/XSL/Transform">

    <xsl:template match="author">
      <html>
        <head>
          <title> Book titles </title>
        </head>
        <body>
          <xsl:apply-templates />
        </body>
      </html>
    </xsl:template>

    <xsl:template match="age">
    </xsl:template>

    <xsl:template match="name">
    </xsl:template>

    <xsl:template match="books">
       <xsl:apply-templates />
    </xsl:template>

    <xsl:template match="book">
       <xsl:apply-templates select="title"/>
    </xsl:template>

    <xsl:template match="title">
      <h4><strong>
        <xsl:value-of select="."/>
      </strong></h4>
      <hr/>
    </xsl:template>

</xsl:stylesheet>
```

Figure 10.17   Result of applying `titles.xslt` to `anAuthorTitles.xml`.

```html
<html>
  <head><title> Book titles </title></head>
  <body>
    <h4> <strong>
      Computing with C# and the .NET Framework
    </strong></h4>
    <h4><strong>
      History of Mathematics
    </strong></h4>
    <h4><strong>
      Advanced Java
    </strong></h4>
  </body>
</html>
```

Figure 10.18   Using a stylesheet to find book titles.

The BIG Picture

Often, receivers of XML data will need to transform it to a format suited to their needs. Moreover, XML focuses on content rather than presentation. We can transform an XML document to HTML for presentation. XSLT (Extensible Stylesheet Language for Transformations) allows us to transform one document to another. We specify the transformations in a stylesheet. The stylesheet follows XML syntax. The transformations use templates that a processor matches against the tags in an XML file.

to the HTML output. Figure 10.17 shows the resulting HTML file, and Figure 10.18 shows the Web page resulting from entering the path to `anAuthorTitles.xml` in the browser address field.

Test Your Understanding

8. List the XSLT tags from the `xsl` namespace that we use in Figure 10.14.

9. Write the unabbreviated equivalent of the `<xsl:apply-templates />` tag.

10. Figure 10.16 includes the

```
<xsl:apply-templates select="title"/>
```

tag. Explain the difference between this tag and the tag

```
<xsl:apply-templates />
```

10.5 Summary

- HTML focuses on presentation, making it hard to determine the information on a page. XML (Extensible Mark-up Language) lets us devise our own tags to reflect the information content. We can pass these standard XML files among various applications to transfer information from one program to another.

- We can use an XML schema to specify the form of a valid type of XML document. We can create a schema in Visual Studio .NET. If we create the schema first, we can use it as a guide when creating XML documents that follow that schema. A valid XML document follows the rules given in its schema. A document can be well-formed without being valid.

- The schema we created defines a pattern that a valid XML document has to follow. If we add an XML file to our project and associate this schema with it, the IntelliSense feature of Visual Studio .NET will prompt us for the correct tags to enter as we create the XML document.

- XML provides a standard format for data. If we take data from the database and put it in an XML file, we can transmit that file to other applications, which can then transform the XML to whatever internal formats they need.

- If we receive an XML document, we can create an `XmlDocument` object and use its features to extract information from the document. The DOM (Document Object Model) API supports the reading of the entire document to make a tree model in memory. We can access nodes of the tree to locate information contained in the XML document.

10.6   Programming Exercises

10.1   Modify Example10-1 to create a schema that requires the `<age>` tag.

10.2   Modify Example10-2 to include only those customers who placed orders for beverages.

10.3   Modify Example10-3 to add the copyright date to the output.

10.4   Modify Example10-4 to omit the age from the resulting HTML.

10.5   Modify Example10-5 to add the copyright date to the output.

10.6   Write a stylesheet to produce an HTML file from `anAuthorTitles.xml` that displays the title and ISBN of each book.

10.7   Write a stylesheet to produce an HTML file from `anAuthorTitles.xml` that displays the author's name and the copyright date of each book.

10.8   Write a Windows application to make a user interface to allow users to choose what information from the `anAuthorStyle.xml` XML document to display. Write a stylesheet to create an HTML file that displays that information.

10.9   Using data from the Northwind database, write a Windows application that lists the company name and contact name for each customer.

10.10   Write a Windows application to create an XML document from the Products data in the Northwind database.

CHAPTER 11

Web Services

Web services use a simple protocol with XML to allow programs to communicate. In this way, an application developed on one platform can use methods of another application running on a different platform at a remote site and perhaps written in a different language. Companies have many applications that need to communicate. A manufacturer might contact parts suppliers to determine availability of needed parts. Using Web services, the search for parts could be done automatically with the manufacturer's program using Web services of the suppliers.

Chapter Objectives:

- Create a client for existing Web services
- Create new Web services
- Create Web services that use data

11.1   Web Service Clients

With Visual Studio .NET, we can easily write a client program to access Web services available on the Internet. We do not need to know the details of the protocol used to communicate with the service. The XMethods site, `http://www.xmethods.net`, contains many Web services that we can try. The XMethods Demo Services listed at the bottom of their page are likely to remain available for some time. We try the Weather-Temperature service that gives the temperature for any zip code area.

We create Example11-1 as a Windows Application. We add a `TextBox` for the user to enter a zip code and a `Button` to submit it to the Web service. We use two `Label` controls, one to label the text box and the other to display the temperature. We set the `(Name)` property of the text box to `enterZip`, the `(Name)` property of the button to `getTemperature`, and that of the label to its

Figure 11.1   Using a Web service to find the temperature.

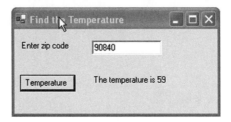

right to display. Figure 11.1 shows the temperature at California State University Long Beach.

11.1.1   Adding a Web Reference

We need to be connected to the Internet to use an external Web service. To refer to the Weather-Temperature Web service in our project, we click the *Project, Add Web Reference* menu item. This displays an Add Web Reference window that includes a text box to enter the address of the Web service. We enter www.xmethods.net and hit the *Enter* key. The frame on the left side shows the XMethods site. We scroll to the bottom where we find the listing of the XMethods Demo Services shown in Figure 11.2. Selecting the

Figure 11.2   Selecting the Weather-Temperature Web service.

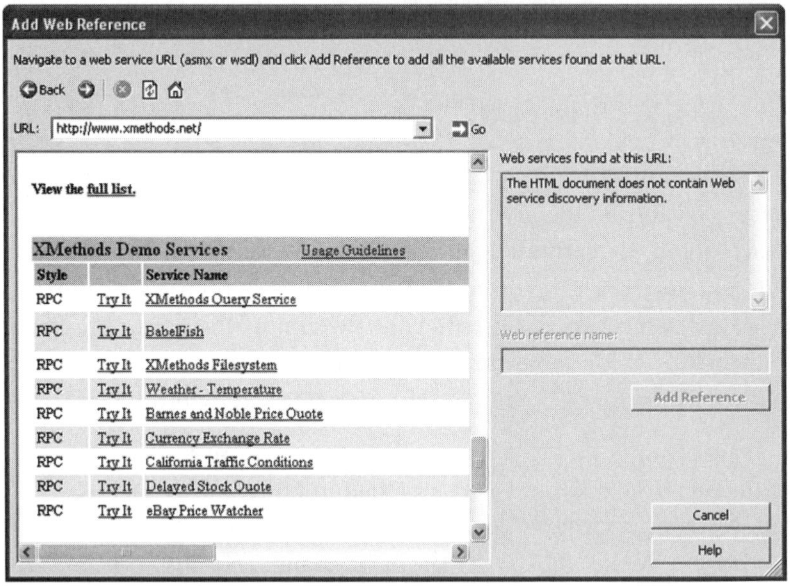

Figure 11.3   The XMethods Weather-Temperature Web service.

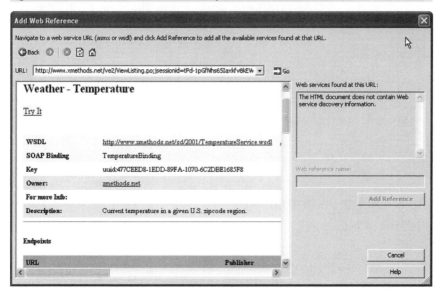

Weather-Temperature Web service displays its Web page on the XMethods site, as shown in Figure 11.3.

The Web Service Definition Language (WSDL) uses XML to describe Web services. We look for the WSDL link on the Weather-Temperature page. It shows the link

```
http://www.xmethods.net/sd/2001/TemperatureService.wsdl
```

which we click. Figure 11.4 shows the Add Web Reference window in our project.

We click the *Add Reference* button to add a reference to this Web service to our project. The Example11-1 folder contains the files for this project. Adding a Web reference creates a Web References folder inside Example11-1. This folder contains a folder called net.xmethods.www, which in turn contains the WSDL file TemperatureService.wsdl, and a C# program, Reference.cs, that exposes the methods of the Weather-Temperature Web service.

We click *Project*, *Add Existing Item*, *Browse*, as shown in Figure 11.5, to find the Reference.cs file, and click *Open* to add it to our project.

Figure 11.4   The WSDL file for the Weather-Temperature Web service.

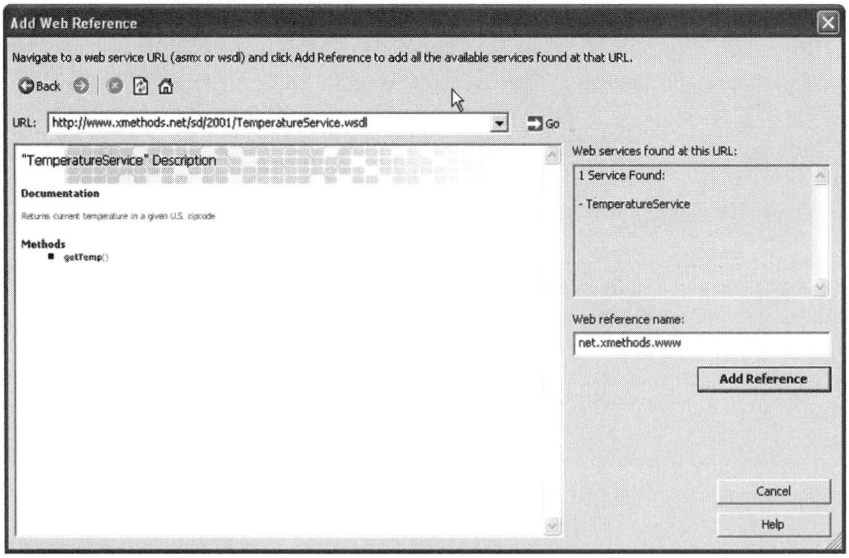

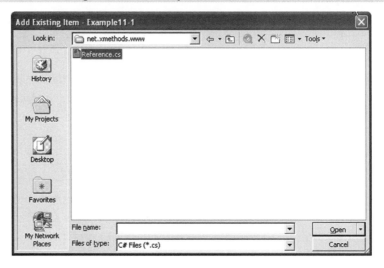

Figure 11.5   Locating the Weather-Temperature code.

The code for Reference.cs shows that it

- is contained in the Example11_1.net.xmethods.www namespace
- defines a TemperatureService class
- defines a getTemp method that has a String zip code parameter and returns a System.Single, which is another name for a float number

When the user clicks the *Temperature* button, we want to pass the zip code that the user entered to the getTemp method and display the return value. Because we are using a Web service, the getTemp method will actually execute on the site of the Weather-Temperature service.

We double-click the button in the Visual Studio .NET design to display its event-handling template and fill in the code as follows:

```
private void getTemperature_Click
                    (object sender, System.EventArgs e)
{
    Example11_1.net.xmethods.www.TemperatureService t
    = new Example11_1.net.xmethods.www.TemperatureService();
    display.Text = "The temperature is "
                    + t.getTemp(enterZip.Text).ToString();
}
```

We first create a TemperatureService object, and then call its getTemp method, passing it the zip code that the user entered. We invoke the ToString method to convert the float to a string to display in the label.

11.1.2   Asynchronous Calls

The getTemp method we used in Example11-1 calls the Weather-Temperature Web service, passes the zip code, and waits for the Web service to return the temperature. We call this synchronous access, because the calling method is synchronized with the Web service. Weather-Temperature is a very simple service, not requiring extensive computation, but one can easily imagine services that might take time to prepare an appropriate response. They may need to contact other Web services, which would prolong the wait. Any network communication is subject to unforeseen delays.

Web services provide asynchronous access to allow the calling program to contact the Web service and then continue further local processing without waiting for the response. The client provides a callback method that the Web service will invoke when it is ready to respond.

The Weather-Temperature Web service has two methods, BegingetTemp and EndgetTemp, which provide asynchronous access. The client calls Beginget-Temp when it makes the request. It passes the zip code and the callback method. When the Web service responds, it invokes the callback method. The callback method calls the EndgetTemp method to get the result.

Example11-2 accesses the Weather-Temperature Web service asynchronously. We create this Windows Application project in the same way we

Figure 11.6   Making an asynchronous request.

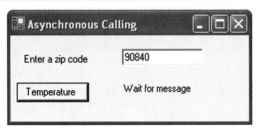

created Example11-1. When the user clicks the *Temperature* button, the event handler calls the BegingetTemp method and displays a message in a label telling the user to wait for a message box giving the temperature. The event handler finishes execution.

**Figure 11.7
The response to the client.**

Meanwhile, the Web service finds the temperature for the submitted zip code and calls the callback method, which calls the EndgetTemp method to get the result and displays it in a MessageBox. This Web service does not take long to respond, so the message box appears soon after the request, but other services will not always be so quick. We use a MessageBox here, but the callback method could write the result to a file or a log, which the user could inspect to get the result. Figure 11.6 shows making an asynchronous request, and Figure 11.7 shows the response to the user.

11.1.3   The Event Handler and the Callback Methods

When the user clicks the *Temperature* button, we want to send the zip code that the user entered to the Weather-Temperature Web service. Because we are not waiting for the Web service to find the temperature, we also send it a callback method that the Web service will call when it is ready to send the reply with the temperature at the requested zip code. Double-clicking on the *Temperature* button in the Visual Studio .NET design displays its event-handling template, which we complete to give

```
private void getTemperature_Click
                    (object sender, System.EventArgs e)
{
    Example11_2.net.xmethods.www.TemperatureService t
      = new
        Example11_2.net.xmethods.www.TemperatureService();
    AsyncCallback callback
                        = new AsyncCallback(Zip_Callback);
```

```
    t.BegingetTemp(enterZip.Text, callback, t);
    display.Text = "Wait for message";
}
```

The four statements of the getTemperature_Click method

- create an instance of the TemperatureService class

- create an AsyncCallback callback, passing it the name of the call-back method

- call BegingetTemp

- place a temporary message in a label

We explain each of these in turn. The first statement creates an instance of the TemperatureService class provided in the Reference.cs file when we added the Web reference to the Weather-Temperature service to our project. The TemperatureService class contains the three methods that we use in Example11-1 and Example11-2: getTemp, BegingetTemp, and EndgetTemp.

The second statement creates the callback we need to pass to the Web service for the callback. The AsyncCallback callback is defined in the System namespace. It specifies the pattern that an asynchronous callback should have. We pass it Zip_Callback, a method that follows that pattern and whose code we discuss later in this section.

The third statement requests a temperature from the Web service by calling BegingetTemp, passing it three arguments. The first argument is the zip code. The second argument is the callback that the Web service will use to respond when it is ready. The third argument is the service object that will be returned with the result during the callback.

The fourth statement displays a message in a label, so the user is prompted to expect a delayed response. We need to write the callback method in the code-behind file that also contains getTemperature_Click. Its code is

```
private void Zip_Callback(IAsyncResult result)
{
    Example11_2.net.xmethods.www.TemperatureService t
    = (Example11_2.net.xmethods.www.TemperatureService)
                                result.AsyncState;
    float temperature = t.EndgetTemp(result);
    MessageBox.Show("The temperature is " + temperature);
}
```

The BIG Picture

With Visual Studio .NET we can easily write a client program to access Web services available on the Internet. We do not need to know the details of the protocol used to communicate with the service. The XMethods site, http://www.xmethods.net, contains many Web services that we can try.

The Web Service Definition Language (WSDL) uses XML to describe Web services. When we add a Web reference, Visual Studio .NET creates a C# file that exposes the Web service methods for us to call in our application.

In addition to synchronous access, Web services provide asynchronous access to allow the calling program to contact the Web service and then continue further local processing without waiting for the response. The client provides a callback method that the Web service will invoke when it is ready to respond.

The `Zip_Callback` method follows the pattern required by the `AsyncCallback` type. It has a parameter, `result`, of type `IAsyncResult`, which represents the result of an asynchronous operation, and a `void` return type. When the Weather-Temperature Web service calls the `Zip_Callback` method, it will pass a result of this type. The `AsyncState` property of `result` provides the response containing the information about the asynchronous operation. In this case, that includes the temperature. The first statement of the `Zip_Callback` method casts the `AsyncState` value to the `TemperatureService` type we are using, so we can call the `EndgetTemp` method to get the temperature.

The second line calls the `EndgetTemp` method that gets the temperature from the `result` parameter. The third line displays the temperature in a `MessageBox`.

Test Your Understanding

1. What does WSDL stand for?

2. Explain the difference between a synchronous and an asynchronous call to a Web service.

11.2   Creating a Web Service

Visual Studio .NET makes it easy to create a Web service. In Example11-3, we create a Web service that provides a `Reverse` method. The client submits a string, and the Example11-3 service returns the reversed string to the user. We open Example11-3 as an `ASP.NET Web Service` template. Visual Studio .NET provides a design page, but we do not use it in this example. Web services operate behind the scenes and do not need a user interface, but in a later example we will add nonvisual components to the design page. Figure 11.8 shows the design page with a link at the bottom to switch to the code view.

We click this link to change to the code page with the default file name of `Service1.asmx.cs`. Visual Studio .NET creates the code template to include a sample Web service method that is totally commented out. It is there to show what needs to be done. That code is

```
// WEB SERVICE EXAMPLE
// The HelloWorld() example service returns
//    the string Hello World
// To build, uncomment the following lines then
//    save and build the project
```

Figure 11.8 The Web service design page.

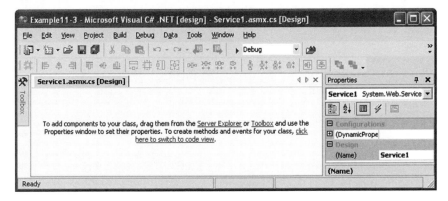

```
// To test this web service, press F5

//          [WebMethod]
//          public string HelloWorld()
//          {
//                return "Hello World";
//          }
```

The key feature to note is the Web service attribute, [WebMethod], included before the method. Adding this attribute enables the method we write to be available as a Web service.

The code for the Reverse method we add is

```
[WebMethod]
public String Reverse(String s)
{
    int size = s.Length;
    char[] c = new char[size];
    for (int i=0; i<size; i++)
        c[i] = s[size-1-i];
    return new String(c);
}
```

To reverse a string, we first find its length. We then create an array of characters of that same size and copy the characters starting from the end of the string to the beginning of the array, so that the array will hold the reverse of the original string. Figure 11.9 shows this process for the string s, where s = "tomato". The loop starts with i=0, so the first copy is

```
c[0] = s[size-1];
```

Figure 11.9   Reversing a string.

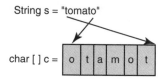

String s = "tomato"

char [ ] c = | o | t | a | m | o | t |

Because size is 6, that becomes

c[0] = s[5]

which copies the ending 'o' of the string s to the first position of the array c.

11.2.1   Testing the Web Service

We can test by pressing the *F5* key or by clicking the *Debug, Start* menu item in Visual Studio .NET, or we can enter `http://localhost/Example11-3/Service1.asmx` in the address field of Internet Explorer. Any of these methods brings up a page with a link at the top labeled `Reverse`. Clicking this link displays the text box shown in Figure 11.10 in which we can enter a string to reverse. Entering `tomato` and clicking the invoke button produces the response of Figure 11.11.

Figure 11.10   Testing the Reverse service.

Figure 11.11   The response from the Reverse service.

The response in Figure 11.11 is an XML file. Inside the `<string>` tag we see the reserved string, `otamot`. Next, we will write a client for this service that will allow users to access it.

11.2.2   A Client for the Reverse Service

Example11-4 will provide a form, shown in Figure 11.12, in which the client can enter a string. Pressing a button will contact the `Reverse` service of Example11-3 and display the reversed string in a label.

We create Example11-4 as a `Windows Application` project and add a button, two labels, and a text box to the form. We set a few properties, including the `BackColor` and `Text` of `Form1`. We set the `(Name)` property of the `TextBox` to `enterString` and its `Text` property to the empty string. We change the `(Name)` of the `Button` to `reverse` and its `Text` to *Reverse*. The `Label` to its right gets a `(Name)` of `display` and an empty string `Text`.

Example11-4 needs to refer to the Web service of Example11-3. To add this reference, we click `Project, Add Web Reference` and enter

```
http://localhost/Example11-3/Service1.asmx
```

Figure 11.12   A Client for Reverse service.

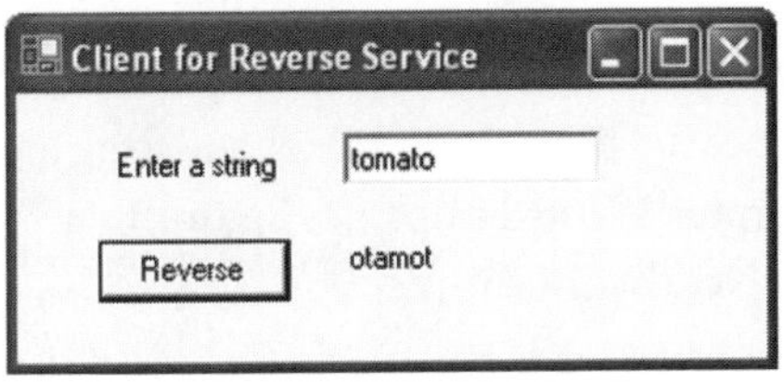

The BIG Picture

Visual Studio .NET makes it easy to create a Web service. Adding the [WebMethod] attribute enables the method we write to be available as a Web service.

We can create a client automatically or build one ourselves. The three ways to create a client automatically are by pressing the *F5* key, by clicking the *Debug, Start* menu item in Visual Studio .NET, or by entering the Web services URL in the address field of Internet Explorer. Creating a client ourselves provides a nicer display of the results.

in the Address box that appears in the Add Web Reference window. When the service is loaded, we click the *Add Reference* button.

To display the event-handler template for the Reverse button, we double-click the button in the Visual Studio .NET design. We add code, so the completed event handler is

```
private void reverse_Click
                 (object sender, System.EventArgs e)
{
    Example11_3.localhost.Service1 r
        = new Example11_3.localhost.Service1();
    display.Text = r.Reverse(enterString.Text);
}
```

In the event handler we create an instance of the Web service and call its Reverse method, passing it the string entered in the text box. We display the reversed string in a label. Example11-4 uses the synchronous call to the service, but the BeginReverse and EndReverse methods are available for asynchronous calling.

Test Your Understanding

3. With what attribute do we prefix a method to enable it as a Web service?

11.3   Accessing Data

A Web service can retrieve data from a database. Example11-5 contains a Web service with methods GetEmployees returning the names and titles of the Northwind employees, and GetProducts returning the names and quantities of the Northwind products.

11.3.1   Creating the Web Service

We create Example11-5 as an ASP .NET Web Service. To build the Web service, we will need one data adapter to get the employee data and another to get the product data from the Northwind database. We will use a DataSet to hold the data to return to the clients of this Web service.

To start, we click the Data tab in the Toolbox and drag an OleDbAdapter to the form. The Data Adapter Wizard pops up. Figure 11.13 shows the screen in which we select the Northwind connection.

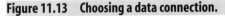

Figure 11.13 Choosing a data connection.

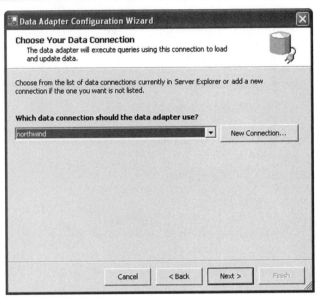

We click *Next* and accept the default *Use SQL statements* in the Choose a Query Type screen that appears next. In the Generate the SQL statements screen we click the *Query Builder* button. Figure 11.14 shows the Add Tables screen in which we select Employees and click *Add* and *Close*. From the Employees box we select FirstName, LastName, and Title and click *OK*.

The Query Builder screen of Figure 11.15 shows the Employees table. We need to select the fields with which we wish to fill the data set that the Web service will return to the client. From the Employees box we select FirstName, LastName, and Title and click *OK*. This finishes building the query and returns to the Generate the SQL statements screen.

We could immediately accept the work of the query builder and click the *Next* button. Optionally, by clicking the *Advanced Options* button we can disable the generation of commands we will not be using. In Example11-5, we click *Advanced Options*, uncheck the *Generate Insert, Update, and Delete statements* box, and click *OK* before clicking the *Next* button in the Generate the SQL statements screen. To complete the configuration of the data adapter, we click *Finish* in the View Wizard Results screen.

Figure 11.14   Selecting the Employees table.

Figure 11.15   Selecting Employees fields.

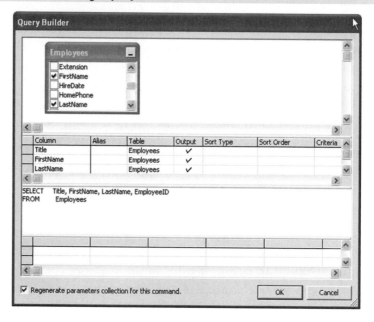

We change the (Name) property of the data adapter that appears in the design to employees and the (Name) of the data connection that appears to northwind.

Similarly, we add a second OleDbDataAdapter and use the Data Adapter Wizard to configure it to use the northwind connection. In that process, we build the query to use the Products table and its ProductName and UnitsInStock fields. We change the (Name) property of this data adapter to products.

We adjust the ConnectionString property value for the northwind connection, if necessary, to

```
Provider=Microsoft.Jet.OLEDB.4.0;Password="";User ID=Admin; Data
Source="C:\Program Files\Microsoft Office \Office10\Samples\Northwind.mdb"
```

The Data Source path may vary on other systems.

We need to add the code for the GetEmployees and GetProducts methods that we will expose as Web services for clients to use. Each method will return a DataSet containing the data that the client can display. When we drag a DataSet control from the Toolbox to the design, the Add Dataset window of Figure 11.16 appears. We select Untyped dataset and click *OK*. In the design view, we change the (Name) property of this data set to northwindData.

We click on the *View*, *Code* menu item and add the code for the GetEmployees and GetProducts methods.

Figure 11.16   Adding a data set.

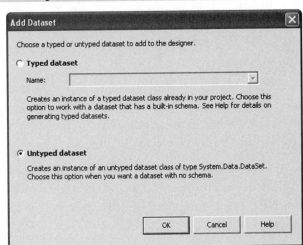

```
[WebMethod]
public DataSet GetEmployees()
{
    employees.Fill(northwindData);
    return nortwindData;
}

[WebMethod]
public DataSet GetProducts()
{
    products.Fill(northwindData);
    return northwindData;
}
```

The [Web Method] attribute identifies each method as a Web service. Each method has a DataSet return type. The GetEmployees code uses the Fill method of the employees data adapter to fill the northwindData data set with employee data. The GetProducts code uses the Fill method of the products data adapter to fill the northwindData data adapter with products data.

Next, we need to create a client to use these Web services.

11.3.2 Creating a Client

In Example11-6, we create a client that allows the user to find either Northwind employees or products. We create Example11-6 as a Windows Application project and add two Button controls and a DataGrid. We set the Text property of the first button to Employees and set the Text of the second to Products. We change the (Name) property of the *Employees* button to employees, the (Name) property of the *Products* button to products, and that of the data grid to display.

We click the *Project, Add Web Reference* menu item to add a reference to the Web service we just created, entering http://localhost/Example11-5/Service1.asmx in the Address box in the window that appears. We click the *Add Reference* button to add this reference to the project.

To access the Web service of Example11-5 from this project, we implement the event handlers for the buttons. Clicking on the *Employees* button in the Visual Studio .NET design, we complete the code in the template that appears, to give

```
private void employees_Click
            (object sender, System.EventArgs e)
```

Figure 11.17 Using a Web service to get Northwind data.

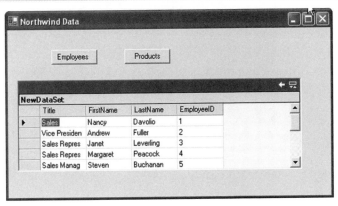

```
{
    Example11_6.localhost.Service1 service =
        new Example11_6.localhost.Service1();
    display.DataSource = service.getEmployees();
}
```

We create an instance of the Web service and call the GetEmployees method to return a DataSet that we assign as the DataSource property of the DataGrid. In the event handler for the second button, we call the GetProducts method of the Web service. The code is

```
private void products_Click
                (object sender, System.EventArgs e)
{
    Example11_6.localhost.Service1 service =
        new Example11_6.localhost.Service1();
    display.DataSource = service.GetProducts();
}
```

Figure 11.17 shows the user obtaining the names and titles of Northwind employees.

Test Your Understanding

4. What does a Web service client need to add to its project to link to the Web service?

The BIG Picture

A Web service can retrieve data from a database. The client adds a Web reference to a Web service and is able to call its methods.

11.4   Summary

- Web services use a simple protocol with XML to allow programs to communicate. In this way, an application developed on one platform can use methods of another application running on a different platform at a remote site and perhaps written in a different language.

- With Visual Studio .NET, we can easily write a client program to access Web services available on the Internet. We do not need to know the details of the protocol used to communicate with the service. The XMethods site, `http://www.xmethods.net`, contains many Web services that we can try.

- The Web Service Definition Language (WSDL) uses XML to describe Web services. When we add a Web reference, Visual Studio .NET creates a C# file that exposes the Web service methods for us to call in our application.

- In addition to synchronous access, Web services provide asynchronous access to allow the calling program to contact the Web service and then continue further local processing without waiting for the response. The client provides a callback method that the Web service will invoke when it is ready to respond.

- Visual Studio .NET makes it easy to create a Web service. Adding the [WebMethod] attribute enables the method we write to be available as a Web service.

- We can create a client automatically or build one ourselves. The three ways to create a client automatically are by pressing the *F5* key, by clicking the *Debug, Start* menu item in Visual Studio .NET, or by entering the Web services URL in the address field of Internet Explorer. Creating a client ourselves provides a nicer display of the results.

- A Web service can retrieve data from a database. The client adds a Web reference to a Web service and is able to call its methods.

11.5   Programming Exercises

11.1   Modify Example11-1 to display the date and time when the temperature is displayed.

11.2   Modify Example11-2 to display the date and time when the temperature is displayed.

11.3   Modify Example11-4 to display the reversed string in a MessageBox.

11.4   Modify Example11-5 to add a GetShippers method that returns a DataSet containing the Northwind Shippers data.

11.5   Modify Example11-6 to add a Button to display the Shippers data added in Exercise 4.

11.6   Create a Web service that returns the amount that will result if a given initial amount is deposited at a specified interest rate for a specified number of years, if the interest is compounded yearly.

11.7   Create a Web service that returns a random lucky number between 1 and 47.

11.8   Pick a service from the www.xmethods.com site and write a client to access that service.

11.9   Create a client that uses the Web service of Exercise 7. The client selects the number of lucky numbers desired from a ComboBox and presses a Button to display the numbers in a Label.

11.10   Write a client to access the Web service of Exercise 6. The client enters the initial amount in a TextBox and displays the resulting amount in a Label.

11.11   Write a client that accesses the Web service of Exercise 6 asynchronously. The client enters the initial amount in a TextBox and displays the resulting amount in a MessageBox.

11.12   Write a client that accesses the Reverse service of Example11-3 asynchronously.

11.13   Write a Web service to display the Northwind Orders data. Include the Order ID, the Customer, and the Shipped Date.

11.14   Write a client to use the Web service of Exercise 13. Display the data in a DataGrid control.

CHAPTER 12

Mobile Applications

Devices such as cellular phones and personal digital assistants (PDAs) are becoming an ever larger part of the computing landscape. These devices vary in capabilities, most importantly in the size of the display and the amount of memory available. Devices with limited capabilities can execute Web applications in which the code for the application resides on the server and a micro browser executes the client on the small device. Devices with more capabilities can run stand-alone applications using the .NET Compact Framework, a version of .NET design for mobile devices.

Visual Studio .NET 2003 includes the ASP .NET mobile controls. We use Visual Studio .NET 2003 in this chapter.

Chapter Objectives:

- Build simple mobile applications
- Store data on the device
- Access Web services from mobile applications

12.1 Introduction

In this section we give an overview of .NET development for mobile devices.

12.1.1 Mobile Devices

Many types of devices have computing capability and run .NET applications. These devices vary greatly in computing power and features. A handheld computer may have about the same capability as a desktop machine. Typically, however, its capabilities are more limited, necessitating some changes in application development. Mobile phones usually have less memory and a smaller screen than handheld computers. Personal digital assistants come in various sizes with differing capabilities. Pagers and other devices may also be programmable.

12.1.2   Operating Systems

Each device runs operating system software that manages the lower-level interactions with it. Desktop computers may use the Windows XP operating system, but this system is too large for the handheld and pocket mobile devices. Microsoft provides the Windows CE operating system for constrained environments.

Devices vary greatly in the features they support. For example, the screen size differs among devices, and a device may not have a screen at all. A device may have a keyboard similar to the larger desktop keyboards, it may have a limited phone keypad, it may have a keyboard simulated in software, or it may have no keyboard of any kind. And devices vary greatly in the amount of memory available to host applications.

Consequently, the Windows CE operating system must be very flexible. Manufacturers may use those Windows CE modules needed to support the features present on their devices and may omit other unneeded modules. A developer must test applications developed for the Windows CE system on an emulator for the target device to make sure that it runs well on that particular device and does not require any Windows CE capabilities not present on the target device.

To make it easier to develop mobile applications that run on many devices, Microsoft has specified versions of Windows CE for particular classes of devices. The Pocket PC operating system is a variant of Windows CE, including specific modules that must be present on conforming devices. Thus a developer for the Pocket PC system can assume that a Pocket PC will have the specified capabilities. For example, every Pocket PC device has a screen size of 240 × 320.

Because the Pocket PC screen size is small, it cannot display more than one application at a time. It would be inconvenient for the user to close one application before starting another, because that application would have to be started again to continue running later. Thus on the Pocket PC, applications run indefinitely. When the user minimizes an application, it does not terminate but stays alive in the background.

Every Pocket PC device will have these common features, so developers can write one application and expect it to run in a similar manner on all Pocket PC devices. The Pocket PC must have at least 32 megabytes of memory to host data and applications, and 16 megabytes for the system software. Thus developers may provide rich clients that will be installed on the device and run as stand-alone applications without any requirements for network connectivity. Windows CE devices have varying amounts of memory. Devices may use the Web to access applications too large to be installed on the device. Microsoft provides smaller versions of its desktop .NET Framework to develop applications for mobile devices.

12.1.3   The .NET Compact Framework

The .NET Compact Framework is a smaller version of the .NET Framework designed for Windows CE systems. Its class library contains versions of about 25 to 30 percent of the full framework. It includes many familiar Windows user interface controls, which we have used earlier in the book to develop desktop applications. Starting with Visual Studio .NET 2003, the .NET Compact Framework classes are included.

To illustrate, we open a new project by clicking the *File*, *New*, *Project* menu item. Figure 12.1 shows the selection of a Smart Device Application project. Figure 12.2 indicates that we can target either the more specific Pocket PC platform, whose devices all must have at least a common set of resources,

Figure 12.1   Creating a Smart Device Application project.

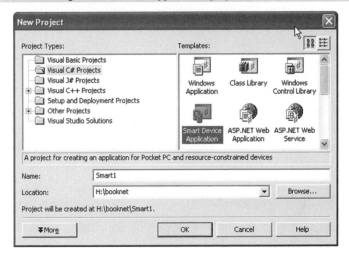

Figure 12.2   Choosing a platform.

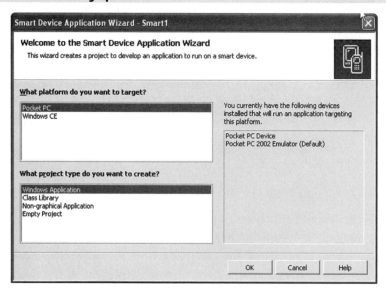

or the more generic Windows CE platform that allows a great variety of device capabilities.

In Figure 12.2, we selected the Pocket PC platform. Figure 12.3 shows the design view that opens when we click *OK*. The Toolbox on the left lists some of the device controls that we can add to the form. The form is the shape of a Pocket PC device. We will see later in the chapter that when we test a Pocket PC application on the Pocket PC emulator, the emulator looks like a typical Pocket PC device.

The other platform choice in Figure 12.2 is the Windows CE platform. But notice on the right of Figure 12.2 that only the Pocket PC emulator is installed for testing Pocket PC applications. No one emulator could model the variety of devices that run Windows CE. Thus to test a Windows CE application, we would need to download an emulator for a specific device from the manufacturer's site. We do not develop stand-alone Windows CE applications in this book, but do develop mobile Web applications for that platform.

12.1.4   Mobile Web Applications

A server hosts a Web application. Typically, the device makes a wireless Internet connection to a Web site. Just as with desktop Web applications,

Figure 12.3   Designing a Pocket PC application.

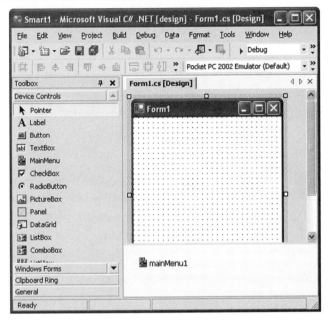

the ASP .NET mobile server controls run on the server sending a Web page to a small browser on the device.

When the device connects to the server it identifies itself, and, based on that identification, the server can vary the page it sends back to the device. The server may take into account the screen size, the availability of color, and other device characteristics in preparing its response. Using .NET, mobile Web applications can adapt to a variety of devices.

To create a mobile Web application, we create a Visual Studio .NET project. In Figure 12.4, we have selected an ASP .NET Mobile Web Application. Figure 12.5 shows the Toolbox that lists a few of the available Mobile Web Form controls that we can drag onto the form at its right.

The Microsoft Smartphone is another specification based on Windows CE. Newer versions of the .NET Compact Framework have the capability to develop applications for Smartphone devices. Because these are currently less common than Pocket PC devices, we concentrate on Pocket PC and generic Windows CE applications in this chapter.

Figure 12.4   Selecting an ASP .NET Mobile Web Application.

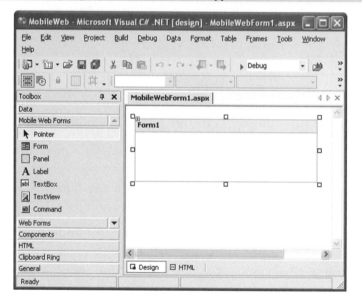

The BIG Picture

Microsoft provides the Windows CE operating system for constrained environments. Manufacturers may use those Windows CE modules needed to support the features present on their devices and may omit other unneeded modules. The Pocket PC operating system is a variant of Windows CE, and includes specific modules that must be present on conforming devices.

The .NET Compact Framework is a smaller version of the .NET Framework designed for Windows CE systems. We will use it to develop stand-alone applications for Pocket PC devices. We will use ASP .NET mobile controls to build Web applications hosted on the server and accessed using a browser on the device.

Figure 12.5   Designing an ASP .NET Mobile Web Application.

Test Your Understanding

1. Which Windows operating system may be installed on devices of varying capabilities?

2. Which .NET class library has been designed for use in mobile device applications?

12.2 A Simple Mobile Web Application

Many of the mobile controls are similar to controls we have used in building .NET Windows and Web applications for personal computers.

12.2.1 Creating a Web Application

Using Visual Studio .NET, we create Example12-1 as an ASP.NET Mobile Web Application project. A simple form appears in the Visual Studio .NET design. The screen area of mobile devices is limited, so we cannot add too many controls. If necessary, we can use additional forms.

The Toolbox, partially shown in Figure 12.5, contains a list of Mobile Web Form controls that we can drag onto a form. For this example, we add a Label and two Command controls. Command controls are like buttons.

We change the Text property of the label to *Have a great day* and its Alignment property to Center. By clicking the plus to the left of the Font property in the Properties window, we display other properties of the current font. We set the Bold property to True. We change its (ID) property to Display.

We also set the Bold property for the Font of each Command to True. The Text of one button is Red and that of the other is Blue. We set their (ID) properties to MakeRed and MakeBlue. We change the BackColor of each Command to reflect its text.

When the user clicks a command, we want to change the color of the label's text to the color indicated by the command. We need to write code to handle the event generated when the user clicks a Command. Double-clicking the command in the Visual Studio .NET design displays the event-handling method for that command. We add a line to each to change the ForeColor property of the label. The code is

```
private void MakeRed_Click
                    (object sender, System.EventArgs e)
{
    Display.ForeColor = Color.Red;
}
private void MakeBlue_Click
                    (object sender, System.EventArgs e)
{
    Display.ForeColor = Color.Blue;
}
```

Clicking the *Debug, Start* menu will test the Web page in the desktop Internet Explorer browser. Starting with the 2003 edition, Visual Studio .NET includes an emulator for a Pocket PC, which serves as a test model for the actual device. Clicking the *Tools, Connect to Device* menu item displays a `Connect to Device` window that permits a choice of two platforms, `Pocket PC` or `Windows CE`.

The Pocket PC option represents a specific version of the Windows CE platform that is designed primarily for personal information management devices with more memory and screen area than some of the smaller mobile devices. Windows CE .NET is a more general platform targeting a wide array of devices.

12.2.2   The Windows CE .NET Emulator

Choosing the Windows CE platform displays the screen of Figure 12.6. We chose the Windows CE .NET Emulator.

Pressing the *Connect* button displays the generic screen of Figure 12.7. We would need to download specific device emulators from manufacturers to get device screens that refer to specific hardware devices running Windows CE. Clicking the Internet Explorer icon displays the generic device browser. We enter the address, on our system, of Example12-1,

`http://192.168.1.100/Example12-1/MobileWebForm1.aspx`

to display the Web application of Example12-1, shown in Figure 12.8. In the URL, we use the address of the local machine we are using, `192.168.1.100`. To find this address, we could execute the `ipconfig` command in a command window.

Figure 12.6   Choosing a device or device emulator.

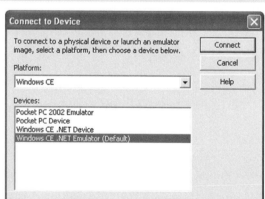

Figure 12.7   The Windows CE .NET Emulator.

Figure 12.8   The generic Windows CE browser.

When we shut down the emulator, we get a dialog that gives us a choice of saving the emulator state or turning off the emulator. We choose to turn off the emulator.

12.2.3   The Pocket PC 2002 Emulator

To use the Pocket PC emulator instead, we choose it in the `Connect to Device` screen. Because the Pocket PC refers to a specific type of device, the emulator is able to represent it more closely. Figure 12.9 shows its start-up appearance.

To configure the Pocket PC emulator to connect to the Internet, we click on the *Start*, *Settings* menu item, then on the `Connections` tab, and finally on the `Connection` icon. Settings will vary depending on the configuration of the host computer. The uppermost combo box gives a choice of `Internet Settings` or `Work Settings` to connect to the Internet. The author selected `Work Settings` to use a broadband connection that is always on. The `Internet Set-`

Figure 12.9   The Pocket PC emulator.

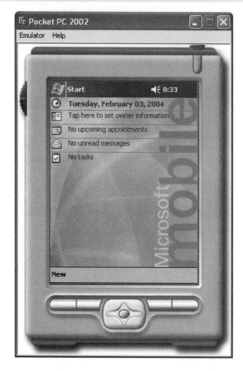

tings choice permits the entry of a dial-up number. After completing the configuration, we click the circular ok in the upper-right corner of the emulator, and the X at the upper right of the Settings screen. We only need to configure once.

To run Example12-1, we click the *Start* menu shown in the upper-left corner of Figure 12.9. Because Example12-1 is a Web application, in the list that appears we click the Internet Explorer item to use the local browser. Figure 12.10 shows the emulator running Pocket Internet Explorer.

We click the *View*, *Address Bar* menu item in the lower-left corner and then enter the address of Example12-1. A keyboard appears, provided to model data entry with a stylus. We can use the mouse with the emulator keyboard. To browse the site, we click the button with the green arrow at the right of the address, as shown in Figure 12.11. Figure 12.12 shows Example12-1 running on the Pocket PC emulator.

Figure 12.10   The Pocket PC emulator running Internet Explorer.

Figure 12.11   Browsing a Web application.

Figure 12.12   Example 12-1 in the Pocket PC emulator.

The BIG Picture

We can add various Mobile Web Controls to a Web application. We can test Web applications in the Windows CE .NET emulator, which provides a generic browser, or in the Pocket PC emulator, which resembles a Pocket PC device.

Test Your Understanding

3. Which device type, Windows CE or Pocket PC, includes devices with more limited resources?

12.3   A Smart Device Application: Appointment List

In this section we create an application that resides on a Pocket PC device. Example 12-2 will allow the user to update a schedule of appointments. The device will store the appointments and allow the user to view the list and to add or delete appointments. The simple user interface could be enhanced with additional effort. The Pocket PC simulator includes an appointment scheduler, so Example 12-2 is meant only to introduce Pocket PC application building.

We create Example 12-2 as a Smart Device Application. In the Smart Device Wizard that appears, we target the Pocket PC platform and create a Windows

Application project. The Toolbox in the Visual Studio .NET design contains a list of device controls that includes Label, TextBox, MainMenu, CheckBox, RadioButton, PictureBox, Panel, DataGrid, ListBox, ComboBox, ListView, TreeView, TabControl, HScrollBar, VScrollBar, Timer, DomainUpDown, NumericUpDown, Track-Bar, ProgressBar, ImageList, ContextMenu, ToolBar, StatusBar, OpenFileDialog, SaveFileDialog, and InputPanel.

12.3.1   Using Tabs

Example12-2 uses a TabControl with two tabs. The first tab lets the user add a new appointment, and the second tab shows the appointment list. We drag a TabControl from the Toolbox to the form. Right-clicking the mouse on it displays a menu in which we click the *Add Tab* item. Repeating this step, we add the second tab. We use the Properties window to set the Text property of the first tab to Add and the text of the second to View.

To permit the user to select an appointment time, we drag a combo box, two radio buttons, and a label onto the Add tab. The user selects the hour from the combo box and AM or PM from the radio buttons. We set the (Name) property of the combo box to time, that of the AM radio button to am, and that of the PM button to pm. We also drag a text box and a label to this tab so that the user can describe the appointment briefly, and we set the (Name) property of the text box to description.

We click *Debug*, *Start* to run the application. Figure 12.13 shows the Add tab that appears when this application starts running. Notice that the controls appear above the keyboard that the user has displayed by clicking the keyboard icon in the lower-left corner. A button allows the user to add an appointment. We set its Text property to *Add Appointment* and its (Name) property to add.

We add a ListBox to the View tab to display the list of appointments and a Save button to allow the user to save the updated list of appointments in an XML file. We set the (Name) property of the list box to appointments and that of the *Save* button to save. The application will initialize the list box with the current list of appointments when it loads. In Example12-2, we do not keep the list in chronological order or include dates. These features are left as exercises for the reader.

When the user clicks the *Add Appointment* button, the event handler adds the appointment to the list box. Double-clicking on the button in the

Figure 12.13   Adding an appointment.

Visual Studio .NET design displays the template for the event handler. With our added code it is

```
private void add_Click
                (object sender, System.EventArgs e)
{
    String amOrPm = "";
    if(am.Checked)
        amOrPm = " AM -- ";
    else
        amOrPm = " PM -- ";
    appointments.Items.Add(time.SelectedItem
                + amOrPm + description.Text);
}
```

The event-handling code for the button sets the amOrPm string to either AM or PM depending upon which radio button the user checked. Then it adds to the list box a string composed of the time followed by the description the user entered in the text box.

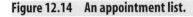
Figure 12.14 An appointment list.

Figure 12.15 The list saved as an XML file.

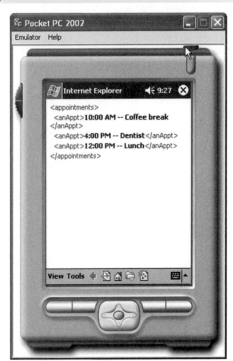

12.3.2 Saving the Appointment List

When the user clicks the Save button in the View tab, the event handler saves the list of appointments as an XML file. Figure 12.14 shows the list containing three entries. When the user clicks the *Save* button, the event-handling code creates an XmlDocument containing the list items and saves it on the device under the name Example12_2.xml.

To view Example12_2.xml, we click the X in the upper-right corner to minimize the application. Then we click the *Start, Programs* menu item, double-click the File Explorer icon, and click the arrow in the upper-left corner to show the My Device folder. We click on My Device and double-click Example12_2 to display it. Figure 12.15 shows this XML file.

The event-handling code for the *Save* button is

```
private void button2_Click
                (object sender, System.EventArgs e)
{
    System.Xml.XmlDocument xml
            = new System.Xml.XmlDocument();
```

```
System.Xml.XmlElement top
        = xml.CreateElement("appointments");
xml.AppendChild(top);
foreach (String s in listBox1.Items)
{
  if (s != ")
  {
    System.Xml.XmlElement appt
              = xml.CreateElement("anAppt");
    appt.InnerText = s;
    top.AppendChild(appt);
  }
}
xml.Save("Example12_2.xml");
}
```

The first line of the event-handling code creates the XML document. The next two lines add the root tag <appointments> to the XML document. The foreach loop takes each string from the list box, adds it as the text of an <anAppt> tag, and makes that tag a child of the root. The last line saves the completed document on the device.

12.3.3   Initializing the Appointment List

When the user starts the application we want to load the Example12-2.xml file and add each appointment it contains to the ListBox in the View tab. Double-clicking on the form displays the template for the Form1_Load method. We add our code to the template, so the completed method is

```
private void Form1_Load(object sender, System.EventArgs e)
{
    if (System.IO.File.Exists("Example12_2.xml"))
    {
      System.Xml.XmlDocument doc
              = new System.Xml.XmlDocument();
      doc.Load("Example12_2.xml");
      System.Xml.XmlElement root = doc.DocumentElement;
      System.Xml.XmlNodeList item
                  = root.GetElementsByTagName("anAppt");
      for (int i = 0; i < item.Count; i++)
          appointments.Items.Add
                    (item[i].FirstChild.OuterXml);
    }
}
```

The code starts by checking that the file exists. Until the user saves an appointment list, this file probably will not be available. When it is, we create a new `XmlDocument` and load the file into it. The `DocumentElement` property holds the root element of the document. That would be the `<appointments>` tag in our example.

Next we get a list of all `<anAppt>` tags that are nested in this root. These form an `XmlNodeList`. The `Count` property contains the size of that list. We use a `for` loop to get each item from the list of `<anAppt>` tags. The `FirstChild` property of each holds an `XmlText` node that contains the text inside the `<anAppt>` tag, which is the appointment we want to add to the list box. The `OuterXml` property gets the content of the tag, which is the text we want to add to the list box. The `Items` property contains the collection of items in the list box. The `Add` method adds an item to this collection.

The BIG Picture

The Toolbox in the Visual Studio .NET design contains a list of device controls that we can use to build smart device applications. Using a `TabControl` lets us break the user interface into multiple screens to best use the limited size of mobile devices. We can save data in an XML file stored on the device.

Test Your Understanding

4. In designing a smart device application, why might we choose not to add controls to the lower part of the screen?

5. Which method can we use to find all the `<anAppt>` tags in an XML document?

12.4 Accessing Web Services

If we have configured our Pocket PC to connect to the Internet, we can access Web services from it. Example12-3 lets the user choose whether to access the `Temperature` Web service hosted on `www.xmethods.com` and discussed in Chapter 11, or the `Reverse` Web service hosted locally and developed in Chapter 11. Figure 12.16 shows the initial screen in which the user has selected the `Temperature` Web service and entered a zip code.

We create Example12-3 as a Smart Device Application. From top to bottom, the device controls we add to the form and the properties we set for each are

```
Label
    Text        Choose a web service

Radio Button
    Text        Temperature
    (Name)      temperature
```

Radio Button

    Text   *Reverse*

    (Name)   reverse

Label

    Text   an empty string

    (Name)   message

TextBox

    (Name)   enter

Button

    Text   *Submit*

    (Name)   submit

Figure 12.16   Selecting a Web service.

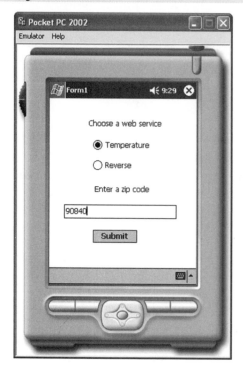

The lower Label is initially blank. When the user checks the Temperature radio button, we display *Enter a zip code* in this label. Double-clicking on this radio button in the Visual Studio .NET design shows the template for the event-handling method. We add the code to set the Text property of the Label so that it becomes

```
private void temperature_CheckedChanged
                    (object sender, System.EventArgs e)
{
    message.Text = "Enter a zip code";
}
```

When the user checks Reverse, we display *Enter a string to reverse* in the label. The event method to change the label is

```
private void reverse_CheckedChanged
                    (object sender, System.EventArgs e)
{
    message.Text = "Enter a string to reverse";
}
```

12.4.1 Adding Web References

To enable our Pocket PC program to use a Web service, we need to add a Web reference to it to our project. To refer to the Weather-Temperature Web service in our project, we click the *Project, Add Web Reference* menu item. This displays an Add Web Reference window that includes a text box to enter the address of the Web service. We enter www.xmethods.net and hit the *Enter* key. The box on the left side shows the XMethods site. We scroll to the bottom and select the Weather-Temperature Web service.

The Web Service Definition Language (WSDL) uses XML to describe Web services. We look for the WSDL link on the Weather-Temperature page. It shows the link

```
http://www.xmethods.net/sd/2001/TemperatureService.wsdl
```

that we click. We click the *Add Reference* button to add a reference to this Web service to our project.

Example12-3 needs to refer to the Reverse Web service of Example11-3. To add this reference, we click Project, Add Web Reference and enter

```
http://192.168.1.100/Example11-3/Service1.asmx
```

in the Address box that appears in the Add Web Reference window. When the service is loaded we click the *Add Reference* button. When developing using the .NET Compact Framework, we need to use a numerical address, 192.169.1.100 on the author's machine, instead of localhost.

The *Submit* button will submit the data to either Web service. In its event handler we determine which radio button the user checked and call the corresponding Web service. The code is

```
private void submit_Click
                     (object sender, System.EventArgs e)
{
    if (temperature.Checked)
    {
      Example12_3.net.xmethods.www.TemperatureService t
        = new
        Example12_3.net.xmethods.www.TemperatureService();
      message.Text = "The temperature is "
                     + t.getTemp(enter.Text).ToString();
    }
    else if (reverse.Checked)
    {
      Example12_3.WebReference.Service1 r
              = new Example12_3.WebReference.Service1();
      message.Text = r.Reverse(enter.Text);
    }
}
```

If the user checks the temperature radio button, we create an object to access the Temperature Web service and display the result of the call of the getTemp method that returns the temperature in the zip code entered.

If the user checks the reverse radio button, we create an object to access the Reverse Web service and display the reverse of the string entered. Figure 12.17 shows a successful use of the Reverse service.

Test Your Understanding

6. What do we need to add to a project to enable a Pocket PC program to use a Web service?

The BIG Picture

If we have configured our Pocket PC to connect to the Internet, we can access Web services from it. To enable our Pocket PC program to use a Web service, we need to add a Web reference to it to our project.

Figure 12.17 Using the Reverse Web service.

12.5 Summary

- Devices with limited capabilities can execute Web applications in which the code for the application resides on the server and a micro browser executes the client on the small device. Devices with more capabilities can run stand-alone applications using the .NET Compact Framework, a version of .NET design for mobile devices. Many of the mobile controls are similar to controls we have used in building .NET Windows and Web applications for personal computers.

- Starting with the 2003 edition, Visual Studio .NET includes an emulator for a Pocket PC, which serves as a test model for the actual device. The Pocket PC option represents a specific version of the Windows CE platform that is designed primarily for personal information management devices that have more memory and screen area than some of the smaller mobile devices. Windows CE .NET is a more general platform targeting a wide array of devices, including cell phones.

- If we have configured our Pocket PC to connect to the Internet, we can access Web services from it. To enable our Pocket PC program to use a Web service, we need to add a Web reference to it to our project.

12.6 Programming Exercises

12.1 Modify Example12-1 to allow the user to choose either the Red, Green, or Blue colors for the text.

12.2 Modify Example12-2 to keep the appointments with the earlier ones listed first.

12.3 Modify Example12-2 to include dates for the appointments.

12.4 Modify Example12-3 to include a list of zip codes for the user to choose from.

12.5 Write a Web application that will allow the user to get a list of lucky numbers from 1 through 49. The user should select how many numbers are desired. The numbers should be randomly chosen.

12.6 Write a smart device application in which the user can enter a name and phone number and store them on the device. The user can choose from a list of names to retrieve the associated phone number from stored memory.

12.7 Write a smart device application that will allow the user to choose from two Web services at the `www.xmethods.com` site and to use whichever service was selected.

12.8 Write a Web application that allows the user to choose a zip code and returns a list of three restaurants located in that zip code.

CHAPTER | 13

Crystal Reports

Crystal Reports for Visual Studio .NET is the standard reporting tool for Visual Studio .NET. We can host reports on Web and Windows platforms and publish Crystal reports as Report Web Services on a Web server. Visual Studio .NET includes Crystal Reports for Visual Studio .NET.

Chapter Objectives:

- Create a simple report
- Add features to a report
- Use data sets as a report source
- Expose reports as Web services
- Enable users to interact with a report

13.1   Creating a Simple Report

Example13-1 builds a Windows application to display Northwind product data. We start by clicking *New*, *Project*, selecting the Visual C# Projects project type and then the Windows Application template. Choosing the Location and entering Example13-1 in the Name field, we click *OK*. Before adding controls to the form, we will create a report.

13.1.1   Adding and Creating a Report

To add a report to the project, we click on *File*, *Add New Item*, select the Crystal Report template, and click *Open*, which displays the Crystal Report

Figure 13.1   Crystal Report Gallery.

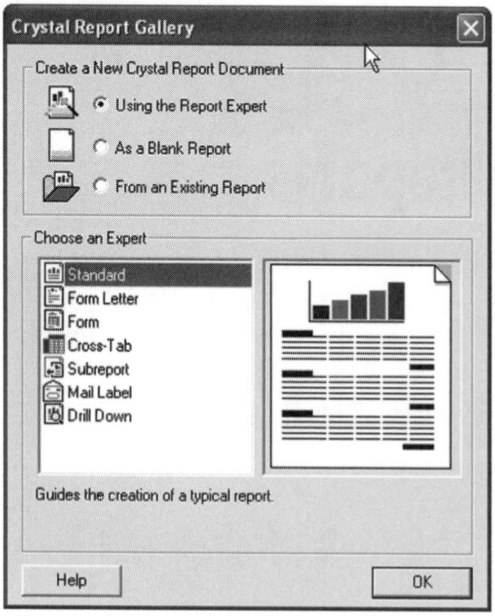

Gallery screen shown in Figure 13.1. The three choices for creating a Crystal Report document are:

Using the Report Expert	Guides report creation. Adds choices to Report Designer
As a Blank Report	Opens the Report Designer
From an Existing Report	Uses the same design as another report

The choices for the report expert are:

Standard	Typical report
Form Letter	Letter combining text and data
Form	Includes a letterhead or logo; used for invoices
Cross-Tab	Contains a summarized grid
Subreport	Contains a second report
Mail Label	Contains multiple columns for address labels
Drill Down	Displays summary and reveals details by drilling down

Figure 13.2   The Standard Report Expert.

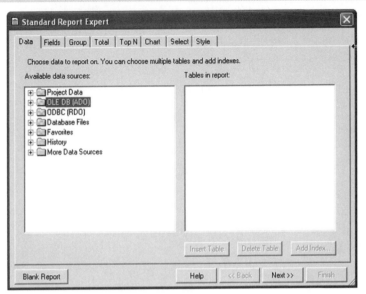

Example13-1 accepts the defaults using the report expert with the standard report. Figure13-2 shows the Standard Report Expert screen that appears. It has eight tabs that allow many report building options.

Because we want to use Northwind data, we select the OLE DB (ADO) data source. Clicking on the plus sign, +, at its left displays the OLE DB Provider screen. We select Microsoft Jet 4.0 OLE DB Provider and click *Next*. In the Connection Information screen in the Database Name field, we browse to find the path to Northwind.mdb and click *Next*. We click *Finish* in the Advanced Information screen.

The display returns to the Standard Report Expert screen that now shows the Northwind database as an OLE DB (ADO) data source. Clicking on the plus sign, +, to the left of its Tables item shows a list of the tables in the Northwind database. We select the Products table and click the Insert Table button to add Products to the Tables in report list on the right side of the screen.

Clicking Next displays the Fields tab of the Standard Report Expert shown in Figure 13.3, in which we have selected the ProductId, ProductName, UnitPrice, and UnitsInStock fields. We held the *Ctrl* key down while making selections to allow multiple selections. Clicking the *Add* button moves the four

Figure 13.3   Selecting fields.

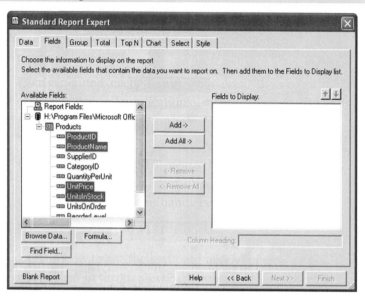

selected fields to the Field to Display column on the right side. Then we click *Finish*.

The project for Example13-1 now contains a CrystalReport1.rpt tab that has five sections: Report Header, Page Header, Details, Report Footer, and Page Footer. For this report, the Page Header section shows a date field in the upper right and column headings for each of the four columns. We increase the width of the date field to fully display the date.

The Details section shows the four pieces of information contained in a typical row of this report. In both the Page Header and the Details sections, we decrease the width of the ProductName field and move the UnitPrice and UnitsInStock fields to the left to make them visible with less horizontal scrolling.

13.1.2   Viewing the Report

The Toolbox contains a CrystalReportViewer control that we drag onto the form. Increasing its size in the Visual Studio .NET design makes it easier to view the data. We change its (Name) property to viewer.

We can easily configure this viewer to display the data for the entire Products table. Clicking on the CrystalReportViewer in the design and opening

Figure 13.4   Display information for all products.

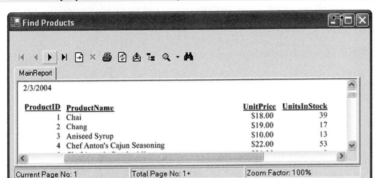

the Properties window, we browse to set the ReportSource property to the
path to the CrystalReport1.rpt report contained in the current project. We
set the DisplayGroupTree property to False because we are not grouping data
in this report. Figure 13.4 shows how the report looks so far. To allow the
viewer to resize when the user resizes the form, we change its Anchor property to anchor it to all four edges of the form.

13.1.3   Filtering

To make the report more useful, we can allow the user to choose a Company-
Name from the list of Suppliers and filter the data to only report Northwind
products from that supplier. We add a ComboBox to allow the user to select a
CompanyName and change the report to only display Northwind products
from the chosen company.

We drag a Label and a ComboBox onto the form, set the Text property of the
Label to Select a Supplier:, set the Text property of the ComboBox to the
empty string, and set its (Name) property to supplier. We anchor each of
these controls to Top only rather than Top, Left.

To display the current list of Suppliers, we will connect to the Northwind
database. We add an OleDbDataAdapter to the form and set its (Name) property to northwindAdapter. We use the Data Adapter Configuration Wizard as
in earlier chapters. In the Add Table screen of the Query Builder, we choose
the Suppliers table. In the CheckBoxList of Suppliers, we select CompanyName

and `SupplierID` as the fields to include in the query. We click the *Data, Generate Dataset* menu item to generate a data set to hold the query results and change its (`Name`) property to `suppliersData`.

We will fill the data set when the form is initialized. Double-clicking on the form itself displays the `Form1_Load` template. We add C# code, so it becomes

```
private void Form1_Load(object sender, System.EventArgs e)
{
    oleDbDataAdapter1.Fill(suppliersData);
}
```

We need to display this data set in the combo box. We do this by setting the `DataSource` property for `comboBox1` to `suppliersData.Suppliers`. We would like to display the company name in the combo box but use the corresponding supplier id to find the products from that supplier. To do this, we select the `ComboBox` and in the `Properties` window set the `DisplayMember` property to `CompanyName` and the `ValueMember` property to `SupplierID`.

When the user selects a company name, we want to alter the report to display only products from the selected supplier. We double-click on the `ComboBox` to display the event-handler template and fill in the code, to give

```
private void supplier_SelectedIndexChanged
                    (object sender, System.EventArgs e)
{
    viewer.SelectionFormula
        = "{Products.SupplierID} = "
            + supplier.SelectedValue;
    viewer.RefreshReport();
}
```

The first line of code sets the `SelectionFormula` property of the `CrystalReportViewer`. The selection formula determines which records are selected for the report. We require that the `SupplierID` of the product be the same as the `SupplierID` corresponding to the `CompanyName` that the user selected in the `ComboBox`. To write the condition we enclose `Products.Suppliers` in braces. Figure 13.5 shows the form with the report. The second line of code refreshes the report to reflect the new selection formula.

Test Your Understanding

1. What choices of report type do we have when using the Report Expert?

The BIG Picture

We used the Report Expert with the Standard format. We use a Crystal-ReportViewer control to view a report. We can filter data by setting the SelectionFormula property.

Figure 13.5　Selecting products from one supplier.

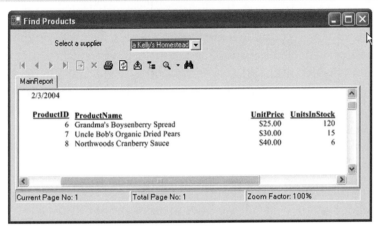

2.　Which property of a CrystalReportViewer control holds the path to the report it displays?

3.　Which property of a CrystalReportViewer control can we set to enable the report to choose which rows of data to display?

13.2　Adding Features to a Report

We can arrange the report by groups, add column subtotals, and add computed fields. Special formatting can highlight or distinguish selected rows. The report of Example13-2 illustrates these features using the OrderDetails table from the Northwind database.

Following the steps used in creating the report of Example13-1, we create a Windows Application project. To add a report to the project we click on *File*, *Add New Item*, select the Crystal Report template and click *Open*, which displays the Crystal Report Gallery screen. Example13-2 accepts the defaults using the report expert with the standard report.

13.2.1　The Data Tab

Because we want to use Northwind data we select the OLE DB (ADO) data source in the Standard Report Expert screen that appears. Clicking on the plus sign, +, at its left displays the OLE DB Provider screen. We select Microsoft Jet 4.0 OLE DB Provider and click *Next*. In the Connection Information screen in the Database Name field, we browse to find the path to Northwind.mdb,

C:\Program Files\Microsoft Office\Office10\Samples\Northwind.mdb

on our system, and click *Finish*.

The display returns to the Standard Report Expert screen, which now shows the Northwind database as an OLE DB (ADO) data source. Clicking on the plus sign, +, to the left of its Tables item shows a list of the tables in the Northwind database. We select the Order Details table and click the Insert Table button to add Order_Details to the Tables in report list on the right side of the screen.

13.2.2   The Fields Tab

Clicking Next displays the Fields tab of the Standard Report Expert. We click the *AddAll* button to add all five fields to the report. We would like to add a column showing the total cost of each order detail before the discount is applied. To do this we click the *Formula* button and enter the name Cost in the text box that appears. Figure 13.6 shows the formula editor that appears.

We want to compute the cost using the formula

Cost = UnitPrice * Quantity

To build this formula, we start by double-clicking Order_Details.UnitPrice in the Report Fields column. This displays it in the area below. Then we click the plus sign, +, to the left of Arithmetic in the Operators column to

Figure 13.6   The formula editor.

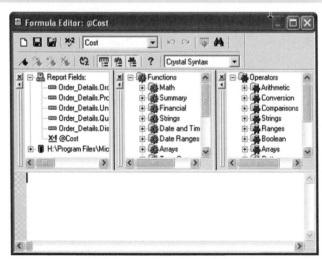

Figure 13.7 A formula for the cost.

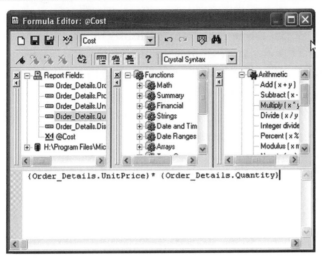

show the arithmetic operators. Double-clicking Multiply adds the multiplication operator to the formula. To complete the formula, we double-click Order_Details.Quantity. Figure 13.7 shows the completed formula.

We click the third button from the left in the Formula Editor to save the formula and close the editor. In the Standard Report Expert, we select the Cost field and click the *Add* button to add it to the Fields to Display list on the right.

13.2.3 The Group Tab

Clicking *Next* displays the Group tab. We will group by the amount of discount, so we select Order_Details.Discount and click *Add* and then *Next*. A combo box allows four choices for the sort order: in ascending order, in descending order, in specified order, and in original order. We select in descending order and click *Next*.

13.2.4 The Total Tab

The Total tab displays a screen that enables us to choose one or more fields to summarize. We choose to summarize the Cost field, making sure that it is the only field in the Summarized Fields list on the right. The Summary Type combo box contains a large number of choices for the type of summary. These include sum, average, maximum, minimum, and count among many others. We choose sum for this example.

13.2.5   The Remaining Tabs

The Top N tab allows various options for sorting the groups in the report. We do not use this tab and click *Next* to display the Chart tab. In the Type tab we select the Pie chart. We do not use the Data and Text tabs to configure this chart.

Clicking *Next* displays the Select tab. We do not wish to select fields to appear in the chart, so we click *Next* to display the Style tab. We enter the title *Northwind Order Details* for this report and click *Finish*.

13.2.6   Viewing the Report

We add a CrystalReportViewer to the form. Clicking on the CrystalReportViewer in the design and opening the Properties window, we browse to set the ReportSource property to the path to the CrystalReport1.rpt report contained in the current project. To allow the viewer to resize when the user resizes the form, we change its Anchor property to anchor it to all four edges of the form. Figure 13.8 shows the pie chart at the head of the report and the start of the listing of order details with 25% discount.

Figure 13.8   The Order Details **report.**

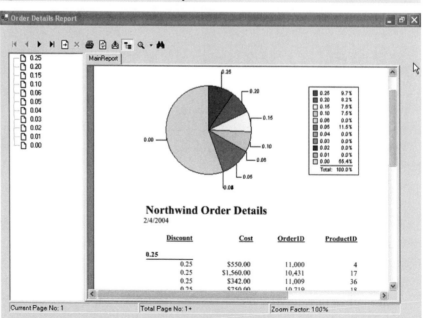

Figure 13.9   Another section of the Order Details report.

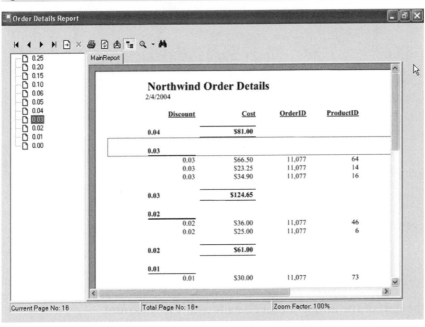

On the left, we can choose the section of the report to view by selecting a discount rate. The report shows the cost (before the discount is applied) of each item, and the total cost of all items at a given discount rate appears at the end of the section listing items at that rate. Figure 13.9 shows the section containing the items with a 3% discount rate.

Test Your Understanding

4.   List the tabs in the Standard Report Expert and describe the function of each.

The BIG Picture

We can arrange the report by groups, add column subtotals, and add computed fields. Special formatting can highlight or distinguish selected rows. Various tabs in the Report Expert help us to configure a report with additional features.

13.3   Reports via the Web

We can view a report from the Web, publish it as a Web service, and access that Web service report from a Windows application.

13.3.1   Viewing a Report in a Web Form

We create Example13-3 as an ASP.NET Web application. We add a Crystal-ReportViewer control to the Web form. To load the report, we add code to the

Figure 13.10   Viewing a report on the Web.

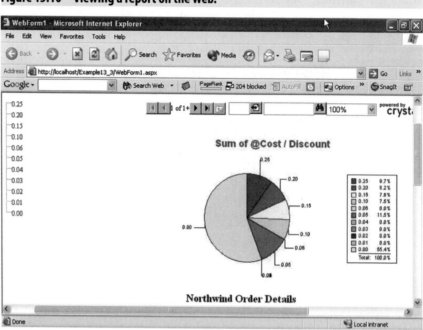

Page_Load method, which we can access by clicking the WebForm1.aspx.cs tab. If that tab is not showing, we show it by clicking the *View, Code* menu item. In the Page_Load method, we need to set the ReportSource property for the viewer. We will view the report of Example13-2. The Page_Load method code is

```
private void Page_Load(object sender, System.EventArgs e)
{
  CrystalReportViewer1.ReportSource
    = "c:\\booknet\\ch13\\Example13-2\\CrystalReport1.rpt";
}
```

Entering http://localhost/Example13-3/WebForm1.aspx in the browser displays the report shown in Figure 13.10.

13.3.2   A Web Service Report

We create Example13-4 as an ASP.NET Web Service. We will publish the Order Details report of Example13-2 as a Web service. In the Visual Studio .NET design, we click the *File, Add Existing Item* menu item and browse to find the report of Example13-2.

To enable this report as a Web service, we first click the *View, Solution Explorer* menu item. Then in the Solution Explorer we right-click on the report entry, `CrystalReport1.rpt` in this example, and click *Publish as web service*. Visual Studio .NET adds a `CrystalReport1Service.asmx` file to the Solution Explorer, which provides the report as a Web service.

13.3.3   Accessing the Web Service

To access the Web service we created in Example13-4, we create Example13-5 as a Windows Application. We click the *Project, Add Web Reference* menu item to add a reference to the Web service of Example13-4. We enter

`http://localhost/Example13-4/CrystalReport1Service.asmx`

in the `Address` field of the `Add Web Reference` screen, and click the *Add Reference* button when it appears.

To view the Web service report, we add a `CrystalReportViewer` control to the form. Double-clicking on the form displays the `Form1_Load` method in which we set the `ReportSource` property of the viewer to an instance of the Web service. The code is

```
private void Form1_Load(object sender, System.EventArgs e)
{
    crystalReportViewer1.ReportSource
      = new Example13_5.localhost.CrystalReport1Service();
}
```

Figure 13.11 shows the Windows application of Example13-5 displaying the report obtained from the Web service of Example13-4.

Figure 13.11   An Order Details Web service client.

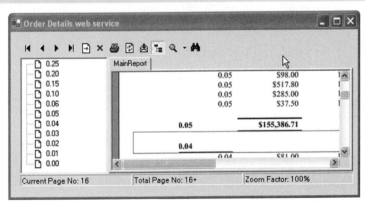

The BIG Picture

We can view a report from the Web, publish it as a Web service, and access that Web service report from a Windows application.

Test Your Understanding

5.   Which C# method do we use to initialize a Web application?

6.   Describe the steps used to publish a report as a Web service.

13.4   Summary

Crystal Reports for Visual Studio .NET is the standard reporting tool for Visual Studio .NET. We can host reports on Web and Windows platforms and publish Crystal reports as Report Web Services on a Web server. Visual Studio .NET includes Crystal Reports for Visual Studio .NET.

The Report Expert displays a set of tabs that we use to configure reports. The `CrystalReportViewer` control enables us to view a report from a Windows application or a Web form. By using the Data Adapter Configuration Wizard, we can incorporate information from a database in a report.

13.5   Programming Exercises

13.1   Modify Example13-1 to filter the data by the category of the product rather than the supplier.

13.2   Modify Example13-2 to show the discounted total cost rather than the gross total cost.

13.3   Modify Example13-2 to group by the quantity rather than the discount rate.

13.4   Write an application that displays a Crystal Report showing the Northwind customers. It will list the company name, address, and country. Group by country.

13.5   Write a Web application that will view the report of Exercise 1.

13.6   Allow the user to filter the report of Exercise 4 by Contact Title. The user will select a contact title from a `ComboBox` and the report will display only those customers with the selected title.

13.7   Enable the report of Exercise 3 as a Web service and write a Web application that accesses that Web service.

13.8   Add a pie chart to the report of Exercise 4.

APPENDIX A

C# Keywords

abstract	as	base	bool	break
byte	case	catch	char	checked
class	const	continue	decimal	default
delegate	do	double	else	enum
event	explicit	extern	false	finally
fixed	float	for	foreach	goto
if	implicit	in	int	interface
internal	is	lock	long	namespace
new	null	object	operator	out
override	params	private	protected	public
readonly	ref	return	sbyte	sealed
short	sizeof	stackalloc	static	string
struct	switch	this	throw	true
try	typeof	uint	ulong	unchecked
unsafe	ushort	using	virtual	void
volatile	while			

APPENDIX B

Operator Precedence Table

Primary	[ ] . () ++ -- new
Unary	++(prefix) --(prefix) + - ~ ! (T)x
Multiplicative	* / %
Additive	+ -
Shift	<< >>
Relational	< > <= >= is
Equality	== !=
Bitwise, Logical AND	&
Bitwise, Logical XOR	^
Bitwise, Logical OR	|
Conditional AND	&&
Conditional OR	||
Conditional	?:
Assignment	= += -= *= /= %= >>= <<= &= ^= |=

APPENDIX C

The ASCII Character Set

The first 32 characters and the last one are control characters. We label those control characters that we use in the text.

0		32	blank	64	@	96	`
1		33	!	65	A	97	a
2		34	"	66	B	98	b
3		35	#	67	C	99	c
4		36	$	68	D	100	d
5		37	%	69	E	101	e
6		38	&	70	F	102	f
7		39	'	71	G	103	g
8	\b	40	(	72	H	104	h
9	\t	41	)	73	I	105	i
10	\n	42	*	74	J	106	j
11		43	+	75	K	107	k
12		44	,	76	L	108	l
13	\r	45	-	77	M	109	m
14		46	.	78	N	110	n
15		47	/	79	O	111	o
16		48	0	80	P	112	p
17		49	1	81	Q	113	q
18		50	2	82	R	114	r
19		51	3	83	S	115	s
20		52	4	84	T	116	t
21		53	5	85	U	117	u
22		54	6	86	V	118	v
23		55	7	87	W	119	w
24		56	8	88	X	120	x
25		57	9	89	Y	121	y
26		58	:	90	Z	122	z
27		59	;	91	[	123	{
28		60	<	92	\	124	|
29		61	=	93	]	125	}
30		62	>	94	^	126	~
31		63	?	95	_	127	

ANSWERS

Chapter 2

1. Size, 300 × 300
3. BackColor, Cursor, Font, ForeColor, RightToLeft, and Text occur in all three.
   BackgroundImage and FormBorderStyle are Form properties only.
   BorderStyle and TextAlign occur in TextBox and Label.
   Lines and ScrollBars occur only in TextBox.
   Image, ImageAlign, ImageIndex, ImageList, and UseMnemonic occur only in Label.
5. The Form fills the entire screen.
7. Fill
9. It remains at the left end of the screen.

Chapter 3

1. CheckedChanged
3. LinkBehavior
5. The user would only be able to select one of the five radio buttons, and not one from each group.
7. The Normal value provides a square box for the user to check. The Button value omits the square box and requires the user to click the check box like a button.
9. SelectedIndexChanged
11. Timer
13. Set the DecimalPlaces property to 2.
15. Hold the Ctrl key down and press the S key.
17. FileName
19. ShowDialog

Chapter 4

1. a, b, f, g, and j are valid. c, d, e, and k use invalid characters. h starts with a digit, i is a keyword.
3. name, type
5. int
7. a. I like

   to write C# programs.
   b. Ali Baba said, "Open, Sesame!"
   c. Find 3\4 of 24
9. a. 3456.79
   b. 0.00
   c. 0.10
   d. 1234567890.99
   e. −234567.77
11. a. 345,678.9%
    b. 0.0%
    c. 9.9%
    d. 123,456,789,098.7%
    e. −23,456,776.5%
13. George   George
    where there are eight spaces in between
15. a. 4
    b. −19
    c. 4
    d. 9
    e. −2
    f. 0
    g. 8
    h. −3
    i. 1
17. a. 234 < 52
    b. 435 != 87
    c. −12 == −12
    d. 76 >= 54

19. x=5 assigns 5 to x. x==5 tests whether x is equal to 5.

21. Many correct answers are possible, for example

    a. x=2, y=7

    b. x=0, y = any integer

    c. x = 20, y = any integer

    d. x=11, y =0

Chapter 5

1. a, b, and c. if (x == 12) y += 7;

3. a. if (y <= 6)

       z += 5;

    b. if (x != 0)

       y+=5;

     else

       z = y + 9;

5. String category = "";

   if (amount >= 1 && amount <= 99)

     category = "Contributor";

   else if (amount >+ 100 && amount < 499)

     category = "Supporter";

   else if (amount >= 500 && amount <= 999)

     category = "Patron";

   else if (amount >= 1000)

     category = "Benefactor";

7. a. 8

   b. 7

   c. 6

   d. 7

9. a. 9

   b. 6

   c. 7

   d. 9

   e. 8

   f. 9

   g. 9

11. a. } should be)

    b. test condition must be **bool** valued

    c. =! should be !=

13. a. does not terminate

    b. terminates

    c. does not terminate

15.
```
int sum = 0;
for(int i = 1; i <= 10; i++)
    sum += 1;
```

17.
```
int sum = 0;
for(int i = 9; i >= 3; i--)
    sum += i;
```

19. 28

21. 26

23. 55

25. 0

27. 72

Chapter 6

1. a. 9

    b. 3

3. Count

5. a. 1

    b. 4

    c. 4

    d. −1

    e. 6

    f. −1

7. System

Chapter 7

1. `ProductID` is unique for each product, whereas two or more products may have the same `ProductName`.

3. `System.Data.OleDb.OleDbDataReader`

5. `DataGrid`

7. `Diagram`, `Grid`, `SQL`, and `Results`

Chapter 8

1. Hypertext Transfer Protocol (HTTP)

3. Hypertext Markup Language (HTML)

5. To link to another document.

7. The code behind the file contains the C# code that initializes the page and the event-handler methods.

9. MultiLine

11. −1

13. `OleDbCommand`

15. `AutoPostBack`

17. `IsPostBack`

Chapter 9

1. `ControlToValidate`

3. `MaximumValue`, `MinimumValue`, and `Type`

5. Both are valid

7. `ControlToCompare` and `ControlToValidate`

9. Set the `Type` property to `Double`

11. (123)456-7890 or 123-456-7890

Chapter 10

1. They are all well-formed

3. The schema of part (a) is valid.

5. `DataSet`

7. `DocumentElement`

9. `<xsl:apply-templates></xsl:apply-templates>`

Chapter 11

1. Web Service Definition Language
3. [WebMethod]

Chapter 12

1. Windows CE
3. Windows CE
5. GetElementsByTagName

Chapter 13

1. Standard, Form Letter, Form, Subreport, Mail, Label, and Drill Down
3. SelectionFormula
5. Form1_Load, where Form1 is the name of the form.

INDEX

SYMBOLS
! 102
!= 100
% 96
%= 99
&& 101
* 96
*= 99
+
    addition 96
    concatenation 60
++ 99
+= 99
- 96
— 100
-= 99
/ 96
/* 99
< 100
<= 100
== 100
> 100
>= 100
_ 81
|| 101

A
anchoring, 25, 27-28, 39
AND, 101-102
arguments, 73
arithmetic expressions, 84, 96-100
arrays, 139-149
    Length property, 140
    variables, 148
ASCII, 82, 88, 335
ASP .NET, 195
assignment, 81, 83-84, 87, 99
associativity, 98
attributes, 11

B
BASIC, 11
binary operator, 96
block, 112-113, 134
bool, 88
BorderStyle, 43-44
    FixedSingle, 43
    Fixed3D, 44
break statement, 124
browser, 198, 200, 216
Button, 34-38
    BackColor, 36
    Click event, 37
    Text, 35

C
C, 10, 11
C#, 1, 11
    case-sensitive, 81
    expressiveness, 12
    features, 12
    flexibility, 12
    power, 12
    productivity, 12
    safety, 12
C++, 11
case, 123
char, 88-89
character set, 82
characters
    escape, 88
    special, 88-89
CheckBox, 53-58, 62
    Appearance, 54
    BackgroundImage, 54
    CheckAlign, 54
    CheckChanged event, 55-56
    Checked, 143-144
    FlatStyle, 55

Image, 54
ImageAlign, 54
TextAlign, 54
class method, 152
client, 195, 216
    client-side validation, 237
COBOL, 10
code, 22-23
code behind, 195, 202-203
collection
    of links, 49-50
ColorDialog, 75-77
    Click event, 76-77
    Color, 76
ComboBox, 61-62
    DropDownStyle, 61
    Items, 62
command
    database, 169, 175-176, 179
CompareValidator, 235
    ControlToCompare, 236
    Operator, 235
compilers, 9
components, 11, 12
concatenation, 60
condition, 110
conditional operators, 101-102
connection
    database, 169, 173-174, 179
constants, 87
constructor, 147, 164
context-sensitive help, 37-38, 39
controls, 2
    adding, 19-25
    moving, 33-34
    positioning, 25-33
    sizing, 33-34
Crystal Reports, 7, 317-330
    adding features, 323-327
    as a Web service, 328-330
    creating, 317-320
    CrystalReportViewer, 320-321
    filtering, 321-322
    reports via the Web, 327-330

SelectionFormula, 322
viewing, 320-321, 326-328

D
data adapter, 169, 179
    Configuration Wizard, 180-182,
        187
Data Form Wizard, 183-187
data link properties, 174
data provider 173
data reader, 169, 176
data set, 169, 179, 182-183
data source, 179
database, 169-192
    connected model, 173-179
    disconnected model, 179-187
    introductory example, 4-5, 6
    multiple tables, 187-191
    Web access, 208-216
DataGrid, 179, 182-183, 187
    AutoFormat, 209
    DataBind method, 210
    DataSource, 182
DataSet, 182-183, 187
    ReadXml method, 262
DateTime
    Now, 67
DateTimePicker, 63-64, 67
    Format, 63-64
    MaxDate, 64
    MinDate, 64
    ShowUpDown, 64
decimal, 87-88
decrement operator, 99, 100
do statement, 133-134
docking, 25, 31-33, 39
Document Object Model (DOM),
    260-263
double, 87, 88

E
editors, 9
emulator
    for Pocket PC, 302, 304-306
    for Windows CE, 302-303

event-driven programming, 1-8, 14
event handlers, 1
  CheckChanged, 44-45, 55-56
  Click, 37, 70, 75, 76-77
  code, 22-23
  LinkClicked, 46-47, 50
  SelectedIndexChanged, 59-61
  TextChanged, 23
  Tick, 66-67
execution, 24-25
Extensible Markup Language
  See XML
Extensible Stylesheet Language
  (XSL), 263
Extensible Stylesheet Language for
  Transformations
  See XSLT

F
F1 key, 38, 39, 143
Field width, 92
file dialogs, 72-75
flow diagram
  for, 129
  if, 111
  if-else, 112
  nested if-else, 119
  while, 126
Focus method, 145
FontDialog, 24, 77-78
  Click event, 77
for statement, 128-130
form, 2
  BackColor, 18
  Text, 18
Format method, 89, 90, 92, 156
format specifiers, 90-92
formatting, 89-92
formatting strings, 89, 95
FORTRAN, 10

G
GroupBox, 42, 47

H
hardware, 8-9
help, 37-38
hidden code, 164
high-level languages, 9-10
history
  of programming languages, 10-11
HTML, 5, 195, 196-200
  anchor, 197
  attributes, 197
  image, 197
  limitations, 247-248
  tags, 196-198
HttpResponse, 216
Hypertext Markup Language
  See HTML

I
identifiers, 81, 87
if statement, 110-111, 116
  nested, 117, 124
if-else statement, 111-112, 116
  nested, 117
  pairing, 119
increment operator, 99
indexer, 152, 162
InitializeComponent method, 146
instance, 163
instance method, 152
instruction set, 9
int, 83, 87, 88
IntelliSense, 23-24, 256
Internet Explorer, 46
Internet Information Server (IIS), 200

J
Java, 10, 11
JavaScript, 238

K
key
  database, 171
keyboard shortcut, 69
keywords, 82, 87, 331

L

Label, 21-22, 39
    AutoSize, 24
    BorderStyle, 43
    Dock, 32
    Font, 24
    ForeColor, 24
    Name, 21
    Text, 21
    TextAlign, 29
Length, 60
library classes, 162-164
LinkLabel, 45-47
    LinkBehavior, 48
    LinkClicked event, 46-47, 50
    LinkLabel.Link.LinkData, 50
    Links, 49
LinkLabelLinkClickedEventArgs, 50
    Link, 51
    Link.LinkData, 51
ListBox, 58-61, 62, 141-142
    Items, 58-59
    Item.Add method, 178
    multiple selections, 141-142
    SelectedIndexChanged event, 59-61
    SelectedItem, 60
    SelectedItems, 142
    SelectionMode, 59
    Sorted, 59
ListItem Collection Editor, 204
Load method, 177, 183
logical complement, 102
loop termination, 127-128

M

MainMenu, 68-70, 78
meaningful names, 21, 32
MenuItem
    Click event, 70
    Shortcut, 69
menus, 68-70
MessageBox, 86
metadata, 11, 12
Microsoft Access, 170
middle tier, 169, 195

mobile applications, 6, 295-316
mobile devices, 295-296
mobile operating systems
    Pocket PC, 296, 300
    Windows CE, 296, 300
mobile Web applications, 298-306
    creating, 301-302
mobile Web form controls
    Command, 301
    Label, 301
MonthCalendar, 64

N

namespace, 162-163
.NET
    Compact Framework, 295, 297-
        298, 300
    components, 12
    class library, 162-164
new, 164
newline, 87
Northwind, 170-172
NOT, 102
null, 164
NumericUpDown, 65, 67
    DecimalPlaces, 65
    Maximum, 65
    Minimum, 65
    ThousandsSeparator, 65
    Value, 65

O

object, 163, 164
OleDbCommand, 175-176
    CommandText, 175-176
    Connection, 175
    ExecuteReader method, 178
OleDbConnection, 173
    ConnectionString, 174
    Open method, 178
    Close method, 178
OleDbDataAdapter, 180
    Fill method, 183
OleDbDataReader, 170
    Close method, 178

GetDecimal method, 178
GetString method, 178
Read method, 178
OpenFileDialog, 72-73, 77
    FileName, 72
    ShowDialog method, 72
operating system, 9
operator precedence, 103
OR, 101, 102
overloading, 154

P
Panel, 41
Parse method
    double, 105
    int, 86
PictureBox, 52-53, 62
    BorderStyle, 53
    SizeMode, 53
    Visible, 160
pixel, 19
Pointer option, 20
precedence, 97-98, 103, 333
PrintDialog, 75, 77
    Click event, 75
PrintDocument, 75
private, 146, 163
Process, 46
    Start method, 46
processor, 8, 9
project, 16-17
    closing, 25
    code, 23
    creating, 26
    design, 23
    tabs, 23
Properties
    autohiding 19
    buttons, 17-18
    categories, 17
    changing, 18-19
    window, 17-18, 27, 38
property, 152, 162

Q
query, 171-172
Query Builder tool, 172, 176, 181-182

R
RadioButton, 41-45
    CheckChanged event, 44-45
    Font.Bold, 43
    group, 41, 47-48
Random, 146
    Next method, 146
random numbers, 145-146
RangeValidator, 231, 235
    ControlToValidate, 232
    ErrorMessage, 232
    MaximumValue, 232
    MinimumValue, 232
    Type, 233
reference, 148, 164
reference types, 139
RegularExpressionValidator, 239
    expression types, 239
    ValidationExpression, 240
relational databases, 170-172
relational operators, 100-101
RequiredFieldValidator, 227
    InitialValue, 228
    ControlToValidate, 228
Response, 216, 224
    Redirect, 218
    redirecting, 216-217
RichTextBox, 70-71, 77
    LoadFile method, 71, 72
    RichTextScrollBars, 71
    SaveFile method, 71, 74
    ScrollBars, 71
    WordWrap, 71
RichTextBoxStreamType, 73

S
SaveFileDialog, 72, 73-75, 77
    FileName, 75
    ShowDialog method, 72
schemas, 251-257
    creating, 252

tag types, 251
search, 144
server, 195, 216
session tracking, 195
Smalltalk, 10
smart device application, 306-311
    accessing Web services, 311-315
    saving data, 309
    using tabs, 307-309
software, 9-10
SqlDataAdapter, 180
Start page, 15-16
StatusBar, 66, 67
String, 150-162
    Chars, 152
    declaration, 151
    Format method, 89, 90, 92, 156
    immutable, 158
    IndexOf, 150, 154-155
    Length, 150
    methods, 152-157
    Replace, 155
    Substring, 153
    ToLower, 153
    ToUpper, 33, 151
    Trim, 153
StringBuilder, 158-159
    Append, 159
Structured Query Language (SQL), 171
switch statement, 122-124
System.Diagnostics namespace, 46

T
TextBox, 20-21, 39
    Anchor, 27
    Cursor, 21
    Dock, 32
    event-handling code, 22-23, 30
    Name, 21
    Property categories, 21
    Text, 21
three-tiered architecture, 195
Timer, 66-67
    Interval, 66
    Tick event, 66-67

Toolbox, 12-13, 19-20, 39
    autohiding, 19
    categories, 19-20
ToLongDateString, 65
ToString, 51, 60, 90, 91
ToUpper, 33
types, 87-95, 139-164
    validation data types, 232

U
unary operator, 96
Unicode, 82
Uniform Resource Locator (URL), 199
UNIX, 10
using, 163
utility programs, 9

V
validation controls, 5, 8, 227-244
ValidationSummary, 243
variables, 81, 82-83, 87
    declaration, 82
    initialization, 83
    local, 86
    name, 82
    type, 82
Visual Basic, 11
Visual Studio .NET, 12-13
    code generation, 23
    design, 12
    documentation, 142-143

W
Web applications, 5-6, 195-225
    creation, 200-201
    execution, 24-25
    multiple forms, 216-224
    virtual directory, 201
Web forms
    adding, 218
    DataTextField, 219
    FlowLayout, 201, 211
    GridLayout, 201
    hidden state, 220-221
    initializing, 219-220, 223

IsPostBack, 220, 224
    Page, 216
    pageLayout, 201, 211
    PageLoad method, 210
Web Matrix, 200
Web reference, 276-279
Web server
    hosting, 200-201
Web server controls, 5, 7, 200-208
    AutoPostBack property, 213, 217
    Button, 202
    CheckBoxList, 204
    checking required fields, 227-231
    code behind, 202-203
    comparing values, 235-239
    Label, 202
    ListBox, 204
    RadioButtonList, 206
    range checking, 221
    Response property, 216, 218
    summarizing validation errors, 243
    TextBox, 202, 204
    validating expressions, 239-242
Web Service Definition Language
        (WSDL), 277, 282
Web services, 6, 8, 275-292
    accessing data, 286-291
    AsyncCallback, 281
    AsyncState, 282
    asynchronous calls, 279-282
    callback method, 279
    clients, 275-282, 285, 286
    creating, 282-285
    IAsyncResult, 282
    synchronous call, 286
    testing, 284-285
    WebMethod attribute, 283, 286
while statement, 126-127

Windows applications, 2-4
    closing, 25
    creating, 15-19, 26
    maximizing, 25
    minimizing, 25

X
XML, 12, 247-272
    attributes, 250
    comment, 250
    document creation, 256-257
    from data, 258-262
    prolog, 249
    syntax, 248-250
    tags, 250
    transforming, 263-271
    validate, 257
    using schema, 256-257
    valid, 255-256
    well-formed, 250
XmlDataDocument, 259, 261
XmlDocument, 261
    DocumentElement, 262
    Save method, 259
XmlElement, 261
    GetElementsByTagName, 262
XmlNode, 261
    FirstChild, 262
XmlNodeList, 261
    Count, 262
XmlText, 261
XSLT, 263-271
    apply-templates, 265, 267
    processing instruction, 264
    stylesheet, 263
    template, match 265
    text, 267
    value-of, 267

Outstanding New Titles:

Computer Science Illuminated, Second Edition
Nell Dale and John Lewis
ISBN: 0-7637-0799-6
©2004

Programming and Problem Solving with Java
Nell Dale, Chip Weems,
and Mark R. Headington
ISBN: 0-7637-0490-3
©2003

Databases Illuminated
Catherine Ricardo
ISBN: 0-7637-3314-8
©2004

Foundations of Algorithms Using Java Pseudocode
Richard Neapolitan and Kumarss Naimipour
ISBN: 0-7637-2129-8
©2004

Artificial Intelligence Illuminated
Ben Coppin
ISBN: 0-7637-3230-3
©2004

The Essentials of Computer Organization and Architecture
Linda Null and Julia Lobur
ISBN: 0-7637-0444-X
©2003

A Complete Guide to C#
David Bishop
ISBN: 0-7637-2249-9
©2004

A First Course in Complex Analysis with Applications
Dennis G. Zill and Patrick Shanahan
ISBN: 0-7637-1437-2
©2003

Programming and Problem Solving with C++, Fourth Edition
Nell Dale and Chip Weems
ISBN: 0-7637-0798-8
©2004

C++ Plus Data Structures, Third Edition
Nell Dale
ISBN: 0-7637-0481-4
©2003

Applied Data Structures with C++
Peter Smith
ISBN: 0-7637-2562-5
©2004

Foundations of Algorithms Using C++ Pseudocode, Third Edition
Richard Neapolitan and Kumarss Naimipour
ISBN: 0-7637-2387-8
©2004

Managing Software Projects
Frank Tsui
ISBN: 0-7637-2546-3
©2004

Readings in CyberEthics, Second Edition
Richard Spinello and Herman Tavani
ISBN: 0-7637-2410-6
©2004

C#.NET Illuminated
Art Gittleman
ISBN: 0-7637-2593-5
©2004

Discrete Mathematics, Second Edition
James L. Hein
ISBN: 0-7637-2210-3
©2003

http://www.jbpub.com/

JONES AND BARTLETT PUBLISHERS
BOSTON   TORONTO   LONDON   SINGAPORE

1.800.832.0034

Take Your Courses to the Next Level

Turn the page to preview new and forthcoming titles in Computer Science and Math from Jones and Bartlett...

Providing solutions for students and educators in the following disciplines:

- Introductory Computer Science
- Java
- C++
- Databases
- C#
- Data Structures

- Algorithms
- Network Security
- Software Engineering
- Discrete Mathematics
- Engineering Mathematics
- Complex Analysis

Please visit http://computerscience.jbpub.com/ and http://math.jbpub.com/ to learn more about our exciting publishing programs in these disciplines.

http://www.jbpub.com/

JONES AND BARTLETT
PUBLISHERS
BOSTON   TORONTO   LONDON   SINGAPORE

1.800.832.0034